KV-194-056

Contents

Introduction

When I first compiled *Students' Money Matters* back in 1992 (this is its 14th edition), student loans were being introduced for the first time, and I felt there was a need for such a publication. I opened the book then by saying: 'When it comes to money, there is no doubt that for most UK students going on to higher education things are tough and are likely to get tougher.' I was right. But I had no idea then just how tough the going was to get and how sweeping the changes would be over the next 16 years. If this book was needed then (and it certainly was popular), it is even more essential today with the introduction of top-up fees. Unless your family has a bottomless purse, or you have a private income, getting through university financially is going to tax your ingenuity to the full.

But don't let this put you off university. It is still the great experience it always was. Students will have fun. The social scene is as active as ever. Students are resourceful by nature, and most are managing to get by financially. Certainly they are leaving university with massive debts to pay off, but remember, as a graduate with a good degree you are likely to earn considerably more during your lifetime than you otherwise would. Estimated starting salaries for graduates for 2008 range from around £20,000 to £35,000 with a median figure of £24,000 (source: AGR Graduate Recruitment Survey 2008, Winter Review), and graduates tend to earn around 20–25% more than A level school leavers over a lifetime – much more for those with a degree in medicine or engineering (Report published by Universities UK 2007). But it's the financial hurdle of the next three to four years that you have to get over first, and this is where *Students' Money Matters* can help.

How *Students' Money Matters* can help you

In this new edition of *Students' Money Matters*, we investigate the means and methods by which students can support themselves while studying for a degree, HND or other HE qualification. It is aimed primarily at students starting their HE studies this year (2008–2009) and beyond.

The book does not set out to argue the rights and wrongs of the financial situation students find themselves in nor, in fact, to tell you what to do. The aim of *Students'*

Money Matters is to give helpful information and advice, and to point out the pros and cons to be considered when seeking loans, overdrafts, work experience, jobs, a roof over your head, etc. It is for you to weigh up the evidence and information and make your own decision – because what's right for you could be totally wrong for somebody else.

However, it does include comments from employers, university tutors, careers advisers and, above all, students. As you might expect, the undergraduates with whom we discussed students' financial situation were very forthright in their views. These have been included, uncensored. There is nothing more valuable or illuminating than a report from the battlefield.

Here's how the book is organised:

- Chapter 1, entitled 'That's the way the money goes', looks in detail at how students spend their money. An important section gives information on how much it is likely to cost you to live as a student in different parts of the country, plus detailed budgets from several students so you can get a picture of your likely expenses. There is information on the cost of university accommodation and a number of actual students' budgets showing exactly how the money goes.
- Chapter 2: now you know how much you are going to need, the second chapter takes a good look at where the money is likely to come from. Topics covered include: top-up fees, loans to cover fees, maintenance loans, grants, and bursaries.
- Chapter 3: so, the funding is out there, how are you going to get hold of it? This chapter looks at applying for loans and grants, means-testing, paying back your debts, additional hardship funds and why parents have never had it so good.
- Chapter 4 provides advice for students who fall into special categories (such as Scottish and Welsh students, mature students, students from abroad), and the financial and social implications of studying for part or all of your degree abroad are discussed.
- Chapter 5 deals with working and earning money during your course. A high proportion of students work during vacations, and a growing number work during term time.
- Chapter 6 takes time out with a gap year and provides full information on organisations to contact plus a special section on the student travel scene.
- Chapter 7 highlights one possible source of additional finance – sponsorship – and looks into how to apply and what you should look out for.
- Chapter 8 focuses on other sources of funding such as scholarships, trusts, charities and professional institutions and has tips on how to approach different funding bodies.
- Chapter 9 examines funding for postgraduates.
- Chapter 10: 'Budget like a bastard' was the advice given by a first-year student at Northumbria University in our student research. With that in mind, the final chapter of *Students' Money Matters* gives you all the information you need to budget without it becoming a burden. It also includes useful information on how the banks can help you with overdrafts, loans and freebies – in fact the bank is the students' friend.

How to use this book

To produce *Students' Money Matters* we drew up a list of all the questions we thought you, as a student, would want to ask about financing your studies. We then set about finding the answers. As a result, the book is written largely in the form of a dialogue. The answers given have been kept as short, simple and direct as possible. We've cut through all the red tape and official jargon. Where we felt that you might want to dig deeper into a topic, alternative reference material has been suggested, along with appropriate organisations you can contact.

Occasionally you will find that information has been repeated. This is to help you, the reader, find the information you need quickly, rather than having to flick from one section to another.

Students' Money Matters has been written in a logical order. You will probably find the next question is the one you would want to ask. However, it is a reference book, and readers need to be able to dip into it, seeking answers to questions as they arise. To help you find the section you require quickly there is a contents list and an index. The contents list covers the main points addressed. In addition to the index, each chapter opens with a list of the main topics covered. If your exact question is not there, turn to the section covering that topic and you will probably find the answer. In the unlikely event you don't find the answer, do contact us – we are always interested in hearing of any omissions. Throughout the book you will also find useful nuggets of information such as thrift tips from current students.

Money, especially the lack of it, can be a depressing subject. We hope you'll find *Students' Money Matters* an illuminating, helpful and amusing read, and that the information given will make your time at university or college less worrying and a lot more fun.

In the last edition we asked for your comments, criticisms and suggestions for the next edition. These are included here along with updated facts and figures taken from new surveys of the student scene, in particular the Royal Bank of Scotland Student Living Index. But nothing is static, least of all the pecuniary plight of students, so please keep those comments coming. It is only by being vigilant and keeping in touch with 'campus correspondents' that we can pass on the right information to those who follow. Our thanks in helping prepare this book must go to all those students who were an invaluable source for so much of the information – and also to the employers and financial and higher education institutions who have given vital assistance in the research of the material.

Gwenda Thomas

That's the way the money goes

How much is it going to cost you to be a student?

So how much will it cost you?

As much as you have, and probably a lot more. Students have always been hard up, but never more so than now.

In the last year there have been numerous stories in the press about students having to give up their degree courses because they just couldn't make ends meet. Drop-out rates in some universities are worryingly high – average around 22%. But we do have over a million first-degree students in higher education in the UK at the moment, and though there was a slight drop in new students with the introduction of top-up fees, since then – the numbers have been steadily rising. How are these students managing?

Many factors can affect your financial situation. Some students are luckier – or perhaps more determined – than others in:

- ⦿ Raising additional finance
- ⦿ Managing to work as well as study
- ⦿ Choosing to study in cheaper parts of the country
- ⦿ Finding additional bursary funding

- Living at home
- Being excellent money managers.

While others ...

- Find that money slips through their fingers like water
- Are great socialisers and imbibers
- Take courses for which they have to buy expensive equipment or books, or need to travel
- Have expensive tastes and hanker after all the good things in life
- Have a wide range of hobbies and interests
- Study in expensive areas such as London.

Obviously you should not pick your course on the basis of where the living is cheapest, but it is as well to know what costs you are likely to face. This first chapter looks at what it is likely to cost you to gain higher qualifications. But first ...

What makes so many of you do it?

Last year around 522,000 people applied for higher education courses in the UK. What is the great attraction? Why did they want to forfeit the chance of having money in their pockets to become near-penniless students and increasingly get into debt?

Here are some reasons given by students taking part in the *Students' Money Matters* research:

'I want to get a job I enjoy.'
'To improve my job prospects with the hope of getting a varied career. I'm not a 9 to 5 person.'
'I wanted to continue learning; university was the obvious path.'

If we asked everyone now studying in universities and colleges across Britain, we'd get thousands of different answers. Most would be positive, but not all:

'I don't rate uni at all. I wish the government would encourage people to do something they are good at and not waste money and time pushing people into a place they don't want.'
Law and Japanese student, Oxford Brookes

Many, however, would say money – or the potential for earning it. And there is no doubt a degree can help increase your earning power. Graduates can expect to earn on average 20–25% more than A level students over a lifetime – and much more if they study medicine or engineering – according to a recent report published by Universities UK.

But whatever your reason for studying, it's going to be hard going financially for the next few years. How are you going to manage?

Fact check

What makes a student decide on a university?

Key factors:

- quality of teaching 54%
- reputation of course 44%
- reputation of the institution 43%
- teaching methods 35%

Less important factors:

- how seriously the institution takes global development issues 6%
- environmental issues 5%

Future Leads Survey based on research carried out with 25,000 university applicants by Forum for the Future and UCAS and sponsored by Friends Provident.

What will university cost?

Fees – will I have to pay them?

Yes – but not the whole fee and not if you're a Scottish student studying in Scotland (more of that later in Chapter 4). Most students who started their course in or after 1998 have had to pay something towards the cost of it. But in 2006 the maximum tuition fee per annum was hiked up to £3,000. With year on year 'inflationary' rises, this year it will be £3,145. Not surprisingly, this move has aroused a great deal of passion among students:

Absolutely ridiculous and should be stopped immediately if the government wants a well-educated population in 50 years' time.
1st year Geography and Economics student, UCL

If there are too many students for the government to support, decrease the number of unis.
2nd year Human Sciences student, UCL

Ridiculous. It's OK for richer students, their families can help them out, and for poorer students who get large grants. It's those in the middle who are left with big financial pressures.
1st year Law student, Oxford

Students shouldn't have to pay at all to have an education. The government should invest in the country's future.
3rd year Fashion Design, Marketing and PR student, Huddersfield

It will put students off doing longer degrees such as Medicine.
5th year Medical student, UCL

It is ironic that the government is driving at higher education for the masses with a 50% target and yet they make it harder financially for students to get there.
3rd year Biology student, Durham

But others had a different point of view. However, it was difficult to find many first-year students actually paying the fees who had opinions like these:

For students considering 'Mickey Mouse' courses, this may be sufficient deterrent.
2nd year Medical student, UCL

Reasonable!
1st year Multimedia Technology student, Huddersfield, who expects to face a debt of £24,000 on graduation

As far as I can see, it is necessary for universities to increase their income by charging higher fees.
3rd year English student, UCL

Think it's a good idea as it will improve the quality of education.
2nd year MChem student, Huddersfield

Necessary and to be implemented as soon as possible.
3rd year Biological Sciences student, Oxford

Harsh but understandable if universities want to compete.
2nd year Geography student, Oxford

Good: they might return the prestige of degrees.
2nd year Music Technology and Audio Systems student, Huddersfield

Your living expenses

These have to be paid for largely by you. More maintenance bursaries are being given by the government and universities than ever before, so there is more help available, especially for low-income families (see Chapter 2 for full details). Managing is not going to be easy, though it shouldn't be impossible. But wherever your money comes from, it's you who will have to eke it out and make ends meet. So here are the facts.

Accommodation – the major demand on your finances

Accommodation will probably soak up half your income. If it's full board in university accommodation you are looking at over three-quarters of your total income.

Finding the right place to live is important, especially in your first year. It can affect your whole attitude to your college, your course, your study, the town or city where you are staying, making the right friends, and whether you actually do well. If it's half an hour's walk, or a bus ride across town, to get to the library, you may think twice about going there. If you're stuck in a bedsit with a grumpy landlord and no other students around you, the weekends could be very long and lonely. Halls are generally thought to be the best for first years, but they aren't right for everyone:

It is impossible to get a decent night's sleep because of noisy students returning after a night out.
1st year Arts student, Robert Gordon University

Occasionally you'll hear people running along the corridor at two in the morning. But mostly people are considerate.
Modern Languages student, Cambridge

Most institutions give first-year students first claim on halls of residence and most students jump at the chance. It gives you a circle of ready-made friends and a great social life. But for some students, living with a hundred or so other people, sharing bathrooms, meal times, TV programmes, problems, passions – even bedrooms – can be an unbearable strain. Others thrive on the camaraderie. Criticising mixed halls, one student told us:

'Coping with an ex-boyfriend over cornflakes and coffee at 8am is something not to be endured.'

Where can I get information and help?

College prospectuses will generally give you details about halls of residence, though these may not be altogether bias-free. Students' unions may also have a view – ask if there's an alternative prospectus or students' union handbook. If it has to be accommodation in the private sector, ask for the university approved accommodation list.

Above all, check out the accommodation for yourself if you can when you make your first visit.

Look at:

- Cost
- Whether rooms are shared
- Eating arrangements – is it full board, half-board, kitchen/do-it-yourself?
- Facilities provided
- Distance from college
- Transport availability – plus frequency and cost
- Shops.

The college accommodation office is responsible for placing students in halls of residence, and will send you details once you've accepted a place. It will also help you to find rented accommodation.

Accommodation in halls of residence

What will it cost?

Costs vary significantly between different types of accommodation and different universities, with much higher costs in the London colleges in particular. Be aware that the number of meals per day, the number of days per week that meals are served and the number of weeks in the academic year can vary between institutions. Some establishments offer accommodation other than the norm, such as en-suite, up-to-the-minute facilities or out-of-town accommodation.

When comparing university self-catering accommodation in halls of residence with the rented sector, remember that with college accommodation gas and electricity are probably (but not always) included. This is unlikely to be the case in the rented sector.

Will I have to share a room?

Possibly. In some colleges you may have to share a room for one or two terms. If you do have to share, you will probably be sent a questionnaire designed to find out what sort of person you are and the kind of person you could live with. Typical questions are: Would you want to share with a smoker (where it's still allowed)? Are you an early riser? Do you like to go to bed late and get up late? Are you a party person? What kind of music do you like – is there any kind you can't stand?

Honesty is the only way to harmony. Even if you are easy-going about smoking, do you really want to sleep in a smoky atmosphere? And, although your intentions may be very laudable at the moment, how are you going to feel about your room-mate stomping around at eight in the morning when you've been out partying until two?

Halls are great except you don't get to pick who you live with; sharing a flat with six other people can be a nightmare,

*especially when food goes missing and the kitchen becomes
a garbage site.*
1st year Management Studies student, Middlesex

*I'd never shared a room with anyone before and didn't really
like the idea. At first it was strange, but after a couple of weeks
you got used to it. Having someone around most of the time
is fun.*
1st year Economics student, St Andrews

*I thought I wouldn't like sharing a room, but actually it's nice
to have someone to come home to.*
1st year Modern Languages student, Durham

Cash crisis note

Students in the South East, but studying outside London, are thought to be suffering
particularly badly, as they are being asked to pay London-equivalent rents while not
qualifying for the larger student loans given to students who study in the capital.

*I strongly believe the London Weighting should be further
increased. My loan has never done more than barely covered
my accommodation and that has made everything really,
really stressful. If I hadn't found a job I don't know what I
would have done.*
3rd year Mathematics student, UCL (job: football statistician; pay: £15 ph)

University managed accommodation costs

		per week
Average rent		£82.00
	London	£99.71
	Wales (cheapest location)	£67.03
	Self-catering en-suite	£86.00
	Self-catering shared	£67.00
	Full board	£105.00
	NUS/Unipol Accommodation Costs Survey, December 2006	

Fact file

Among the lowest weekly rents for halls of residence offering two meals (or possibly more) a day was £57 at University of Chester, while the highest was a staggering £275 at the Regent Street Business School, London.

Among the lowest rents in university accommodation with no food was £30 at Northumberland College and the highest with no food was £275, again at the Regent Street Business School. So, as you can see, there is a great deal of variation in costs.

Most universities offer a range of costs for their accommodation, so the highs and lows can be misleading. For example, Chester students can find they are paying over £75 just for accommodation with no food.

The rent for college accommodation usually includes heating and lighting, and you generally only pay for the weeks you are there, which is not the case in accommodation rented in the open market. As the figures quoted here are for 2006–2007 you may well find your costs are higher.

Information based on *University and College Entrance Big Guide* 2007

What's it going to cost?

Most of the figures given in this section on what students are likely to have to pay are based on the Royal Bank of Scotland Student Living Index Survey August 2007 carried out amongst students in 27 major university towns throughout the UK and it revealed some interesting facts.

How much is rented accommodation going to cost?

Average outside London: £73 per week; average in London: £102 per week.

While on average students throughout the country, excluding London, are paying £73 per week, the average rents among students in London were predictably higher than anywhere else, at around £102 per week. Oxford was also high at £88 per week followed by Aberdeen at £84 per week. You could pay less if you're living outside the centre, but remember you would then have travel costs. Among the cheapest places to rent were Sheffield and Leicester at £59 per week. These are of course average figures; there were pockets of the country where rents varied considerably.

Don't forget that on top of rent you are likely to have utilities (gas, electricity, water) to pay for. The Student Living Index Survey estimates these costs will be around £15 a week, which is something you probably won't have to pay in university accommodation. Full details of rents in different parts of the country are shown on page 107.

Cash crisis note

If you are renting in the private sector remember an upfront deposit may have to be paid – average £232 (NUS/Unipol Accommodation Costs Survey).

Action

Check out the length and terms of your contract. A recent survey of university students found that more and more landlords were asking students to sign 52-week contracts for accommodation. This means they are paying rent during the Christmas, Easter and three-month summer vacations, when they are likely to be at home – something you don't have to do in university accommodation.

Another problem we encountered was that students who have to undertake a placement away from their university, such as medical students, may find they are paying for accommodation away for a couple of months while still paying for the accommodation in their university town.

Advice note

From one who knows. 'If your landlord won't fix something, take a photograph of the problem so you have evidence that it's not your fault. With this in hand, the landlord will find it difficult to play the trick of docking your deposit when you leave. Our curtain railing has come down and the landlord won't fix it. But he won't pull a fast one over us.'

Law student, Northampton

Possible problems when renting accommodation

- 'Exploding shower, broken-down washing machine, dangerous housemates.'
  3rd year Entertainment Crafts student, Cleveland

- 'Entertaining unwanted visitors – cockroaches from the café downstairs.'
  1st year Modern European Studies student, Thames Valley

- 'Lodgings miles from anywhere. Buses stopped at 7pm so late study and going out meant paying for a taxi home.'
  2nd year Engineering student, Brunel

- 'I'm living with my landlord and a horde of mice – they eat everything – the mice that is!'
  3rd year Mental Philosophy student, Edinburgh

Advice note

Landlords who don't give deposits back should be a thing of the past in England and Wales. A new tenancy scheme has been introduced. Check www.direct. gov.uk/en/TenancyDeposit/index.htm for full details before handing over your deposit and check that your landlord is adhering to the new law. Of course, if you trash the place, you can't expect to see your money back – it works both ways.

⦿ 'Heating non-existent! We all wear gloves and thick socks around the house and jumpers in bed. But the mice are quite content.'
   3rd year Creative Imaging student, Huddersfield

⦿ 'I'm living with thieves. My mail has been opened and "things" taken out.'
   2nd year Music Technology and Digital Media student, Huddersfield

But it's not all complaints:

⦿ 'Our landlord is very sweet; he bought us a huge packet of biscuits for Christmas.'
   2nd year Psychology student, Queen's University, Belfast

⦿ 'Our landlord is ace. When the security system started beeping at 1am, he came out to fix it.'
   2nd year Law student, Reading

Alice's story

Problem: my bedspring broke. Sleep was impossible. Exams were looming. I needed rest but my landlady was very slow to get things done. Strategy was called for. I invited the landlady over and got her to sit on the bed while we talked. I asked her if she was comfortable, and she had to agree she was not. I then asked her if she would like to sleep on the bed – every night. A new bed arrived within four days.

Should I take out insurance?

That's something only you can really decide.

A recent survey completed by Endsleigh shows that, on average, students now take £4,200-worth of belongings to university, and this is not going unnoticed by thieves. These possessions are often highly valuable and portable, for example laptops, iPods and mobiles. If you lost them, how would you replace them?

Insurance is another drain on your resources, but it could be money well spent and save a lot of heartache. Endsleigh receives some £350,000-worth of claims from students during their first month at uni, which is fairly substantial.

If you are living in halls you may find there is a comprehensive policy covering all students and this is included in your rent bill.

If you are living in rented accommodation, the landlord of the house or flat you rent should have the premises covered by insurance for fire and structural damage, but this is unlikely to cover your personal possessions. Students tend to keep open house, and because people are coming and going all the time security is often lax. If you do have a lot of expensive possessions it might be worthwhile considering taking out your own insurance, especially if you carry your expensive belongings about. Ask yourself: What would it cost me to replace my iPod, stereo, TV, DVD player, camera, gold watch, PC, course books, whatever? Compare that with an outlay of, say, £30 a year. Rates for personal insurance depend on where you live. It costs more if you live in a big city than a sleepy rural town. In a crime hot spot, rates can be prohibitive.

Everybody round here hires a TV so if it walks it's covered by the TV rental company. The same goes for washing machines and all other appliances.
1st year student, Liverpool University

We had a microwave and sofa cushions stolen! But mainly it's computers, TVs, stereos.
3rd year Genetics student, Birmingham

Are you covered by your parents' insurance?

If you are, that is obviously the cheapest form of cover, but don't assume that your possessions are covered by your parents' home insurance once you go to uni. Some standard home insurance polices specifically exclude students – I wonder why? Get your parents to check the small print.

You can also take out insurance to cover the fees you have paid, just in case you are ill – or worse – and can't complete your year.

NatWest offers a choice of packages to students: their basic 'budget' policy starts from £17. This covers your possessions against theft, burst pipes, fire, storm, vandalism and flood: while in your room; at your parents' home(s); in direct transit to and from home at vacations; and in locked storage on campus at any time. Items automatically included are cover for your landlord's property for fire and theft damage up to £5,000, college property on loan up to £250 and accidental death of parent or guardian up to £5,000. Cover can be extended to include desktop computers, accidental damage, vacation cover, legal expenses and rental protection. The NatWest comprehensive 'peace of mind' policy includes all these benefits and a lot more. For more details check out www.natwest.com/studentinsurance. The same insurance is also available from the Royal Bank of Scotland. See details on rbs.co.uk/studentinsurance.

Endsleigh, who specialise in helping students, offer student possessions insurance starting at £16 for £2,500-worth of cover for halls of residence, and £25 for £2,500-worth of cover off-campus in a 'good' area.

They also offer the option of special portable computer equipment cover for either Room Only or All Risks. Room Only (excluding accidental damage) starts at just £2 per £100 worth of cover rising to £7 per £100 of cover in dicey areas. All Risks cover starts at £6 per £100 worth of cover rising to £11 per £100 of cover in the worst areas (prices correct at November 2007).

Do you make music? Whether you play in an orchestra or drum for a rock band, or whether it's part of your course, for pleasure or to make extra money, if you lost that valuable guitar, violin, double bass or cello you'd be stuck. Insurance rates vary depending on whether you are in the UK or travelling in Europe, and what kind of instrument you have. Endsleigh offer flexible cover against theft and accidental damage for any musical instrument subject to a minimum premium of £20. The cost of cover in the UK starts at £1 per £100 for orchestral instruments (such as violins or double basses) and cover is also available for non-orchestral instruments. There is a choice of where cover can operate: UK only; UK and up to 30 days in the EU; and anywhere in the world. Shop around to get the best cover before making a decision.

Where to live?

Halls, rented accommodation with friends, at home? We asked some students what they thought.

Living in halls – Stephen's story

Stephen is a second year History student at Christ's College, Cambridge. He chose to do a second year living in halls because: 'It's easier and cheaper too. All the food is prepared for you and everything is provided.

'You pay a fixed rent for the room, and then have a card to pay for your food and bar costs. You decide how much you want to load onto your card. If it isn't enough, you then pay it off the next term. In my first term I put £250 on my card. Since then it has been £300 a term. My rent this year is £700 a term.

'In my first year I had a bedroom and a sitting room all to myself with a shared bathroom down the passageway. It was fantastic especially when my younger brother and his friends came to stay, and excellent if you wanted to study. However, I discovered when I went knocking on my neighbours' doors, most of the students in my block were third years and didn't really want to know a fresher. But I soon found my way to the freshers' block which was only minutes away.'

So, Stephen was in fact spared the noisy corridors at night, the great blasts of pulsating music, and friends calling at all hours of the day and night which is often the pattern of first year student life.

Most of Stephen's social life centres on the college. 'You just meet up with friends in the college bar. There is always someone there you know.' Asked if they had parties, he explained: 'There is an old nineteenth century rule that says no more than five people should gather together in one room, but some rules are there to be broken, so, yes, we do chill out together.'

This year Stephen's accommodation is not quite so spacious. In fact it is more like a cell with a desk, bed and wardrobe. It is en-suite, which sounds great, until you start negotiating to get into the bathroom. 'The room is so small if you are not careful you can get trapped in a corner when you open the door. Because of the room size I tend to work in the library which actually means fewer distractions, I get more work done and I am doing better academically this year, which has to be good.'

See also 1st year Cambridge student Nadia's budget on page 31.

Sharing a flat – Matt's story

Matt is a second year Forensic Science student at Nottingham Trent.

'You could say there are eight of us living in this flat – 3 boys, 4 girls and a ghost. The building is a converted telephone exchange, and it has a chequered history. Extraordinary things went on there – including a suicide. I can't say I have actually seen an apparition, but I've certainly heard a lot of creaks, bangs and strange laughter.'

The telephone exchange has been expensively modernised into a block of eight large flats. Matt's flat has a kitchen with a large dining area plus a TV and seven large bedrooms with en-suite bathrooms.

There are no bills to worry about: all the utilities are included in the rent which, at £84.99 each a week, isn't exorbitant for Nottingham. Unlike most places, the contract is for 48 weeks. Sounds perfect!

But this isn't a happy household. 'Things go missing,' says Matt – 'champagne, wine, saucepans, sauces from the fridge – and it isn't the ghost. What really bugged me, it was my champagne.

'There is no togetherness. We each cater for ourselves, which is an expensive way to live. My food bill alone is £25 a week. If only people could be bothered to put their dirty dishes in the dishwasher or put out the rubbish now and again, it would help.'

Matt's advice: 'Get the whole sharing thing sorted before you move in and don't air your grievances on Facebook: it just makes things worse.'

In contrast, Emma's experience couldn't be more successful.

Sharing a house – Emma's story

Emma is a second year student at Durham University studying Modern Languages.

'There are five of us living in the house – three girls and two boys. We all met in halls last year so we're already good friends. We have three bedrooms upstairs for the girls, plus a bathroom and two bedrooms and a shower downstairs for the boys. There is also a large kitchen/living-room.

'One of the girls has a boyfriend so she generally eats with him; the rest of us cater together – which is the cheapest way. We girls make a list and go out and do the weekly shop which is then delivered. Cost £10 – £15 a week each. On top of that we have THE KITCHEN MUG, a kind of kitty into which we all put £5 every two weeks to buy general stuff for the house.

'I am not sure how it works, but it does. It is not arranged; there is no cooks' rota; it just happens. One person will cook and we all eat. Once I cooked for everyone for a week, and then did nothing for weeks.

'I can't say I'm a good cook, but when you are hungry (and we always are), people will eat anything. We eat a lot of pasta, rice and frozen vegetables. Sausage and mash is a great favourite. Not a madly healthy diet, but it's cheap. One memorable occasion I cooked a roast dinner.

'All utility bills are divided by five and we have a special utilities bank account into which we pay the money. Getting the housework done is more of a struggle to organise. But we are all good friends so eventually it happens.

'The great joy of this house is that you have your own space. But you are never lonely. Go down into the kitchen and there is always someone there. Maybe it's the atmosphere here, maybe it's because we have the space, but people are always dropping in. We don't arrange parties – we don't have to. It happens. My bill for socialising has crashed from around £500 in my first term last year when I lived in halls, to a mere £170, and I am still having a great time.'

Thrift tips

'Book travel in advance. I travelled from Durham to London for £10.'

2nd year Modern History student, Durham

'Work as a TV extra or catalogue model.'

3rd year Psychology student, Wolverhampton

'Sell your work.'

3rd year Visual Studies student, Norwich School of Art and Design

'Use your hobby – I photographed a family on holiday and pocketed €100.'

Wolverhampton student

Drinking tips

'Make your own beer – it's fun, cheap and tasty.'

3rd year Digital Media student, Wolverhampton

'Organise parties at home and get others to bring the drink.'

2nd year Journalism, Film and Media student, Cardiff

'Drink cider rather than beer – it's cheaper and takes less to get you drunk.'

4th year Biochemistry student, Oxford

'Become teetotal. Impossible? Try the next tip.'

3rd year Design student, Wolverhampton

'Learn to drink slowly.'

3rd year English student, Wolverhampton

Living at home – Christopher's story

Christopher studied Business Administration at the University of the West of England, Bristol.

'Money – that is why I decided to go to the nearest university and live at home. My parents didn't charge me rent. I ate with the family most of the time (I have two younger brothers) and I guess it is much easier: not so much to worry about, things like internet connection, doing the washing, running out of food. It worked because my parents are pretty free and easy. They just let me get on with it and do my own thing.

'Of course there were drawbacks – mainly in my social life. Many people make their friends at uni, not so much on their course, but from living in halls. I found it difficult making friends and entering into the life of the university. I lived about 25 miles away and only drove in when I had lectures. I took a gap year before uni so I found I was older than many of the students in my year. The first year for many students is their first time away from home and they go wild. I had done all that.

'My biggest expense was petrol – £30 a week – and insurance on my car. I took out a student loan – around £3,000 a year – and had a job in a sausage shop during the holidays – in a busy week I could earn around £264. I drew £50 a week spending money from the bank during term time and found I was never short of cash. What's more I had no debts.

'Would I advise students to live at home? Probably not. I felt I missed out on student life, but if you want an easy, trouble-free, debt-free existence, there is a lot to be said for it. It's a matter of personal choice. I don't regret my decision.'

More and more students are choosing universities where they can continue to live at home because it is cheaper. In fact 69% of students responding to our 2007 survey said they knew of someone who had decided to study in their own home town for financial reasons. As you will see in the next chapter, the amount of loan you can borrow if you live at home is smaller, but then that means less debt. For some students, this idea would be unthinkable. Going to university is all about gaining independence. But if that results in you having to abandon your course because of debt then you could be back where you started – at home! It's worth thinking about.

Do I have to pay Council Tax?

Students are largely exempt from paying Council Tax. Certainly, if you live in a hall of residence, college accommodation, student house or somewhere in which all the residents are students, you will be exempt. If you live in a house where there are already two adults, your presence does not add to the bill. If you live in a house with one adult, that person will not lose their 25% single occupancy discount, providing they can supply proof that you are a student.

However, things are never quite that simple, as Paul Hubert, the welfare officer at Leeds Metropolitan University, pointed out to us. 'Frequently,' he said, 'students in external accommodation do not spot the problems coming and these can prove intractable.' Some examples:

- A full-time student moves into a house shared with non-students, and housemates expect them to contribute to the Council Tax bill.

- The flatmate who drops out of their course during the summer and fails to claim benefit.
- The part-time student who thought they would be exempt.
- The student/postgrad who is writing up work and is refused student status by local authorities.

If in doubt, go to your university welfare officer – they are usually on the ball.

Other living expenses

While your accommodation will probably take at least half of your available resources, how are you going to spend the rest?

Food

Average: £21.60 eating in, £16.30 eating out per week.

Once you have a roof over your head, the next major expense is food, and here the RBS Student Living Index Survey showed that costs were fairly similar throughout the country, with an average weekly food bill of £37.90. However, when we started to look at individual areas within the UK the picture changed. The hungriest students, with an average weekly spend of £45.80 for eating in and out were in London followed very closely with an average weekly spend of £44.06 in Glasgow. For frugal living go to York where students' average spend is £29.42 (£17.60 in the supermarket and another £11.80 on food out).

⭐ **Social spenders**

	Weekly spend
Belfast	£56.70
Leeds	£50.40
Brighton	£49
Nottingham	£46.40
Southampton	£46.20
Oxford	£45.80
Manchester	£45.30
Cardiff	£44.60
Bath	£43.90
Liverpool	£43.50

Source: RBS Student Living Index Survey 2007

Thrift tips

... for hungry students:

'Give dinner parties and charge.'

2nd year Industrial Relations and Modern History student, St Andrews

'Make your own sandwiches for lunch and sell them to friends.'

1st year Medicine student, Cambridge

'Get to like pasta!'

4th year Psychology student, Paisley

'If each of your friends brings a potato, carrot, leek you've got a great stew for next to nothing.'

1st year Music, Huddersfield

Socialising/entertainment

Going out – average: £15.80 per week

Alcohol – average £27.10 per week

The RBS Student Living Index Survey didn't assess how good a 'good time' students were having, or how often they went out, but on average students spend £42.90 per week on clubbing, pubbing, gigs, cinema and drinking. The biggest spenders, with bills of around £56.70 per week were to be found in Belfast, followed by Leeds with a weekly bill of £50.40 and Brighton with an average weekly spend of £49. However, if you just look at the alcohol consumption then top of the list is still Belfast with an average weekly spend of £35.20, followed by Southampton – average spend £32.30 and then Cardiff filling up to the tune of £31.30 a week.

The most abstemious students can be found at Sheffield with an average weekly alcohol bill of £19.50 while the stay-at-homes are to be found in Canterbury with an average weekly spend of only £11.40 a week on going out. But they don't hold back on the alcohol, spending on average £24.50 a week.

Drink – what will it cost?

Students told us in the *Students' Money Matters* Survey 2007 that the average price of the cheapest alcoholic drink was £1.47 and the cheapest non-alcoholic drink was 54p. But when it came to students' favourite drinks the average rose to £2.02.

★ Most popular drinks	
Region	*Drink*
Oxbridge	G&T, Coke, Archer's and lemonade, Guinness
London	G&T, red wine, cocktails
Southern England	cider
Midlands and Wales	snakebite
East Anglia	snakebite, beer, vodka and lemonade, wine
Northern England	vodka and lemonade
Scotland/Northern Ireland	wine

Cash crisis note

2007 A level/Highers students were a little out of kilter in estimating their potential alcohol spend, putting it at £17.31 a week when in reality it was more likely to be £15.40 a week, according to the NatWest Students Money Matters Survey. However, the RBS Student Living Index put the figure at £27.10 a week.

Books and course materials

Average: £9.30 a week.

All students said they spent more on books in the autumn term and in their first year than at any other time. Some reported that they'd then taken to using libraries instead of buying, as books were so expensive. It is difficult to give an average figure for books, because what you need to buy depends on your course and how well stocked your college library is in your subject. It's worth checking this out before starting your course if you can. As a very general guide, the average figure was £9.30 a week (RBS Student Living Index).

Book check

Your university or college may have a second-hand bookshop. Find out before you start purchasing: books are very expensive. Check out your college library. Is it well stocked in books on your subject? Is it close to where you study and where you live? Try looking at www.uni-trader.co.uk, a website started up by a student at Durham University, which works a little like the student noticeboard. Students with things to sell – especially textbooks – put them on the site. Initially launched in Durham in 2004, then expanded nationwide, each university has its own designated area so you can start by trying to buy – or sell – locally. As well as textbooks we found other useful stuff for sale: electric guitars, a swivel chair, toaster, mini fridge, dissection kit, juggling balls, a vintage 'head-bopping' car dog (a must for all university students) for just £3, and a Ford Escort a snip, or possibly a liability, for just £399.

I'm currently on the most expensive course – 3D Design. The financial strain of coping with the cost of materials is hindering my design capabilities and interfering with my studies; the annual cost of course equipment is £200.

Photocopying, library costs and fines etc.

Average: £4 per week.

Many universities provide a photocopying card which eases the cost. For those on courses where study covers topics in a wide range of books the cost can be considerable. On average £4 a week was spent on photocopying and library costs.

Field trips

Up to £800.

Geography, Biology, Zoology, Law, Fine Art, Graphic Design, Sculpture, IT, English, Textile Design, Drama, Psychology, Urban Studies and Planning – on all these courses field trips may be a compulsory component and could cost anything from £20 to £800. Actual cost depends on the course you are taking so an average would be meaningless.

Geology is becoming very expensive. I have two compulsory field trips a year costing £150 each.
3rd year student, Durham

Mobile phones

Average: £12.90 per week.

Most students today have a mobile. New deals have brought mobile phone bills down, but phone costs are still averaging £12.90 a week. More and more students are relying on their mobiles rather than paying for a landline. Highest spenders according to the RBS Student Living Index were students at Canterbury where bills averaged £15.50 a week.

Best-dressed regions	
Region	Average spend per week
London	£26.90
Midlands	£20.96
Wales & South West	£18.85
Scotland & Northern Ireland	£18.27
Oxbridge	£17.33
	RBS Student Living Index

Best-dressed universities (of 27 looked at)	
University	Average spend per week
London	£26.90
Leeds	£26.50
Leicester	£26.20
Dundee	£22.20
Belfast	£21.60
Cardiff	£21.50
	RBS Student Living Index

Clothing

Average: £18.50 a week.

On average students spend £18.50 a week on clothes, which is an increase on last year. The best dressed universities of the 27 the RBS Student Living Index Survey looked at were London who spend an average of £26.90 a week followed closely by Leeds at £26.50. The university least bothered sartorially was Lancaster with a weekly bill of £11.10.

Want to cut the cost of your phone bill?

Certain 08 numbers (0844, 0845, 0870 and 0871, for example) masquerade as being the same as local calls when in fact they may not be as cheap as you think, and may not be covered by the 'cost-saving' phone deal you have in place. Certainly many mobile phone packages are excluded from freephone numbers such as 0800 and 0808, so you pay the going rate for calling these numbers. To find the cheapest way to phone an 08 number log on to saynotoo870.com. They might give you an alternative local number, or show how your call can be routed in a different way.

Internet

An expense for many students is the internet. Figures last year varied enormously – from £5 to £75 a term so a meaningful average was difficult to give especially since so many students said they didn't know what they spent, or it was provided by their university. Those in halls of residence often find broadband is included in their rent. A broadband connection can mean a monthly bill of around £20 but in most houses this would be shared. Look for the special offers, and if you are hoping to hop from one special offer to another make sure there are no tie-in clauses in the contract.

So – where is the cheapest place to study?

Our research this year suggests that students in the North of England are high in the league for money management followed by those in Wales and the South West. The most expensive place to study is, of course, London.

Travel during term time

Average: £10.70 per week

To survive, it seems you need to be fit. Students said that walking was their main way of getting about. For many, however, travel was a significant cost, with students in London experiencing the most severe problems in terms of expense (average £15.60 a week) and time taken to get to lectures. At the other end of the scale Edinburgh students seemed to have the lowest weekly bills at £5.30. Our average figure of £10.70 includes taxis. Students studying Medicine and based in London can be the hardest hit, as training often involves attachments to other hospitals, which may be as far as 40 miles away (check with your local authority to see if you are entitled to financial help with transport). Scottish students can claim extra for travel as a grant if costs exceed £155 a year.

About a fifth of students are thought to own a car or motorcycle. This estimate includes many mature students, who tend to drive longer distances during term. Our research showed last year the average cost of petrol per week during term time was £12. Cycling seems to be much less popular than it was a few years ago. Students complained that cycling was dangerous, and another gripe was having their bicycles stolen – even being mugged for a mountain bike. Students cited pollution and traffic congestion as problems.

Travel check

◉ The frequency of university and local bus services. A huge number of students complained of the infrequency and unreliability of bus services and the fact that they didn't run at night.

'... and when the buses do come they are often so full they don't stop. It's quite common to be late for lectures.'
2nd year International Tourism and Management student, Robert Gordon University

◉ The last bus. A number of students complained that in many cities bus services finish early, with no regular service after 10.30pm – a major problem for sociable students in outlying districts. Check on this when choosing accommodation; you don't want to find ...

'The last bus was at 7pm. Even a modest social life was impossible.'
Law student, Bristol

◉ What the area is like at night. An increasing number of both male and female students in many more universities said it was dangerous to walk alone at night: these included students from Huddersfield, Staffordshire, London, and many more. Many also said taxis were expensive.

'Taxis can cost £4 for a three-minute journey after midnight.'
3rd year English student, St Andrews

'You need a car in Bradford; walking even in the early evening is dangerous. Somebody just up my road had a gun pulled on them. Fortunately most students don't have much money.'
2nd year Technology and Management student, Bradford

But there were more positive comments:

'Taxis are in good supply in Bangor and a journey across town is cheap.'
2nd year Psychology student, Bangor

How much will it cost to get to your college from your family home and back again during the year? Average: £12.90 per week spent on longer trips.

If you live in Exeter and decide to study in Glasgow, getting there is going to be a major expense and you won't be popping home very often. But if home is Birmingham and you study somewhere close at hand, like Manchester, it's relatively cheap and you might go home weekly, so an average isn't really meaningful especially as there are some fantastic coach and rail bargains if you book early. In addition, on some courses you will have to go out on field trips. To give you an idea of costs the RBS Student Living Index came up with an average figure of £12.90 per week.

Student budgets around the country

The budgets below are based on research carried out in August 2007 for the Royal Bank of Scotland Student Living Index.

For students living in university accommodation, utilities (gas/electricity/water) are generally included.

Plan your trips home and book early – there are some fantastic bargains. Coaches are generally cheaper than trains, but they take longer and the amount of luggage you can take with you is usually limited. The most popular means of transport for students is the train. However, many students said their parents might give them a lift at the beginning and end of the year when they have a lot of luggage. If you do have to stagger home with your luggage using public transport, remember your costs may have to include taxi fares.

Student budgets around the country

per term (average)	London	Southern England	Wales & South West	Midlands	Oxbridge (Oxford & Cambridge)	North	Scotland & Northern Ireland
Rent	£102	£73	£70	£67	£83	£68	£75
Alcohol	£22.70	£28.47	£28.60	£27.21	£25.35	£26.84	£27.04
Supermarket food shopping	£24.50	£21.54	£23.45	£20.71	£21.61	£20.12	£22.61
Buying clothes	£26.90	£17.20	£18.85	£20.96	£17.33	£17.01	£18.27
Eating out (inc café, restaurant, canteen food etc)	£21.30	£16.78	£13.88	£18.38	£19.64	£14.16	£16.82
Going out (cinema, clubs, gigs)	£19	£15.25	£14.56	£17.22	£15.32	£15.30	£16.03
Utility bills	£16.70	£13.55	£14.15	£16.96	£14.57	£14.31	£17.51
Cigarettes	£15.20	£15.72	£12.86	£16.58	£15.26	£14.66	£14.47
Transport costs for longer trips	£14.50	£12.73	£13.41	£14.05	£10.79	£10.47	£16.15
Telephone/mobile phone bill	£13.10	£13.36	£10.03	£12.42	£9.77	£10.09	£11.04
Day-to-day travel (inc taxis)	£15.60	£11.08	£10.58	£12.29	£9.10	£9.38	£10.70
Buying CDs, DVDs and videos	£12.10	£9.68	£9.74	£10.68	£8.25	£9.83	£9.85
Books and course materials	£12	£8.81	£8.68	£12.46	£9.32	£8.18	£9.10
Laundry/dry cleaning	£7.10	£4.10	£3.93	£5.40	£4.02	£4.04	£4.74
Photocopying/library costs, fines etc.	£6	£4.47	£3.28	£4.40	£3.72	£3.79	£4.14
Total	£328.7	£265.74	£256.00	£276.72	£267.05	£246.18	£273.47

Thrift tips

Don't shop on an empty stomach – it's disastrous.

Shop just before closing and get the bargains.

Watch out for special coach-company offers.

Check that water rates are included in your rent.

Look for special student nights at clubs, theatres, cinemas.

Students' union shops buy in bulk so can give good discounts. Beer, stationery, dry cleaning, even holidays, could be part of their cost-cutting service.

Student rail and coach cards

Both train and coach services offer student reductions, provided you buy their special student cards. These last for a year. One longish journey will more than cover the initial outlay, which is:

Railcard: £24 pa (January 2008)

Reduction: one-third off all rail fares.

Travel restrictions: check with station for full details.

Young Person's Coachcard: £10 pa or £25 for three years if booked on web (January 2007)

Reduction: up to 30%.

Travel restrictions: some journeys cost slightly more at certain times.

Advice note – Travel

- Restrictions on cards can change, so always check what is being offered and when you can travel.
- Look for special reductions: occasionally the rail or coach companies will have special promotions such as half-price student cards, or half-price fares. They may also give discounts on things like CDs or subscriptions to magazines. Check out www.gobycoach.com.

See the table below for some comparative travel costs from London, based on return fare prices in January 2008. Prices quoted include Young Person's Railcard or Coachcard discount.

Typical fares	Train		Coach
	Saver Return	Advanced Purchase Return	Mostly Off Peak booked in advance. £1 booking fee charged
London to:			
Edinburgh	£67.60	From £31.40	£31.50
Newcastle	£65.55	From £25.80	£34.50 (£22.50*)
Manchester	£41.20	From £17.20	£27 (£22.50*)
Nottingham	£33	From £11.90	£18.50
Birmingham	£18.80 depending on route	From £11.90	£17.20
Cardiff	£37.60	From £15.20	£23.50
Bristol	£32.35	From £13.20	£20 (£19.60*)
Exeter	£38.95	From £15.80	£30 (£23*)
*If booked seven days in advance			

Many tickets have special conditions, and advance booking conditions vary. With some rail tickets it is cheaper to buy singles. Train companies operating on the same route have different fares. Check with Rail Information on 0845 748 4950 and ask for a full list of options for the journey you are making. See also www.moneysavingexpert.com, and don't get taken for a ride.

Coach prices: travel on Friday is generally more expensive; reduction if booked in advance.

Can I afford to run a car?

If your only income is the standard funding for students, most rational people would say no. But since so many students do seem to have cars they must be managing it somehow. A recent survey by Reaction UK claimed nearly half of all students own or use a car. Travel from your home to your university will probably be cheaper by car, but you may also find yourself coming home many more times in a term, acting as chauffeur to the party, and taking trips at weekends. And don't underestimate the maintenance bills: they can be astronomical, especially on an old car. Then there's the road tax, currently £115 pa (£63.25 half-yearly) for cars under 1549cc and £180 pa (£99 half-yearly) for the rest. If you are lucky enough to have a car manufactured since March 2001 then you'll be charged according to its CO_2 emission. There are seven different bands and costs range from zero for cars with very low CO_2 emissions to £300 a year (£165 half-yearly) for the mighty 4x4 gas-guzzler. Add to that your MOT and AA/RAC membership, which makes sense if your car has a tendency to break down, and your biggest outlay of all – insurance, which for third party, fire and theft (the cover favoured by most young people), is said to be averaging close to £1,000. According to our research the average spend by students on petrol last year was £169 a term.

How much to insure my wheels?

Two wheels or four, it's not going to be cheap or easy.

Four wheels

Students lucky enough to have a car may find they don't have much luck getting insurance, especially if they are first-time drivers and aged under 21. Try Endsleigh Insurance: in 1997 the NUS, worried that many students who ran cars couldn't afford the cost of insurance cover, asked Endsleigh (an insurance company that they part own) to try to find a way to reduce motor insurance premiums for students – which they did, by up to 30%.

A word of caution: think twice about 'fronting'; that's the old trick of mum taking out the insurance and naming the student as second driver. If there's a claim and it's discovered that the student is really the main driver, you could find the insurance company won't pay up.

Insurance costs vary, depending not just on who you are, but on where you live. Big-city drivers pay a higher premium than, say, those in the country. In London the costs are prohibitive. Endsleigh warns: 'Insurance premiums are based on the address where the car resides for the majority of the year. Therefore, if you are living away from home while studying, you must provide the address where you live for the majority of the year.' So even if it would be cheaper to take out insurance from, say, your parents' home address, think before you do it. Giving false information could lead to claims not being paid.

Two wheels

You might think a bicycle was much easier to insure. But any student intending to take a bicycle to university must think in terms of having it pinched, or at least borrowed without permission. Insurance companies certainly do.

Insurance advice: a good padlock and detachable wheel or saddle should be your first form of insurance. Consider exchanging that expensive mountain bike for something that looks as if it's come off the tip.

Who to try: Endsleigh offers bicycle cover for bikes and fixed accessories up to £1,500 against accidental damage and theft anywhere in the UK and up to 30 days' cover in Europe. Premiums are dependent on the value of your bike and where in the country you live, ranging from £27 for bikes worth up to £149 in a fairly theft-free area, up to £185 for a £1,500 bike in a higher-risk area.

Also try the banks – some offer fairly good deals.

Approximately half of all UK-registered bikes are scooters (about 0.5 million) and they have enjoyed a recent upturn in popularity because of TV stars such as Jamie Oliver. They are often regarded as a cheaper alternative to cars, but remember – they are easily stolen. Some insurers exclude theft cover unless the bike is garaged at night. Immobilisers don't always stop thieves either, as a bike/scooter can be bundled into even a small car.

Endsleigh provides insurance for scooters and small motorbikes. A lot of their enquiries in this area come from students with bikes under 250cc. They offer Comprehensive; Third Party, Fire and Theft; and Third Party cover only.

Green facts

Going green has never been more popular among Britain's students:

- ⊙ 35% reject non-green employers
- ⊙ 67% recycle waste at home
- ⊙ 69% choose to walk or cycle over short journeys
- ⊙ 48% say they try to buy with an environmental conscience
- ⊙ 38% use energy-saving devices such as wind-up radios and low-voltage light bulbs.

Survey by Fujitsu Siemens Computers

So how do so many students manage?

For many students, money is not just a problem – it's the major problem. Even students not in debt and apparently managing fairly well see finance as their biggest worry. But coping on a limited budget is also a test of independence and ingenuity. Here are some money-saving ideas from current students.

' Rent out any extra room space. '
1st year Contemporary Photographic Practice student, Northumbria

' Visit car boot sales to sell, buy and sell again. '
4th year Environmental Science student, Stirling

' Offer to walk the neighbours' dogs for a couple of quid an hour. '
1st year American Studies and Computing student, Wolverhampton

Never be afraid to ask if there is a discount for students. I found my NUS card reduced my swimming sessions from £1.95 to 75p.
Computer student, London University

A lot of websites pay you to fill out questionnaires to receive text message advertising – you can also sign up for offers on sites such as www.britishfreebies.com and find yourself with enough free samples of shampoo for the year.
Sheffield Hallam University student

Try www.moneysavingexpert.com for all kinds of savings. '
3rd year Media and Print Journalism student, Huddersfield

Teach piano.
English student, Oxford

Coach A level and GCSE students.
3rd year Medicine student, Oxford

Facts and figures

- ⊙ Students spend over half of their money on accommodation.
- ⊙ Students taking up university places in autumn 2007 were up by 4.8% on the previous year to 411,971 (UCAS figures).
- ⊙ 22% of full-time students at UK universities fail to obtain a degree (Staying the course, House of Commons Committee on Public Accounts Report 2007–08).
- ⊙ Drop-out rates in some universities reached 35%, but in others, such as Oxford, the figure was 1.4% (HESA figures for 2006/7).
- ⊙ The NUS believes a major cause of drop-outs is financial hardship (NUS Student Hardship Survey). Other reasons include exam failure, ill health and switching courses.
- ⊙ Even at 22% Britain has one of the lowest university drop-out rates for degrees on the global completion table. Japan tops the list with a drop-out rate of just 8%. Ireland is a good second with just 16%. In Germany it's 27% and in America 46%.

How much will you need to survive as a student?

£6,000? £7,000? £8,000? £9,000? £10,000 pa?

The NUS estimated that for the last academic year (2007–2008) students would need £15,214 if living in London and £13,135 in other parts of the country for the 39-week academic year, including fees at £3,070. You'd be lucky if you had that. In fact, based on what you are likely to receive in funding, the NUS suggested a shortfall in funds of £7,408 for students in London and £6,683 for students elsewhere. And that was last year. So in reality you're going to have to survive on what you can get and what you can earn. How much is that likely to be? Read on!

Cash crisis note

A level students thinking of giving university a miss because of debt should remember that, on average, graduates can expect to earn 20–25% more than A level students, which is £160,000 over a lifetime – and much more if you are taking medicine – a cool £340,315 (Universities UK report 2007). However, government research put the figure much higher, at around 45%.

Typical student budgets

Four students show how their money goes, and where it comes from.

Emma, a 2nd year Modern Languages student at Durham

Emma shares a house with four other students – two girls and two boys. There are five bedrooms – three upstairs which the girls have and two downstairs for the boys. There is one bathroom upstairs and a shower room downstairs. They have a large living-room/kitchen. See Emma's story 'sharing a house' on p. 13.

Outgoings	Per Term	Comments
Rent	£1,161	£67 a week × 52. They have a 52 week contract. Paid by parents. TV and broadband inc.
Utilities	£	We are still waiting for the bills
Fees	£1,023	£3,070 a year
Food in	£150	£15 a week – we eat and shop together: it's cheaper – sausage and mash is a great favourite
Kitty	£25	£5 ever two weeks
Socialising	£170	Go out once a week – drinks in college bar. Mostly people drop in at house
Music/ent.	£20	2 DVDs special offer at Tesco
Phone	£75	£25 a month
Debating Society	£50	Life time membership – hope to become a lawyer
Gym Membership	£10	Free at uni, membership at home
Holiday	£485	Skiing in French Alps
Return fare home	£70	To Wales
Books/newspapers – foreign & UK	£200	That covers the whole year
Insurance	£92	
Clothes	£75	
Toiletries	£30	
College ball	£35	Ticket + champagne £25, extra drinks £10
Total	£3,671	

Income	Per Year	Comments
Fee loan	£1,023	£3,070 over the year
Student loan	£1,100	£3,400 over the full year
Parents	£1,161	They pay for my rent
Overdraft	£500	£1,250 available for whole year
Job (term)	£200	Works in college toastie bar 4 hrs per week for £5 ph, £20 a week
Jobs (Vac)	£500	Supermarket over Christmas £5.25 ph
Christmas gifts	£400	
Total	£4,885	

Emma says: 'I was shocked to discover I had an overdraft of £300 at the end of my first term at uni and worked in a local supermarket during the Christmas holiday to pay it off.' This year she says she is keeping better track of her finances. 'I bank online so I can see how and where the money goes. However, by Christmas this year my overdraft was £500. Again I worked over the Christmas to pay it off. Because I live in a house, people are always coming round so I have cut back greatly on socialising.' Despite this, Emma expects her debt to be around £24,000 by the time she graduates.

Matt, a 2nd year Forensic Science student at Nottingham Trent

It was the murder of a local girl in his home town of Croydon that made Matt decide on this subject. 'Forensics played an important part in solving the case.'

Matt lives in a large flat with six other students – four girls and three boys including himself and a ghost (see Matt's story 'Sharing a flat' on page 13). The building is a converted telephone exchange with an interesting history. He has a large en-suite bedroom and shares a large kitchen, which includes an eating area and TV, with his flatmates. The chart overleaf shows how his money goes.

Outgoings	Per Week	Per Year	Comments
Rent	£84.99	£4,079.52	Contract 48 weeks. All utilities are included. Not exorbitant for Nottingham
Mobile	£10	£520	Covers whole year
Internet connection		£25	
Food in	£25	£900	I cater for myself. More expensive than sharing, but I eat better – meat, pasta, veg, fruit – a great impovement on last year's tinned spaghetti and chicken dippers
Food out	£10	£360	
Laundry	£2	£72	Wash and dry £2 on premises
Toiletries	£2.50	£105	
Socialising, entertainment & music	£70	£2,556	Biggest expense. Night out can cost £100+. Mostly goes on drink, pubs and clubs. Go out 2–3 nights a week. Covers socialising in term-time only
Gym membership		£95	Covers whole year
Travel (in town)		£220	Annual travel card. Go anywhere in Nottingham
Travel (home)		£54	£18 return on coach to Croydon, Surrey
Course Equipment		£5	Goggles. Books no cost – mostly from library
Vices: Cigarettes	£8	£416	I have cut back cost as friend brought back a good supply from abroad. Cost covers 52 week year
Clothes		£300	
Gifts		£30	Mostly over Christmas
Holidays	£0	£0	Can't afford them
Fees		£3,070	
Interest on overdraft	£?	£?	Not certain. Have gone over my free interest limit by £40
Total		**£12,807.52**	

Income	Per Year	Comments
Fees	£3,070	
Loan	£4,500	Student loan
Parents	£1,300	They are not expected to contribute, but they do
Grant	£600	From Government
Bursary	£400	From university: £200 in second and then third term
Jobs	£750	So far from working in bar. Job finished. Expect to get another job for rest of year. Anticipated earnings £2,250. Also occasional work as demonstrator in stores showing cameras
Overdraft	£1,290	£1,250 interest free from bank but have had to extend this
Total	£11,910	

Matt says: 'My advice to all new students is to watch the first two weeks. Freshers' week is the killer; many students spend over a grand. By the end of my first term here I was down to having just £7 a week for food. I have done better this year.' If Matt gets another job and reaches his anticipated earnings of over £2,000 he will make ends meet. He expects his final debt when he graduates to be over £20,000.

Your first term

The first term at university is expensive – and it can be the undoing of some students, condemning them to three years of anxiety and debt. Stories abound of students spending £3,000 just on socialising, though funnily enough you never seem to meet anyone who has actually done the spending. But overspending there certainly is, especially during Freshers' week, and once you get badly into debt it's very difficult to get out of it.

Nadia, a 1st year student at New Hall, Cambridge

Nadia is 18 and studying Social and Political Sciences. She lives in halls and has rooms arranged on two floors, a bedroom with two beds upstairs and a sitting-room/dining-room plus kitchen downstairs. 'Bourgeoisie was the reaction of my friends when they first saw it. But it's great for entertaining.' Nadia had asked for the cheapest accommodation possible, but because she has no family to support her and will have to stay in college during the vacations, New Hall gave her a top-grade apartment but at the lower price.

The figures given here are for a nine week term. Life at uni is more expensive for Nadia as she has to exist during the vacation as well.

Outgoings	Per term	Comments
Rent	£1,315.20 Inc. hall charges	The actual rent for my accommodation is £886 per term but I expect to receive a refund of around £200 because I had asked for the cheapest accommodation available.
Mobile phone	£90	£10 a week – nine weeks £90. But remember you pay for this in the vacation as well.
Food in	£350	At Cambridge you have a card to pay for food and drink. I loaded mine with £110 which wasn't actually enough, so I will probably have to pay extra next term. Food cooked in my room cost me a great deal more. I eat a lot in the college restaurant and have attended Forms (formal three course meal) in the dinning room 3 times this term. £8 for a three course meal. Two course meals in the canteen cost around £3.
Food out	£55	Occasionally we go to a restaurant, but not often.
Laundry	£32.40	£2.60 for the washer; £1 for the tumble dryer – once a week.
Toiletries	£25	
Entertainment Socialising	£35 £60	A great deal of the entertainment in uni is free. Friends often bring round bottles of wine and we watch a DVD while quietly drunk. It's cheap and again free. I've been clubbing 5–6 times this term.
Club membership	£85	Life time membership to the Cambridge Union – the centre of my social life. It's not all heavy political debates. I can recommend the Ben & Jerry Ice Cream 'orgy'.
Travel	£120	Second-hand bike currently on the missing list.
Vices	£20	I'm a nutaholic – brazil, walnuts, almonds, sunflower seeds, hemp.
Books	£15	2 books from Amazon. Cambridge is awash with libraries (books, newspapers, political magazines to read for free), essential when on a tight budget.
Laptop	£550	
Clothes	£200	Had absolutely nothing suitable for formal dinners – well that's my story. Spring ball coming up – seen perfect dress – £95.
Walking boots	£20	Free tickets for 4-day break to Inverness.
Gifts	£120	Well it is Christmas!
Fees	£1,023 app	I am paying £3,070 a year.
Total	£4,111.60	

Nadia says: 'I should have kept a budget right from the start, but by the time I realised this, it was too late, and anyway I am not that kind of money watching person. When choosing something, always go for the cheapest: look for the bargains and the freebies, and always ask yourself "do I really need this"? Fact is, you probably don't. You have to be resourceful. You are under pressure, there are targets to be met, and work to do but it's well worth it. You meet so many people from all walks of life and some people here have done so much.'

Income	Per term	Comments
Fees	£1,023	£3,070 pa – Fee loan.
Loan	£1,082	Full maintenance loan.
Grant	£922	I think I am entitled to the full grant.
Bursary	next term	I receive a grant from my college of £3,000 pa paid out in two tranches (£1,500) in the spring and summer terms.
Access to learning grant	(£200)	I expect to receive a £200 rebate on my rent each term as an independent student facing hardship.
Overdraft	£200	I have a free overdraft facility from the bank of £1,200 but by the end of term I had used only £200 of this.
Savings	£0	I worked during the summer in the college restaurant – £6.45 per hour, but I needed every penny to live.
Helena Kennedy bursary	£500	Fund set up to help deserving students with financial difficulties. Each year I will receive £1,000. Teacher at my school put me on to this.
Total	£3,727 (4,927)	If you include a third of her university bursary (£1,000) and her access to learning grant (£200) for rent.

Alex is 19 and has just completed his first term at Loughborough University

He is studying Information Management and Business Studies, a subject he chose because it leaves so many career options open to him. He lives in halls with full catering – that's three meals a day, five days a week. Alex says: 'I chose full catering because you meet so many different people in the canteen, and make so many friends, which is what you need when you first arrive. Some people complain about the food, and yes it is a bit repetitive, but I find it okay.

'Loughborough is a campus university so everything is within walking distance. All the halls of residence are grouped round the dining hall and common room, so there is always plenty going on. There are 12 of us in my halls and sometimes we all do something together. And though the town is small, it is only five minutes walk away.

'At the weekends the students have to cater for themselves. We do have a kitchen with a microwave and kettle, shared between 12, but we tend to eat out. Loughborough is a very student friendly town and there are plenty of cheap restaurants – pasta just £2.60 and it's very good.

'I was surprised at just how much I spent – £1,000 on eating and socialising. You may think you have a great deal of money when your loan comes through, but, believe me, you haven't. Beware the temptations of Freshers' week – at Loughborough it is 16 expensive days.' Alex expects to graduate with a debt of £14,000 – £16,000.

Outgoings	Per Term	Comments
Halls	£1,400	Full catering 5 days a week. Food OK but a bit samey but at least you get fed. Meet new people every day. Own room en-suite. Rent includes room cleaned and bins changed.
Deposit	£180	Annual – Paid against damage to room.
Hall subs	£50	Annual payment.
Food out, socialising, music/entertainment	£1,000	Of this around £500 – £600 went on socialising. SU/halls entertainments – clubs, bars. Eat out at weekends – pasta only £2.60 in town.
Laundry	£33	Machines provided – wash £1.80, dry £1.20 for two goes.
Phone	£100	PAYG not a good idea – too expensive. Need to change this.
Sport – Tennis	£65	Club membership. I also play badminton and squash for halls.
Tennis kit	£88	
Travel – term time	£20	Mostly taxis back at night. Town only 5 min walk away.
Travel home	£40	£20 return – went home twice.
Books	£100	£32 for a book – that's excessive!
Toiletries	£0	Put on Mum's shopping list.
Gifts	£120	Mostly Christmas presents.
Fees	£1,023	Full fee for year £3,070.
Total	£4,219	

Income	Per Term	Comments
Fees	£1,023	
Loan	£1,000	
Parents	£1,646	This also includes £180 deposit against breakages.
Sports kit	£88	
Overdraft	£1,125	Used £300 only of this.
Total	£4,882	

So now you know how much it is going to cost: but where will the money come from? Turn to the next chapter to find out.

Fact file

Great news, guys, it looks as if you are going to be outnumbered yet again. Of the students starting courses in 2007, 54.1% were female and 45.9% were male (UCAS figures)

Where will the money come from?

Main sources of finance for undergraduates

This chapter answers questions on the main sources of finance for students embarking on higher education in 2008–2009.

The information in this chapter is based on the funding package for students starting university in the UK in 2008–2009. Any variations in Scotland, Wales and Northern Ireland and additional help for special case students are covered in Chapter 3.

Top-up fees are here to stay

The arguments are over – top-up fees or, as they are officially called, variable fees, are here to stay for most students and already inflation is hiking them up still further. But while student debt is rising at an unprecedented rate, some ingenious ways have been introduced to help alleviate some of the financial anxieties while you are actually studying. So it's not all bad news.

Student funding – the main points

- ⊙ Universities can charge different (variable) fees for courses, but most do charge the maximum.
- ⊙ The maximum a UK student starting study for a first degree in 2008–09 can be expected to pay in fees is £3,145 pa.

- Welsh domiciled students studying in Wales will pay fees of £1,255 (see page 79).
- Scottish students studying in Scotland do not pay fees at all (see page 76).
- Students can take out a loan to cover their fees, which they will pay back gradually once they have graduated.
- Payback for loans will begin in the April after you graduate if you are earning over £15,000.
- There will be no help with fees for low-income families.
- Maintenance grants of up to £2,835 are available for students on a sliding scale depending on family income. From this year the income scale has been broadened in England so many more students will receive help.
- Bursaries are available from universities, especially for students from low-income families.
- Main source of maintenance income is the student loan, available to all students, max £4,625 – (£6,475 in London).
- Part of the loan is means tested on family income and on the amount of maintenance grant students receive.
- Non-repayable Special Support Grants of up to £2,835 are available for students receiving government support – largely lone parents/disabled students.

Cash crisis note

Remember, every student doesn't get everything. How much support you can receive will depend on three factors:

- where you live
- family income
- where you choose to study.

It's not all bad news

Although fees have gone up dramatically and help with fees has been stopped, you won't have to pay your fees until after you graduate, and then over many years. To cushion the fee blow, grants and bursaries are given – on a sliding scale – to help with maintenance. The real winners are parents, whose assessed contribution has been decreased. But, since parents have generally given more than their assessed contribution, students may well be in luck too.

Should students have to pay for their education?

This book does not set out to argue the rights and wrongs of the students' situation; its function is to provide information. However, not surprisingly, our research revealed strong feelings among students. Here are a few of their more printable comments:

Students will find it hard enough to get a foot into the real world without £30,000+ debt round their neck.
3rd year Physics student, Oxford

Pretty bad idea, but hard to avoid. Higher education needs the money and the government doesn't exactly have any to spare what with these wars on terror.
1st year English student, UCL

It will improve the quality of education.
2nd year MChem student, Huddersfield

It's a cheap way for government to make money out of students.
3rd year Media and Sports Journalism student, Huddersfield

It will encourage students to study at institutes closer to home rather than at the best universities.
2nd year Modern History student, Durham

I feel pressure from the amount of debt that I am in, so to increase that would increase the stress.
2nd year Combined Sciences student, Durham

If they remove the cap on fees, as they are discussing, our future workforce may be non-existent.
1st year Music student, Huddersfield

What the government said:

On average, a graduate earns much more than someone without a degree. Over a working lifetime, that will make a big difference in their income.
(Graduates earn around 45% more than non-graduates – Labour Force Survey 2005.)

Looking at the detail

Am I a special case?

If you fall into any of the categories listed below, check out Chapter 4.

- Scottish students and those studying in Scotland (see page 76).
- Welsh students and those studying in Wales (see page 79).
- Northern Irish students and those studying in Northern Ireland (see page 80).
- Students from another country in the EU or outside the EU (see pages 81, 83).
- Refugees/asylum seekers (see page 84).
- Sandwich/industrial placement students (see page 86).
- Part-time students (see page 87).
- Foundation students (see page 88).
- Second undergraduate degrees at Oxbridge (see page 88).
- Full-time distance learning course (see page 89).
- Attending a private higher education institution (see page 89).
- Nursing/midwifery students (see page 89).
- Healthcare students (see page 89).
- Medical/dentistry students (see page 90).
- Trainee teachers (see page 91).
- Physics students (see page 92).
- Social Work students (see page 92).
- Dance and Drama students (see page 93).
- Married/independent (see page 93).
- Single parents/with a family to support (see page 94).
- Disabled students (see page 94).
- Students studying abroad (see page 97).

Fees – what you pay

How much will I have to pay towards my fees?

Your university will set a price for each course up to a maximum of £3,145 pa. Fees are flexible, but most universities charge the full amount.

However, we did find a few universities that were charging lower fees to 2008–09 entrants. These included:

Institution	Fee
Greenwich	£2,835
Leeds Met	£2,000
Writtle College	£2,835

Who will pay my fees?

You. There will be no help from the your LA* for fees and your parents will not be asked to contribute. What's more, family income will have no bearing on what you pay. Universities can charge what they like for a course up to the maximum of £3,145 pa, and what they ask is what you must pay, but you may take out a loan to cover these fees.

Will every student pay the same fees?

Students from the same country on the same course at the same university will pay the same fees – they are not means-tested – but course fees can vary even in a university. Your university will decide what fees it is going to charge.

Remember: Scottish students studying in Scotland do not pay fees at all, while non-Scottish students who study in Scotland do, but at a different rate to England. Wales also takes an independent line. For full details and reasons why the rates are different, see Chapter 4.

Will top-up fees ever go up?

Yes, they already have. When the top-up fee programme was first mentioned, the government said that fees would not go up before 2010, but the original top-up fee of £3,000 has been given an inflationary lift to £3,070 for 2007–2008 and now £3,145 for 2008–2009. What will happen in 2,010 nobody knows, but there is plenty of speculation in the media and some universities are demanding that fees go up to £7,000.

How you pay – fee loans

Where is a student going to find £9,435 or at worst £12,580 for fees?

They won't, at least not while they are studying. One of the better aspects of the current funding system is the fee loan, which all students can take out. And you don't have to start paying it back until you have graduated and are earning at least £15,000 (see page 65 for full details). So the good news is that students will no longer have to pay fees up front; there will be no getting slung out of uni for not having the money to pay fees. The bad news is that your debt will increase – substantially.

*LA stands for Local Authority in England and Wales. When the term LA is used in this book, please read SAAS for Scotland (Student Awards Agency for Scotland) and ELB (Education and Library Board) for Northern Ireland.

Where will the loan come from?

From the Student Loans Company.

How do I get my loan for fees?

You apply to your local authority at the same time as applying for your maintenance loan and a grant. It is all on the same form. They will then pass this request on to the Student Loans Company, who will then inform you that this has been done. The form is available from www.studentfinancedirect.co.uk or from your local authority by post.

How much can I borrow?

Whatever your course costs, up to £3,145 pa.

Is it means-tested?

No.

What will happen to the money I borrow for fees?

It will be paid direct to your university.

Who can get a fee loan?

UK first-degree students, EU students and those taking a PGCE (postgraduate Certificate in Education).

Is taking out a loan for fees a good idea?

Yes. The big plus about the 'top-up fee' funding system is that, because students can take out a loan to cover their fees, they or their parents will not have to pay fees before they start university or while they are studying. So all of your maintenance loan, anything your parents give you and everything you earn will all go towards living. You should have fewer money worries than your predecessors during your time at university, but your debt will undoubtedly be greater.

If my parents want to pay my fees, can they do so?

There is nothing to stop parents paying your fees. Fees have to be paid at the start of each year. Most universities allow fees to be paid in tranches, but you will need to talk to your university. Some universities will give a discount if fees are paid in full up front.

Advice note

If your parents want to pay your fees but will have to borrow to pay them, it's worth remembering that the loan offered by the Student Loans Company is probably the cheapest money you can borrow, so it might be an idea to come to a family arrangement – you take out the loan for your fees and they pay it off for you.

Who gets help with fees?

Nobody, unless you:

- started your course in 2005 or before
- are a 2005–2006 gap-year student who had an exemption
- are a Welsh student studying in Wales (see page 79)
- are a Scottish student studying in Scotland (see page 76).

What happens if I drop out of my course – will I have to pay fees?

Probably, but there are no hard and fast rules. If you drop out before 1 December you may be all right as your fees won't have been paid by the Student Loans Company before that date. But generally, it will be a matter of discussing it with your university – after all, they have all the expense of providing a place for you.

I want to change my course; what happens about my fees?

Again, it will be a matter of discussion with your university. If you are changing to another course in the same university, fees may not be a problem, but if you are moving to another university it might be more difficult.

Will I be able to get a loan for fees for any course I take at college?

No. Courses for which loans for fees will be given include: full-time (including sandwich) degree, HNC, HND, postgraduate Certificate of Education, school-centred initial teacher training, or equivalent courses undertaken at a UK university, publicly funded college or comparable institution.

Courses for which loans are not available include: school-level courses such as A levels or Scottish Highers, BTEC and SCOTVEC National Awards and City & Guilds courses for those over 19, postgraduate courses (except teacher training), all part-time courses* (except initial teacher training courses), some correspondence and Open University courses.

*See page 87 for details of grants for part-time courses.

What can I do to raise funds to pay my fees if I am unable to get a loan?

1. Talk to your local authority.
2. Talk to the college where you want to take the course.
3. Apply for a Career Development Loan – see page 51.
4. Apply to professional bodies, trusts, foundations, benevolent funds – see Chapter 8.

Advice note

If a fee debt of £9,435+ (£12,580+ for a four-year course) fills you with horror, and well it might, don't abandon your degree aspirations – yet. There are some excellent bursary deals on offer and many students, especially those from low-income families, may find that while studying they are better off than their non-top-up-fee predecessors.

Fast facts on finance

For students starting their course 2008–2009:

Fees	Max £3,145 pa (except in Wales).
Fee Loan	Up to £3,145 pa.
Student loans	£6,475 in London, £4,625 elsewhere, £3,580 living at home (less in your final year); 25% is means-tested on parents' income and maintenance grant received if you have been assessed for a maintenance grant.
Maintenance grant	£2,835 for low-income families (less in Scotland and Wales). Means-tested on family income.
University bursaries	At least £310 pa for those on full maintenance grant (most give more).
Access to Learning Fund (Contingency Fund – Wales; Hardship Funds – Scotland; Support Funds – N. Ireland)	Random distribution; given largely to help with rent and other financial hardships.
Part-time students	Increased levels of fee grants to max of £1,180 plus course grant of £255.
Salary payback threshold for fee and maintenance loans	£15,000.

Maintenance – grants, bursaries and loans

There are three elements to students' maintenance:

- maintenance grants
- university bursaries
- student loans.

Maintenance grants

What are they and will I get one?

Maintenance grants are not new: they have been creeping into the funding system since the year 2000. What is new, though, is the amount – up to £2,835 – and the number of students who will receive them. This is not government generosity, however, but because students no longer receive help with fees. Maintenance grants are means-tested on your or your family's income up to £60,005 but note: this is only in England. At the time of publishing, in Wales, Northern Ireland and Scotland the family income cut off point is much lower – see Chapter 4.

The £60,005 income threshold is only for students who are starting their university course in 2008–09. For students based in England who are already on a course the household income cut-off point for a full grant is £18,360 and a partial grant £39,305.

Maintenance grants for new students in England	
Who receives what in 2008–2009	
Family Income	Grant
£25,000 or less	£2,835
£30,000	£2,002
£35,450	£1,260
£40,000	£998
£50,000	£525
£60,005	£50
More than £60,005	£0

How many students will receive a maintenance grant?

This year around a third of students are expected to receive a full grant, and around a third a partial grant in England now that eligibility has been extended to a family income of £60,005.

When will I get my grant?

It will be paid in three instalments, one at the start of each term.

Who will calculate how much I will get?

Your local authority/Student Loan Company, based on the information you supply on your application form.

University bursaries

Universities have always offered bursaries to good students but never on the scale that they are doing now. The government stipulated that to charge the maximum fee – currently £3,145 pa – universities must sign up to an Access Agreement, which says that students receiving the full £2,835 maintenance grant (i.e. those from low-income families) must be given a further non-repayable bursary of at least £310, making a grand total of maintenance grant and bursary of £3,145 – (the same amount as the full fees) but the bursary could be more.

Some universities are sticking to the guidelines. Others are being far more generous. Many are offering bursaries on a sliding scale to all those receiving a proportion of the maintenance grant and this year, with many more students eligible for a grant, that could be many more students. The average bursary given by universities in 2007–2008 was £1,000 pa for those receiving the maximum maintenance grant. This could be given in kind – e.g. reduced accommodation costs. Even students who don't actually fall into the low-income category are cashing in. Examples are given on p. 45. For up-to-date information check out the bursary map website: http://bursarymap.direct.gov.uk.

Shop around. As you can see, there are some fantastic bursary deals about and every university has a different approach. Finding a university giving generous bursaries could be more cost-effective than trying to find a low-cost course, and probably better educational value too.

Where will the money for bursaries come from?

Universities are setting aside over £350 million from the increased fee money to support students from low-income families, and it is estimated that some 400,000 students will benefit from this. But many universities are already heavily endowed by generous benefactors and have always awarded scholarships, awards and bursaries to selected students.

Where can I find out about university bursaries and scholarships, and what's being offered?

- University prospectuses and websites are a good starting point and should provide plenty of information.
- www.studentsupportdirect.co.uk.
- www.ucas.com.
- http//bursarymap.direct.gov.uk.

There is also more information on university awards and scholarships, including sports bursaries, music scholarships, location scholarships and awards for students from abroad, in Chapter 8 of this book.

King's College London	Whatever level of maintenance grant given will be matched with 50p for every pound received. So grant of £2,765 will be matched with £1,382 bursary. If same criteria used for 2008/9 grant of £2,835 + bursary £1,417.	
University of Bradford 2008–2009 figures	Family income under £40,000	Family income £40,001 – £60,005
	1st yr £500	£400
	2nd yr £700	£500
	3rd yr £900	£600
University of Manchester	All home students from households with income of less than approx £27,120 eligible for a bursary of £1,000 pa. Achievement scholarships of £2,000. Advantage scholarship £5,000 also given.	
University of Cambridge 2008–2009 figures	Students in receipt of full state support will receive a bursary of £3,150 pa. Students in receipt of partial state support will receive bursaries on a sliding scale. Specific college awards are also available.	
Canterbury Christ Church University 2007–2008 figures	£820 for students on full state support. £510 for students on partial state support. £410 for students with household incomes between £38,331 and £46,048.	
University of Central Lancashire 2007–2008 figures	£1,000 where principal earner's salary is less than £60,000 pa. Harris Bursary Fund offers additional support for local students. Excellence bursaries targeting key areas – up to £1,000 pa.	
	If receiving:	Awarded
	76–100% of grant	£1,320
	51–75% of grant	£990
	26–50% of grant	£660
	1–25% of grant	£330
University of Reading 2007–2008 figures	To qualify in 2008–09 household income must be £45,000 or less.	

(TIS)

Cash crisis note

Many students are missing out on bursaries just because they didn't ask. Check with your university if you are entitled to a bursary even if you are not from a low-income family. They are not necessarily given out automatically. See the bursary map at http://bursarymap.direct.gov.uk.

To compare and contrast what universities are offering take a look at *University Scholarships, Awards and Bursaries*, published by Trotman. As well as giving full information about the bursaries now offered by universities to students from low-income families, it lists over 100 institutions offering scholarships, awards and bursaries. Many are for people studying specific subjects, or are travel awards. Subjects vary from the more usual Engineering, History, Geography, Languages, Law and the sciences to the more specialised, such as Cultural Criticism Studies, Paper Science, Rural Studies, Retail and Textiles.

Student maintenance loans

How much can I borrow?

Not enough – at least that is what most students think. The maintenance loan is reviewed annually and generally increased. What you receive is dependent on where you are studying. (Note: the Student Maintenance Loan, usually called the Student Loan, is quite different from the Maintenance Grant. The loan you have to pay back – the grant you don't.) The rates for a full maintenance loan for a full-time student in England, Wales and Northern Ireland in 2008–2009 are shown in the table.

		Full year max available	Final year max available
Students living away from their parents' home and studying:	in London	£6,475	£5,895
	elsewhere	£4,625	£4,280
Students living in their parents' home		£3,580	£3,235
Studying overseas		£5,510	£4,790

When I started uni I didn't think I'd need a student loan. I'd taken a gap year and saved and was getting £500 a year bursary, but I spent about £800 in the first term – well, actually most in the first month – it was outrageous, it really was. Well, let's face it, the first year isn't exactly quiet. Most went on booze, pizzas and more booze. But that first month was probably the best few weeks of my life. I had worked continuously during my gap year, so when I got to uni I hit it hard.
Jono, 3rd year student, Loughborough

Is the loan means-tested?

Yes. Not everybody can take out the full maintenance loan. It is means-tested on your maintenance grant and on family income. So for low-income families part of the grant is paid in lieu of part of the maintenance loan, so those receiving the full maintenance grant, or a high proportion of the full grant, may find they are not entitled to the full loan. Higher-income families, those earning over the £61,061 income threshold, will find a quarter of the loan allocation is means-tested against your income or that of your family. It is hoped that any part of the means-tested loan you do not receive will be paid by your parents or spouse.

This is the maintenance students can expect in England in 2008–2009:

Family Income (£)	Assessed Contribution (£)	Maintenance Grant (£)	Maintenance Loan (£)	Total Grant Plus Loan (£)
Student living at home			**Maximum £3,580**	
25,000	0	2,835	2,320	5,155
30,000	0	2,002	2,320	4,322
40,000	0	998	2,582	3,580
50,000	0	524	3,056	3,580
60,005	0	50	3,530	3,580
61,061	0	0	3,580	3,580
65,000	414	0	3,166	3,166
69,564	895	0	2,685(*)	2,685
Student studying in London			**Maximum £6,475**	
25,000	0	2,835	5,215	8,050
30,000	0	2,002	5,215	7,217
34,450	0	1,260	5,215	6,475
40,000	0	998	5,477	6,475
50,000	0	524	5,951	6,475
60,005	0	50	6,425	6,475
61,061	0	0	6,475	6,475
65,000	414	0	6,061	6,061
70,000	940	0	5,535	5,535
80,000	1,620	0	4,855(*)	4,855
Student studying outside London			**Maximum £4,625**	
25,000	0	2,835	3,365	6,200
30,000	0	2,002	3,365	5,367
34,450	0	1,260	3,365	4,625
40,000	0	998	3,627	4,625
50,000	0	524	4,101	4,625
60,005	0	50	4,575	4,625
61,061	0	0	4,625	4,625
65,000	414	0	4,211	4,211
70,000	940	0	3,685	3,685
72,034	1,155	0	3,470(*)	3,470

*The point at which the 75% non-means-tested part of loan is reached

How the calculations are made

Where students receive a maintenance grant, the amount of loan for which they are eligible will be reduced, pound for pound, by the amount of grant up to £1,260. Any university bursary is not included in this. This means that if you come from a lower-income household you will have a smaller loan to repay. All students will be able to get 75% of the maximum student loan for maintenance.

Where the student is not receiving a grant, the other 25% will be assessed on family income over £61,060.

Cash crisis note

Sixth formers starting university in 2008 expect to pay on average £34,740 for a three-year degree course. This is up from £33,512 last year and includes the new tuition fees according to the NatWest Student Money Matters Survey. However, Vickie, a fourth-year medical student at Liverpool, reckons she will have debts of around £45,000 when she graduates, and she doesn't even have to pay top-up fees.

My academic year is longer than at most colleges – can I get extra money?

Yes. If your course is longer than 30 weeks you can claim for an extra loan, which will be means-tested, for each week you have to attend your course. Weekly rates for 2008–09 are:

London	£103
Elsewhere	£81
Living at home	£53
Studying abroad	£112

Where does the student loan come from?

The Student Loans Company, which is a special company set up by the government to provide loans for students.

Student loans – a few facts

When the student loan was first introduced in 1992 there was uproar. Many thought that higher education in this country should be completely free; others said that students should contribute to the cost of their education. At the time, the loan was around £580. People predicted student numbers would plummet. They were wrong. In fact, while the loan increased year on year, so did student numbers.

But 2006, the first year of the top-up fees, saw a drop in student numbers. Applicants for courses were down by 3% to 506,304. And the number of students actually starting courses was down by 3.6% to 390,809 students (UCAS figures).

Fast forward to January 2008 and, according to UCAS, application figures, which increased in 2007, are already up for 2008 by 6.7% on the same time last year. But it is still early days.

Our research amongst students in December 2006 showed that around 56% of students actually knew of somebody who didn't go to university because of financial reasons, and 69% said they knew someone who had decided to study in their home town to save money.

Whatever your views about funding yourself through university, if you are a student just starting in higher education in the UK, you will probably end up having a hefty loan. Most students – around 80% – already do.

How much do students owe?

In the first year of the Student Loans Scheme, around £70 million was paid out to fund some 180,000 students.

By its tenth anniversary £1,823 million was paid out to 723,000 students.

By 2006–2007 (latest figures), with an estimated 82% of eligible students taking out a loan, the amount being lent had reached £2,954.1 million paid out to around one million students, which all adds up to …

… a massive £18,116.3 million currently being borrowed by some 2.5 million students and graduates. Next year, with the fee loan, these figures will go sky high. Average interest rate: 4.8%. (Sept 2007 – 31 Aug 2008)

How do students feel about debt?

According to a NatWest student survey in August 2007:

Students –

- 77% were worried about the amount of debt they would have on graduating
- 54% of students say they are concerned about debt
- 23% have considered packing in university
- 73% were concerned about the increasing fees.

A level sixth formers considering university –

- 66% say their biggest concern is money
- 54% say they are concerned about workload, keeping up, failing exams.

What students say about debt

When my bank offered an interest-free overdraft I thought the £1,500 was mine to spend. Now I have to think about paying it back. Very distressing!

It is unfair to judge the financial status of a student on the parents' income, since it's the student who will be paying off the debt.

In my first year I spent all my loan in two weeks, so I had to live on noodles for three months. Ugh!

I don't like living at home, but I have to because I'm skint!!!

Student debt is bad enough, but the 'invisible' debt is worse – overdrafts, credit cards, borrowing from family – all of which has to be paid back.

Depression is a problem that hits everyone who lives on a tight budget.

There are students who take a different view:

Generally, studying is an indulgent luxury which improves prospects and so people should take as much responsibility as possible.

Most students don't mind the thought of paying back money once they are earning.

Who can get a maintenance loan?

UK students who undertake full-time first degree or Diploma of Higher Education courses at universities or colleges of higher education. While there is no age limit on students taking out a fee loan, maintenance loans are available to students aged under 60.

I'm an overseas student: can I get a maintenance loan?

No. Even students from the EU who are classified as 'home' students for fees, are not entitled to apply for a maintenance loan. For further details see Chapter 4, page 84.

Are there loans for part-time students?

No. But there is help (see Chapter 4, page 87).

I want to do a second degree – can I get a loan for maintenance and fees?

It depends how long your first course was and the length of your second course. In general, support will be available for students for the length of a course plus one extra year. Say your new course is three years. Add to that one year. Subtract the length of your first course, say three years, and you would receive funding for one year. But if, for example, your previous course was three years and your new course is four years, add another year to that and you would receive funding for two years. Of course it could work the other way, if your previous course was four years and your new course was only three. Then you would end up receiving no funding at all. However, if you are thinking of taking a second undergraduate degree at Oxford or Cambridge you could be in fee loan luck – see Chapter 4, page 88.

I want to change my course: what happens to my loan?

If you change to another course in the same college, your entitlement to a maintenance loan may well stay the same, but your fees could be different. Equally, if you transfer to another college the fees may be different. The major problem arises if you change to a college/course that does not attract student support or there is a break in your studies before you join the new course. It is very important if you transfer from one course to another or withdraw from your current course that you not only discuss this with your college, but also talk to your LA (or the SLC if on the pilot programme) as soon as possible.

I am doing a further education course – can I get a loan?

If you are doing a course that leads to a first degree, HND, HNC, PGCE or NVQ at Level 4 you can get a student loan. The information in this book is aimed mainly at higher education students. Students in the 16–19 age group attending further education colleges may be eligible for financial help through their college.

What are career development loans?

They are designed for people on vocational courses (full-time, part-time or distance learning) of up to two years where fees aren't paid, and you can't get support from your LA. They cover course fees (only 80% given if you are in full employment, 100% if you have been out of work for three months or more) plus other costs such as materials, books, childcare and living expenses. You can apply for £300 to £8,000.

The scheme is funded by a number of high street banks (Barclays, the Co-operative, the Royal Bank of Scotland) and administered by the Learning and Skills Council (LSC), who will pay the interest on your loan during training and for up to one month afterwards. If the course you take lasts more than two years (three years if it includes work experience) you may still be able to use a CDL to fund part of your course. Shop around the different providers and compare the terms offered before making a choice.

For a free booklet on career development loans phone 0800 585505. More information can also be found on www.lifelonglearning.co.uk.

See also Chapter 8 for Other Sources of finance to tap.

> ‘ *Get a job – the student loan seems like a lot of money, but it doesn't cover even the essentials.* ’
> Psychology student, Hull. (See Chapter 5.)

Why are the loan rates lower for the final year?

Because they do not cover the summer vacation. You are expected to be working by then, or can draw Social Security. However, if your final year is longer than 30 term weeks you can apply for more loan for each week. If it lasts 40 weeks or more you can get a loan at the full rate. This is often the case for students on 'accelerated' degree courses. Rates for 2008–2009 are:

	Full year	Final year
Home	£3,580	£3,235
Elsewhere	£4,625	£4,280
London	£6,475	£5,895

Further information

Who to contact/what to read

Contact Student Finance Direct 0845 607 7577 for financial information including information on your loans.

Contact the Student Helpline, 0845 602 0583, between 10am and 4pm for more detailed questions on student finance and eligibility.

Full information about fees, maintenance grants and loans is given in the following free booklets, which you would be well advised to get and study:

For students in England: *A Guide to Financial Support for Higher Education Students in 2008/9* (which is the source for the loan statistics in this chapter). Tel: (booklet) 0800 731 9133; (helpline) 0845 602 0583. Website: www.studentfinancedirect.co.uk. Braille and cassette editions also available.

For students in Scotland: *Student Support in Scotland: A Guide for Undergraduate Students 2008/9*, available from any Scottish university or the Student Awards Agency for Scotland (SAAS), 3 Redheughs Rigg, South Gyle, Edinburgh EH12 9YT. Tel: 0131 476 8212. Email: saas.geu@scotland.gsi.gov.uk. Website: www.student-support-saas.gov.uk.

For students in Northern Ireland: *Financial Support for Students in Higher Education 2008/9*, Student Support Branch, Department for Employment and Learning (Northern Ireland), Rathgael House, Balloo Road, Bangor, Co. Down BT19 7PR. Tel: 028 9025 7710; (for booklet) 0800 731 9133. Website: www.delni.gov.uk.

Getting funding and paying it back

In this chapter you will find information covering:

Applying for grants and loans

You should start thinking about applying for financial support as soon as you have applied for a place on a course. Do not wait until you have a confirmed place on a course: just quote the course you are most likely to attend. Apply even if you don't think you will be entitled to a maintenance grant, as your LA will also assess how much loan you are entitled to and how much your family is expected to contribute (if at all). Remember that the loan is paid by the Student Loans Company, not your LA. Your LA is responsible for means-testing family income. Any problems with your loan should be addressed to the Student Loans Company (see page 70).

There are three important steps to follow:

1. You can apply online at www.direct.gov.uk/studentfinance from March onwards. Or you can get a paper application form from your LA, or download one from the above website.
2. Fill in your application form and return it to your LA by post or on the web. You can find the right address from the above website. Give all the details you are asked for and say whether you intend to apply for a loan. Remember to include your National Insurance number if you want a loan. You might also be asked to send your UK passport or birth certificate as identification.

3. If your application is in order, it will be sent to Student Finance Direct, who will send you details of the support you are entitled to six to eight weeks after you send your application.

Timing is important.

- ⊙ You can apply to your LA from March onwards.
- ⊙ New students – try to return your form no later than 27 June 2008.
- ⊙ Students not providing financial information should apply by 25 April 2008.
- ⊙ Late applications may result in late payments.

If you want to discover what help you are entitled to, check out the online calculator at www.direct.gov.uk/studentfinance.

Pilot application schemes

While the above is the correct procedure for most students, the government is carrying out pilot schemes to assess whether an easier applications procedure can be found. So, if you live in one of the areas listed below, your application will be dealt with by the Student Loans Company (SLC) and you will need to contact the SLC's Customer Support Office on 0845 607 7577 to make your application (SFD Processing Unit, PO Box 89, Darlington DL1 9AZ). This will not affect your entitlement to support in any way.

Local Authorities taking part in the pilot programme:

- ⊙ London Borough of Brent
- ⊙ Darlington Borough Council
- ⊙ London Borough of Hackney
- ⊙ Hartlepool Borough Council
- ⊙ North Yorkshire Council
- ⊙ Redcar and Cleveland Borough Council
- ⊙ Southend-on-Sea Borough Council
- ⊙ South Tyneside Council
- ⊙ London Borough of Southwark
- ⊙ Stockton-on-Tees Borough Council
- ⊙ York City Council

Students based in Wales, Scotland or Northern Ireland should turn to the next chapter for details.

When and how will I get the money?

Your student loan and grant: once you have registered your arrival at university and have started to attend the course your student loan and grant (if applicable) will be paid into your bank account. However, it could take three working days after your college has confirmed that you have arrived for the money actually to reach your bank account, so you may need funds to tide you over. Payments will be in three tranches, made at the beginning of each term.

Your fees: will be paid direct to your university.

Your university bursary: likely to be paid into your bank account by your university. This will generally be paid out in two tranches in the second and third terms. You may need to inform your university that you think you are eligible for a bursary.

Make sure you have filled in the right section on your application form to ensure financial information is passed to your university so they can assess you for a bursary.

Advice note

You will need to have some cash in hand when you arrive at university, since your loan/grant payment will not hit your bank account on the first day and it could in fact be several days before you receive any money.

Panic! My loan and grant cheque hasn't arrived!

It happens – not that often, but it can be dramatic when it does. In an ideal world your cheque should be waiting for you when you arrive at your university or college, but things can go wrong. Some typical reasons we discovered were:

- Local authorities were behind with their workload and have not processed your application.
- You applied late, so the amount of the loan has not been assessed.
- Loans company has been inundated.
- Wrong information on your bank account.
- Didn't give all the information required, e.g. NI number.
- Whatever the reason, it doesn't help the destitute student to eat, so …

What can I do?

- Try the bank. If you already have a bank account, the bank may help you out with a loan – most banks offer free overdrafts to students. Talk to the student adviser at the campus or local branch. This, of course, is no help to the first-year student who needs that cheque to open a bank account, so make sure you have an account before you start your course.
- Try your college. Ask your college for temporary help. Most institutions have what's called a hardship fund set up to cover just this kind of eventuality.
- Try the Access to Learning Fund, which has been set up to help students. Full details are given on page 63.
- Friends? They may well take pity on you when it comes to socialising, buying you the odd drink, but it is rarely a good idea to borrow from friends.

How late can I apply for funding support?

Up to nine months after you have started your course.

Applications can be made at any time during the academic year. The cut-off date for a maintenance loan application is one month before the end of your academic year.

Parents – what to expect

What are parents expected to contribute?

Less than in the past. Since the introduction of the current funding arrangements, and especially now the family income threshold for being eligible for a grant has been raised in England to £60,005, and the family income threshold to receive the full loan has been raised to £61,060, parents are not expected to contribute so much – except in Scotland. Parents are expected to make up any of the means-tested portion of the loan that a student does not receive.

The approximate maximum parents/spouses in England are expected to contribute for one student in the year 2008–2009 is:

- Students studying in London: £1,618
- Elsewhere: loan top-up £1,156
- Living in parents' home: £895.

Note: Scotland has a different system of funding for students, and parents are assessed and contribute substantially more than parents in the rest of the UK. For Wales and Northern Ireland the figures are also different. See Chapter 4.

Note to parents: No parent is expected to contribute more than the maximum means-tested portion of the loan for each student, however high their income – but many do. (See page 57 for details of what you might have to pay.)

It's a fact

Parents are contributing more than ever before:

- almost two-thirds of students receive financial support from their parents
- 26% give a regular amount
- 23% give money as and when needed
- 8% of students receive a lump sum at the beginning of each term
- 4% received a one-off payment at the start of their studies.

NatWest Student Survey, August 2007

How do they calculate how much loan I can have?

The actual calculation of whether and how much your family is expected to contribute towards maintenance, and how much grant you are entitled to, is very complex. It is based on 'residual income': that means what's left after essential expenses have been deducted. The assessment will be on family income, so if both parents are earning, both incomes will be assessed.

So what are essential expenses? It works like this. The LA takes your parents' or parent plus partner's gross income before tax and National Insurance and then subtracts allowances for things like pension schemes, dependants and superannuation payments that qualify for tax relief, and whether you will be receiving any maintenance grant. Having done this they then assess what your household contribution should be. It is not until the family income is over £61,061 that parents are expected to contribute. See table on page 47.

My parents are divorced – whose income will they assess?

Your LA will decide which parent they consider you are living with, and assess their income, while ignoring the income of the other parent.

I have a step-parent – will his income be included?

Yes: the income of a step-parent, if that's the parent you live with, or a cohabiting partner, whether of the same or opposite sex, will be taken into account. However, maintenance received from an absent parent will not be considered as part of the household income when assessing income.

What happens if my parents are not prepared to divulge their income?

You will not be assessed for a maintenance grant and will only be eligible for three-quarters (the non-means-tested portion) of the maintenance loan.

What if I have a brother or sister claiming for a maintenance grant and a loan?

If there are several children in higher education in the family, the grant and loan entitlements are calculated on the same scale as for one student; those parents whose residual income is below £60,061 would not have to contribute for either student and you would both be eligible for a full loan. If the family income is over £60,061 but below £72,034 (£80,000 in London) then parents would find they have to contribute no more than for one student, and any additional loan received would be divided proportionately between the students. Any parental contribution should be divided in the same way. It must also be remembered that any other dependent children they have will come into the calculation. Parents with a higher residual income will have to contribute more. The maximum parents can be asked to pay, regardless of how many children they have at university, is £6,055 if students are under the new top-up fee system.

Does the parental contribution ever change?

It certainly did this year in England as the income threshold for receiving a grant was raised to £60,005. But in general, the threshold at which parents begin to contribute towards maintenance is likely to be raised each year as the loan is increased. But if parental earnings are static they could find they contribute less the following year. Remember, parents are only expected to contribute – nobody can force them.

What if my mum or dad is made redundant?

If your parents' income suddenly drops, then you should contact your local authority or awards branch immediately as you could be entitled to a maintenance grant and more maintenance loan. You should also tell your university since many bursaries are linked to the amount of maintenance grant received.

If my parents can't afford to or won't pay the shortfall in my maintenance loan, is there anything I can do?

No. There is no way that parents can be made to pay their contribution towards your maintenance and fees, and the local authorities will not make up the difference. Equally, they can choose how they give their contribution: cash in hand or paying for something like rent, utility bills, books.

Are there any circumstances in which my parents would not be expected to contribute towards my maintenance?

Yes – if you are:

- 25 or over
- married
- an orphan
- in care
- have been supporting yourself for three years.

Is the debt worth the struggle?

Judge for yourself!

Graduates earn on average 20%–25% more over their lifetimes than A level students which amounts to £160,000 according to a report published in 2006, but how much depends on what you study:

Medicine	£340,315 more
Engineering	£243,730 more

Maths/Combined Sciences	£241,749 more
Environmental Science	£237,935 more
Business and Finance	£184,694 more
Technology	£119,484 more
Education	£114,935 more
European Language	£96,281 more
Humanities	£52,549 more
Arts	£34,494 more

(Figures from a report published by Universities UK written by PricewaterhouseCoopers and London Economics 2006)

Some important questions and answers

I want to go to a university in my home town, but don't want to live with my parents – can I get the full financial package?

Students living at home are eligible for the lower 'living at home' maintenance loan only. There is no regulation preventing you from living away from home, but funding is at the discretion of your local authority.

An increasing number of A level students in the Midlands are said to be considering studying at a university close to home. In fact, according to a survey conducted by Staffordshire University for the Sutton Trust the figure is as high as 56%.

I'm thinking of getting married – will it affect my maintenance grant and loan entitlements?

Yes. Students who get married before the academic year are considered as independent and their support is no longer assessed on their parents' income but on that of their partner, provided he or she is earning enough. This is calculated in a similar way as for parental income.

I'm not married but living with a partner – will this affect my support?

Yes – you will be considered independent in the same way as a married student would be and income will be based on your partner's income.

What is the maintenance loan meant to cover?

Lodgings, food, books, pocket money, travel, socialising – but not fees.

My academic year is longer than at most colleges – can I get extra money?

Yes. If your course is longer than 30 weeks you can claim for an extra loan, which will be means-tested, for each week you have to attend your course. Rates for 2008–2009 are:

- London: £103 per week
- elsewhere: £81 per week
- living at home: £53 per week
- studying abroad: £112 per week.

If your course year is 45 weeks or longer, you will receive a loan based on 52 weeks.

★ **What subjects are up and what subjects are down with students applying for uni in 2007**

Subject	Percentage change	Subject	Percentage change
Up		Down	
Imaginative writing	+26%	American Studies	−4.6%
Range of Biological Sciences including Applied Biological Sciences	+23%	Forensic & Archaeological Science	−4.8%
Business & Administration	+22.2%	Anatomy, Physiology & Pathology	−5.5%
Finance	+18.3%	Crafts	−5.8%
Tourism, Transport, Travel	+17.6%	Production & Manufacturing	−6.1%
Combined Physics/Maths	+17.3%	Medical Technology	−6.7%
Mathematical & Computer Science	+16.3%	Com. Physic/maths science plus arts, humanities and languages	−6.7%
Building	+14.9%	Information Systems	−7.4%
Academic Studies in Education	+14.8%	Comb. Physical Sciences	−7.4%
Planning	+14.8%	Social Studies	−11.8%
		Archaeology	−13.9%

UCAS application figures for 2007

If I work part-time, will it affect my student financial package?

No. Students can work during their course – i.e. undertake vacation work – and the money earned will not be considered when their loan/grant is calculated.

What will happen if I drop out of my course?

You will have to pay off any loans taken out for fees and maintenance. Your LA might also ask you to repay some of the fees they have paid.

Cash crisis note

Avoid being a university drop-out. Around 22% of students dropped out or failed to get a degree at the last count. Freshers who think they've taken the wrong course should beat a hasty path to their course director or their Careers Service for advice as soon as possible. Nothing is set in stone. The critical date is 1 December: the Student Loans Company doesn't actually pay your fees before then.

When is the best time to take out a maintenance loan?

There are three options:

1. When you need it.
2. As late as possible – because it's index-linked to inflation (see page 66).
3. As soon as possible. Some financially astute students take out their student loan, even if they don't need it, and invest it in a good interest-paying account with a bank or building society. These accounts generally pay more than the inflation rate. Make sure you know what you are doing. Check out interest rates first, and ensure you can get at your money quickly and easily if you are likely to need it – some high-interest rate accounts give limited access.

'Because I had sponsorship, had worked for a year before uni and had a Saturday job, I didn't need a student loan, but I took it out anyway, and put it in a good building society account, just in case I wanted to go on to do further study. As it is, my sponsor has offered me a job that's too good to turn down, so I won't need it, but it was nice to have that security cushion there. I haven't checked it out yet, but I think the loan has actually made me money; at least it hasn't cost me anything, which has to be good.'

3rd year student

Cash crisis note

- As your loan cheque will not be banked until you have arrived at your university or college, you will need to have some money of your own to get yourself there, and possibly to maintain yourself until the cheque is cleared. Check out the cost of train fares.

- If you are living in halls of residence, your college will probably be sympathetic if your cheque hasn't arrived and will wait until it does. But don't be too sure about this – check it out. Some colleges will add a penalty to the bills of students who don't pay up on time. And if you run out of money and can't pay your bill at all, you will not be allowed to re-register for the next academic year. If it's your final year, you will not get your degree until the bill is paid.

- If you are living in rented accommodation, you can expect no leniency. Landlords expect to be paid on the dot, usually ask for rent in advance and may request an additional deposit. You will need funds to cover this.

Advice note

Postgraduates are not entitled to a student loan. So if, as an undergraduate, you do not need the loan or all of the loan now, but are thinking of going on to do a postgraduate course, it might be worth your while taking out the student loan and investing it, so the money is there to help you through your postgraduate studies later on. If you are not a financial whiz-kid, take advice. The student loan is a really cheap way of borrowing money but you don't want to build up debt unnecessarily.

Do I have to take out the whole maintenance loan amount?

No. You can take out however much you want, up to the maximum for which you are eligible that year. If you do not apply for the full amount at the start of the academic year you can apply for the rest later.

Will the loan be paid all at once in a lump sum?

No. The loan will be paid termly, in two or three instalments depending on when you apply for it.

Is there any help with travelling expenses?

England, Wales and Northern Ireland: the first £295 of any travelling expenses is disregarded. Above that you can claim a grant for certain expenses if you are: disabled; attending another establishment as part of a medical or dental course; or attending an institution abroad for eight weeks or more as part of your course. (Scottish students see page 78.)

Fact check

Of the students graduating last year:

- 319,260 first-degree students obtained a degree.
- 12% of first-degree students who graduated were part-time.
- 12% of students obtained a first-class degree.
- 57% of first-degree graduates were women.
- 42% of students received a science degree, of whom 50% were women.
- 202,225 students obtained a postgraduate qualification.

(HESA statistics for academic year 2006–2007)

Additional help

Access to Learning Fund

What is it?

This is a special fund available through your college, which provides help to students who may need extra financial support to stay in higher education.

Who gets Access help?

If you are in real financial difficulty this is the source to tap. The fund is open to both full- and part-time students studying 50% of their time on a full-time course. It is there to help those facing particular financial hardship, those in need of emergency help for an unexpected financial crisis and those who are considering giving up their studies because of financial problems. Priority is given to students with children, mature students, those from low-income families, disabled students, students who have been in care, and students in their final year.

Ask for help as soon as you realise you have a financial problem as it takes at least four weeks to assess an Access to Learning Fund application. But in the end I got £200 – a lifesaver when you can't pay your rent.
4th year Astrophysics student, UCL

How much can you get?

That depends on your college. It could be just a few hundred pounds to tide you over a sticky patch, it could be £3,000 plus. Your college will use its discretion. The amount given will depend on a number of factors – your circumstances, how many other students are applying and how much they have in the kitty. You can apply for help more than once in a year.

Wales: similar payments are made through the Financial Contingency Funds (FCFs) scheme.

Scotland: provides help through Hardship Funds.

Northern Ireland: provides help through Support Funds.

Because I have no family and have to spend the whole year in halls, my college will be asking the Access Fund to help out with my rent.
1st year student, Cambridge

Will I have to pay the money back?

Access payments are usually given as a grant, but they could be given as a short-term loan.

'*I tried to get funds from Access but felt I was on trial.*'
Mature student, Physics and Engineering, Heriot-Watt

'*The college hardship fund is a wonderful scheme to help you survive.*'
Mature Midwifery student with four children, Canterbury Christ Church

How do I set about getting money from the Access to Learning Fund?

Apply to your college. Every institution will have a different procedure and different criteria for measuring your needs. You will probably have to fill in a form giving details of your financial situation. Most institutions will have somebody to help and advise you. They may even have a printed leaflet giving you details.

When should I apply for Access funding?

As soon as trouble starts to loom. The fund is limited to the amount that is allocated, so it is largely first come first served. We have heard of institutions that have allocated most of their funds by the end of November of the academic year.

I'm a student from abroad – can I apply for Access money?

Sorry, but no. The Access to Learning Fund is restricted to 'home' students only, so overseas students are not eligible.

Are there any other hardship funds?

Some institutions, and also some students' unions, have resources to help students in real financial difficulty. They all vary depending on the institution, and they will pay out money for a variety of reasons. Funds are generally given when all official avenues are exhausted. Priority is often given to students who are suffering financially because of unforeseen circumstances such as a death in the family or illness. Sometimes small amounts are given to tide you over or to pay a pressing bill. Increasingly, hardship payments are taking the form of an interest-free loan, which can be especially useful if your grant/loan cheque doesn't arrive on time. They may also offer help to students from abroad.

Leeds University Union, for example, offers a range of financial assistance to students who find themselves in difficulty. There is a Fundraising Group, which considers all applications. As most of the money comes from external charitable trusts, their hands are tied to some extent because they are governed by each individual trust's guidelines and criteria. But they do offer much-needed support.

Are there any other allowances, grants and bursaries I could apply for?

Yes. Check the next chapter: you might fall into a special category. Otherwise try Chapter 8, 'Other sources to tap'.

Gordon's story

Latin American Studies student, Glasgow

When I came to university I had an electric guitar, an amp, a bass guitar, a stereo and a camera. In times of financial need these have all had temporary lodging in the pawnshop. Gradually this became less and less temporary so that now I no longer have a bass guitar, a camera or a stereo. The loss of the latter is no great hardship as I have already sold my CDs/DVDs one by one to the second-hand record shop.

Thrift tips

'Try the Access to Learning Fund: it isn't widely advertised. I got £200.'

3rd year Sociology student, Aberdeen

'Try to get your booklist early and be first in line for second-hand books – then sell them back to your uni library later.'

3rd year Physics student, UCL

'Take a gap year and save.'

3rd year Geography Management student, York

'Find food nearing its sell-by date and being sold off cheaply, then freeze it.'

1st year Social and Political Science student, Cambridge

Loans – paying them back

Will I be able to afford to pay back my loans?

It may take a long time, but a system has been worked out that allows you to pay back what you borrowed in line with what you earn.

When do I have to pay back my loans?

You repay nothing until the April after you have graduated, and then only when your income is over £15,000 pa will you begin to pay off the loans. The amount you pay is related to your salary, so whether you have borrowed £1,000 or £25,000, have had a maintenance or fee loan, or both, your monthly repayments will be the same if you stay on the same salary. You will go on paying until the debt is paid off. However, if after 25 years you still haven't paid it all off, the government will write off anything left outstanding (except arrears). Rates are currently worked out at 9% of income over £15,000. So the current scale looks something like this:

Annual income up to	Monthly repayments	Repayment as % of income
£15,000	£0	0
£16,000	£7	0.6
£17,000	£15	1.1
£18,000	£22	1.5
£19,000	£30	1.9
£20,000	£37	2.3
£21,000	£45	2.6
£22,000	£52	2.9
£23,000	£60	3.1
£24,000	£67	3.4
£25,000	£75	3.6

How will I make the repayments?

Repayments will be collected through the Inland Revenue and will be deducted from your pay packet at source. Probably all you will know about it is an entry on your pay slip.

Will I have to pay back more than I borrow?

In real terms, no. The interest rates on loans are linked to inflation, so while the actual figure you pay will be higher, the value of the amount you pay back is broadly the same as the value of the amount you borrowed. The interest rate in the year to August 2007 was 2.4%; the rate from September 2007 to August 2008 is 4.8%. So it does vary.

Will all students graduate with a huge debt?

Most students starting a course now will have to face up to the prospect of starting work with a debt to pay off, and this could be substantially more than the amount totted up under the Student Loans Scheme. According to the NatWest Students Money Matters Survey, school leavers in 2007 estimated that they would graduate with a debt of £34,740 and since they will be paying top-up fees for their full course this could turn out to be a reality. Our research amongst undergraduates in 2007 showed that: 66% of students had overdrafts; some 65% had student loans; 44% had a tuition fee loan; and a massive 90% expected to be in debt either to the bank or to the Student Loans Company, or possibly both, by the end of their course – by anything from a few hundred pounds to over £16,000. (The most quoted figure over £16,000 was £21,000 plus.)

Estimated student debt	
2007–08	
7%	No debt
4%	Less than £1,000
2%	£1,000–£2,000
3%	£2,000–£4,000
4%	£4,000–£6,000
2%	£6,000–£8,000
13%	£8,000–£10,000
15%	£10,000–£12,000
13%	£12,000–£14,000
11%	£14,000–£16,000
27%	Over £16,000

Great news – loan repayment holiday for students

Students starting their course this year 2008–2009, and so start their loan repayments in or after April 2012, will be eligible for a loan repayment holiday of up to five years at any time after they graduate. This means you can put your repayments on hold at any time of your choice. This could be a great help if you are wanting to buy a house, go travelling, have got into debt. As we publish, this only applies to English domiciled students. The rest of the UK is still thinking about the idea.

Cash crisis note

- Check out Chapter 10 on budgeting – it might save you a few sleepless nights.
- Compare current bank overdraft rates for newly qualified graduates.

Do the pay-back rules ever change?

They are reviewed every year to make sure graduates can realistically pay back what they owe. The payback threshold has been £15,000 for the last few years.

Will I be able to pay it all back?

As well as the possibility of graduating with a massive debt, most students graduate to a fairly substantial salary. Starting salaries for graduates with good second-class honours degrees in a blue-chip company in 2008 are expected to be around £24,000 (median figure – AGR Winter Review 2008). If you are earning around £2,000 a month, the repayments won't seem quite so grisly. But will you find a job? Are you going to be a 2:1 success story? Many graduates start work on salaries of less than £16,000. At the time of writing, the employment market for graduates in the UK is said to be slowing down. Deloitte, one of the largest private sector employers of graduates, has seen a 22 per cent rise in the number of graduate applicants which is always a bad sign. But according to the Association of Graduate Recruiters Recruitment Survey, Winter Review graduate vacancies are expected to rise by a massive 16.4% in 2008. Whatever the truth, it's worth remembering that if you can't find work, the Student Loans Company will wait for repayment; the banks, however, may not be so sympathetic, though most do offer special overdraft facilities to graduates, which you should investigate.

I'm a graduate with £20,000 student-loan debts to clear – is my new employer likely to pay this off?

When the loan scheme first came in, many employers thought they might need to offer the 'carrot' of paying off students' loans if they wanted to attract the best graduates. Whether the government was hoping that employers would step in and clear students' debts in this way was a question often discussed in the national press. In fact, at least one major company did draw up contingency plans for a 'golden hello' scheme, and a number of companies we contacted said they were watching the market and their competitors very closely.

Then the recession hit the UK hard, graduate openings were in short supply, and graduates were competing for jobs rather than employers competing for graduates. Employers put all ideas of 'loan pay-off schemes for students' on the back burner. However, market trends and influences change very rapidly. Good-quality graduates are seen to be in short supply again and employers are quite genuinely concerned about the amount of debt graduates have. So the 'golden hello' has quietly materialised. I say 'quietly' because few employers are keen to call it that. According to the 2008 Association of Graduate Recruiters Winter Graduate Recruitment Survey, 33% of their members offer 'golden hellos', and the median level of payout is £2,000.

Cash crisis note

Don't forget, if you're anticipating a 'golden hello', that the taxman will expect his cut.

Where are the big graduate starting salaries to be earned?	
Median starting salaries in 2007 by type of organisation	
Investment banking/Fund Managers	£35,500
Law firms	£35,000
Banking/financial services	£29,000
Consulting/business services	£26,563
IT	£25,500
Telecommunications	£25,000
Accountancy	£24,250
FMCG (Fast Moving Consumer Goods)	£24,000
Energy/water/utility	£22,750
Engineering/industrial	£22,750
Construction	£22,500
Retail	£22,000
Public sector	£20,730

(AGR Graduate Recruitment Survey, Winter Review 2008)

Cash crisis: Girls, is this fair?

You are likely to earn £1,000 a year less than your male counterparts and this is apparent within three years of leaving university according to a major survey on graduate experience published in January 2008 by the Higher Education Statistics Agency (HESA). Whatever happened to equal opportunities?

Can I get out of repaying student loans?

Yes:

- ⦿ If you never earn more than £15,000 a year
- ⦿ If you become permanently disabled
- ⦿ If you die!
- ⦿ After 25 years the loan will be written off.

Is bankruptcy an option?

Not any longer.

A few years ago we reported that some 9,000 students and graduates were considering making themselves bankrupt to avoid debt. New laws making it easier to become bankrupt were being introduced, and in straightforward cases you could probably clear your debts within 12 months.

The government, it would seem, were hot on their heels, moving rapidly to close this obvious loophole in its system of student finance, and today the Student Loans Company tells us that making yourself bankrupt is not an option for clearing your student loan debt. Well, at least your good reputation will be intact.

Cash crisis note

It's official ...

The great British entrepreneurial spirit is not dead and only slightly dampened by rising student debt. The number of students planning to set up their own business after qualifying remains consistent at 4%, or around 30,000 students.

However, student debt is likely to slow down their plans: while 75% of students with ambitions to go it alone would either scale back or defer their plans until their debts were paid off, a brave (possibly foolish) quarter would carry on regardless.

(Survey commissioned by the National Council for Graduate Entrepreneurship (NCGE) in conjunction with Barclays, 2006)

Where can I get more information on student loans?

- ⊙ The Student Loans Company is based at 100 Bothwell Street, Glasgow G2 7JD. It has a free Student Loans Scheme Customer Support Line: 0845 607 7577. Website: www.slc.co.uk. Student Finance Direct website: www.studentfinancedirect.co.uk.
- ⊙ Full information about the Student Loans Scheme is set out in its own leaflet, issued free and updated each year.
- ⊙ There are many anomalies within the scheme that we have not touched on here. For details see 'Further information' at the end of this chapter (page 73). Do also take advice from your local authority and college so that you know exactly what you are getting involved in.

Cash crisis note

72% of sixth formers starting university last summer said they were already worried about the amount of debt they could face while 73% were concerned about the increase in fees; 66% said their biggest concern was money being tight while only 54% were concerned about failing their exams.

(NatWest Student Money Matters Survey)

Is the Student Loans Scheme better than borrowing from the bank?

Most banks and some building societies will give students overdraft facilities on special terms, usually including an interest-free £1,000–£2,000 overdraft facility (see page 55). This is intended mainly to help you during that difficult period when your loan hasn't yet arrived or you've run out of cash at the end of the term. The overdraft is wiped out as soon as the loan cheque arrives. It is better to use the bank's 'interest-free' facility if your financial problems are temporary or you are certain you will be able to pay it back once you graduate. Most banks won't start charging interest on student overdrafts immediately you graduate, giving you time to get a job. This can be several months, but check it out with your bank. Banks also offer students longer-term loans at competitive rates, which should be investigated.

But, in general, banks are not the best bet for long-term borrowing for students – the Student Loans Scheme is, since the interest rate is no more than inflation, and payback is related to your salary and ability to pay. (See details on pay-back arrangements on pages 65–66.)

It's worth remembering, however, that to get a loan you have to have a bank or building society account. As mentioned, if you already have an overdraft with your bank, as soon as the loan hits your account it will automatically be used to pay off the overdraft, so you might not actually find that you have more cash in hand to spend, though you'll certainly have more peace of mind.

The bank is the student's friend

For most students the best thing the bank offers is the interest free overdraft.

But remember:

- ◉ To get the free interest overdraft facility you must tell your bank you are a student.
- ◉ If your overdraft goes over the set free interest limit you will be charged interest.
- ◉ You may be able to negotiate a larger interest-free overdraft, but don't bank on it.
- ◉ Use the bank's free interest limit rather than build up debt on a credit card.

Interest-free loans offered by banks to students in 2007–08:

	Abbey	BOS	Barclays	Halifax	HSBC	Lloyds TSB	Natwest	RBS
1st year	£1,000	£2,750	£1,000	£2,750	£1,000	£1,500	£1,250	£1,250
2nd year	£1,250	£2,750	£1,250	£2,750	£1,250	£1,500	£1,400	£1,400
3rd year	£1,500	£2,750	£1,500	£2,750	£1,500	£1,500	£1,600	£1,600
4th year	£1,800	£2,750	£1,750	£2,750	£1,750	£2,000	£1,800	£1,800

See what else the banks offer in Chapter 10 page 163.

Cash Crisis Health Note

Health check

I'm sick and myopic, and I've got toothache – can I get free treatment?

As a student you don't actually qualify for any help, but as someone on a low income you could qualify for free or reduced:

- dental charges
- glasses
- eye tests
- prescriptions.

Form HC1 ...

... is the starting point, available from high street opticians, the Benefits Agency or post Office. That will probably send you off on a trail leading to form HC2 or HC3; if you haven't received either of these items you will need form HC5, and don't forget to ask the chemist for receipt form FP57 (EC57 in Scotland) to claim for free prescription charges. If you are confused – and who isn't? – then leaflet HC11 (Are you Entitled to Help with Health Costs?) will put you straight on the NHS in general and HC12 on costs – both are available from your Benefits Agency or by phoning 0845 850 1166 (local rates) or 0191 203 5555.

Try to get things going before treatment begins, or at least before you need to pay up. Otherwise, make sure you keep all bills and receipts, as evidence of costs. If after filling in HC1 you are told you are not entitled to any help and you think you are, give the Department of Health a ring on their freephone advice line 0800 917 7711. It could be that the computer is 'confused' as well – it has been known! It can be a long process, but it's often worth the effort.

For immediate medical advice, phone NHS Direct on 0845 4647.

It's serious – I could be off sick for weeks. What should I do?

If you become seriously ill and are likely to be off sick for months then you should obviously let your university department know, but also your LA and the Student Loans Company, since your student loans might be affected if you are off for more than 60 days.

Thrift tips

'Spend time in the library in winter as it's warm and saves on heating bills.'
2nd year Politics and History student, Aberystwyth

'Take all the food you can at breakfast, which is free, and eat it for lunch.'
1st year Medical student living in halls of residence at Dundee

'If you think £1 is nothing, try saving one a day for a year. £365 is two months' rent.'
2nd year Electronics student, Robert Gordon University

Further information

Who to contact/what to read

Contact Student Finance Direct 0845 607 7577 for financial information including information on your loans.

Contact the Student Helpline, 0845 602 0583, between 10am and 4pm for more detailed questions on student finance and eligibility.

Full information about fees, maintenance grants and loans is given in the following free booklets, which you would be well advised to get and study:

- ◉ For students in England: *A Guide to Financial Support for Higher Education Students in 2008/9* (which is the source for the loan statistics in this chapter). Tel: (booklet) 0800 731 9133; (helpline) 0845 602 0583. Website: www. studentfinancedirect.co.uk. Braille and cassette editions also available.

- ◉ For students in Scotland: *Student Support in Scotland: A Guide for Undergraduate Students 2008/9*, available from any Scottish university or the Student Awards Agency for Scotland (SAAS), 3 Redheughs Rigg, South Gyle, Edinburgh EH12 9YT. Tel: 0131 476 8212. Email: saas.geu@scotland.gsi.gov.uk. Website: www.student-support-saas.gov.uk.

- ◉ For students in Northern Ireland: *Financial Support for Students in Higher Education 2008/9*, Student Support Branch, Department for Employment and Learning (Northern Ireland), Rathgael House, Balloo Road, Bangor, Co. Down BT19 7PR. Tel: 028 9025 7710; (for booklet) 0800 731 9133. Website: www.delni.gov.uk.

- ◉ For students in Wales: *A Guide to Financial Support for Higher Education*, National Assembly for Wales, Higher Education Division 2, 3rd floor, Cathays Park, Cardiff CF10 3NQ. Tel: 0845 602 8845. Websites: www.studentfinancewales.co.uk; www.learning.wales.co.uk.

Cash crisis note

Can't face all this debt? There's always The Open University. More and more young people are choosing The Open University as a way around accumulating debt for university. In 2006/07 of all its students, the OU had 20,984 undergraduate students under 25 years of age – the equivalent of a good-sized university. That's more than a three-fold increase in the last eight years. And of those, a third (5,771) were new students, aged 21 and under. The average cost of an OU degree is £3,700. By comparison figures show a three-year degree at a conventional university will cost over £33,000 (news.bbc.co.uk/1/hi/education/6090872.stm). The OU doesn't ask for qualifications to get in.

- Most students in our universities would probably argue the OU route is not so much fun, but then debt isn't a bundle of laughs either. For information check their website (www.open.ac.uk) or phone 0845 300 6090.

★ Lowest drop-out/failed to get a degree rates	
Oxford	1.4%
Royal Veterinary College	1.8%
Royal College of Music	1.9%
Durham	2.8%
Nottingham	3%
LSE	3.1%
Warwick	3.3%
Bristol	4%
Imperial College	4%
St George's Hospital Medical School/Royal Welsh College of Music and Drama	4.1%

(HESA performance indicators for UK universities and colleges – full-time study for courses started 2004/05 predicted, published September 2006)

★ Highest drop-out/failed to get a degree rates	
UHI Millennium Institute	35.3%
University of Bolton	31%
University of Glamorgan	29.9%
Aston University	27.1%
Middlesex University	26.5%
Liverpool Hope University	26.3%
University of Salford	25.4%
London Southbank University	25.3%
North East Wales Institute of HE	25%
Swansea Institute of HE	24.1%

(HESA performance indicators for UK universities and colleges – full-time study, for courses starting 2004/05 published September 2007)

Am I a special case?

Funding for students in special categories

This chapter looks at various special categories and funding options

- Geographical – Scotland, Wales, Northern Ireland, (page 76)
- Where is the best place to live and to study? Check our comparative funding table (page 81)
- Students from abroad (page 81)
- Courses with a difference – sandwich/industrial placements, part-time courses, foundation courses, second undergraduate degrees at Oxbridge, distance learning courses (page 86)
- Attending a private higher education institution (page 89)
- Healthcare courses – nursing, midwifery, paramedics, medicine, dentistry (page 89)
- Specialist courses – teaching, physics, social work, dance & drama (page 91)
- Additional help for specialist groups – mature students, students with dependants, disabled students (page 93)
- Studying abroad (page 97)
- Further information (page 103)

This chapter looks at the funding and extra help that is available for students in special categories. In some cases this is in addition to the funding outlined in the previous chapter; in others it is a completely different system or, sadly, there is no funding at all.

Geographical – Scotland, Wales and Northern Ireland

Not all regions of the UK follow the same student funding system. Scotland, for example, decided to introduce its own no-fees funding solution for its own students soon after the new Scottish Parliament was set up. Now Wales has decided to take a more independent line.

Scotland – what's the deal?

In brief:

- If you live and study in Scotland you pay NO FEES for your university education, and because of EU regulations, this also applies to non-UK EU students.
- Students from the rest of the UK who study in Scotland do pay fees but less than in the rest of the UK.
- Scottish students attending universities in England, Wales and Northern Ireland pay top-up fees of up to £3,145 pa.
- As in the rest of the UK, those paying fees will be able to get a loan to cover their fees.
- All students studying in or outside Scotland can apply for a maintenance loan.
- Non-repayable bursaries will be given to students from low-income families. These will replace part of the loan so you will not incur too much debt.
- The graduate endowment, previously paid by Scottish and EU students who study in Scotland, has been abolished: a saving to students of over £2,000.
- Better off Scottish parents are assessed to contribute more than in the rest of the UK.

I'm a Scottish student studying in Scotland

If you are a Scottish student studying in Scotland you are eligible for:

Student's loan	Min.	Max.
Living in parental home	£590	£3,570
Living elsewhere (amount depends on family income and bursary; loan rates for final-year students are slightly lower)	£890	£4,510
Non-repayable Young Students' Bursary (means-tested on family income of up to £33,330; full YSB paid if family income £18,825 or less)	Up to £2,575	
Additional loan for students from low-income families (on family income up to £21,210)	Up to £590	
(Loan money for Scottish students studying in Scotland is paid out monthly)		

Extra loan for longer courses

If your course is longer than 30 weeks and 3 days you can claim for additional loan:

Living in parents' home £53 per week

Living elsewhere £81 per week

I'm a part-time student: will I get any help?

Yes, and better than in the past. From Autumn 2008 a £500 part-time HE fee grant will be given to new and existing part-time students who earn £18,000 or less and are studying 50% or more of a full-time degree course. This is a fee grant and will replace the current £500 loan which has been abolished so you won't have to pay it back.

See chart on page 87.

I'm a Scottish student studying outside Scotland

If you are studying in the UK but outside Scotland you will have to pay the full fees demanded by the university for your course, up to £3,145 pa.

To help finance your studies you are eligible for:

Student fee loan to cover fees (not means tested)	Up to £3,145	
Non-repayable means-tested bursary (on family income up to £33,330; full bursary given where family income £18,825 or less)	Up to £2,095	
Student maintenance loan	**Min.**	**Max.**
Living away from home in London	£890	£5,565
Studying elsewhere	£890	£4,510
Studying outside Scotland but living at home	£590	£3,570
(The maintenance loan is based on family income and bursary received; loan rates for final-year students are slightly lower)		
Additional loan for students from low-income families (on family income up to £21,210)	£590	
You may be eligible for a bursary from your university: see page 44.		

Extra loan for longer courses

If your course is longer than 30 weeks and 3 days you can claim for additional loan:

Living in parents' home £53 per week

Living elsewhere £81 per week

London £103

What parents in Scotland are expected to pay

This table will give some idea of what Scottish parents could be in for.

But, remember, students in families where the residual income is up to £33,330 should be receiving an income assessed Young Student's Bursary.

Residual income	Assessed contribution
£23,660	£45
£25,000	£194
£30,000	£749
£35,000	£1,305
£40,000	£1,861
£45,000	£2,416
£50,000	£2,985
£55,000	£3,755
£60,000	£4,524
	(NB figures for a spouse are slightly higher)

Families with a residual income below £23,660 are not expected to contribute.

A deduction of £190 will be made from the assessed contribution for every dependent child other than the student. No parent is expected to contribute more than £4,675 pa for one child studying in London or £3,620 pa if the student is living away from home and studying anywhere else, and £2,980 pa if the student is living at home, however much they earn. These figures are based on the full loan minus minimum loan that a student can take out. If there is more than one child at university the maximum contribution a parent can be expected to make is £7,795 pa, regardless of how many offspring they have at university. Although Scottish parents may look with envy at parents in the rest of the UK, who will be assessed to contribute considerably less than those in Scotland, English students will be accumulating a great deal more debt than their Scottish counterparts.

Travel for Scottish students

If living away from home, three return journeys per year to your place of study can be claimed for, plus additional term-time travel to and from your institution. (This does not include students whose parents live outside the UK.) The first £155 of any claim will be disregarded. Only the most economical fares will be allowed. (Cost of student railcard or bus pass may also be reimbursed.)

I'm a student from outside Scotland studying in Scotland

If you are from outside Scotland you will pay a set fee of £1,775 pa. This may seem like a lot less than the £3,145 students are paying in other parts of the UK, but the reasoning is that Scottish degree courses last four years whereas degrees in the rest of the UK generally last three years. If you multiply £1,775 by four you'll see you're paying a lot less than the £9,435 some students will have to find. But Scottish universities will be under no obligation to pay bursaries to students from lower-income families and are unlikely to do so. The rest of your funding will follow the English pattern, so see Chapter 2 for details on fee loans (page 39), maintenance grants (page 43) and maintenance loans (page 46). Fees for Medicine, see page 90.

Wales – what's the deal?

Welsh students studying in Wales

The Welsh Assembly, like the Scottish Parliament, has decided to take an independent line on fees. While UK students from outside Wales will have to pay in full the top-up fees asked by universities, students who normally live in Wales and choose to study in Wales, along with EU students, will receive a fee grant of £1,890 pa to offset part of the fee. This is not means-tested, does not have to be repaid and will have the effect of keeping the fees Welsh students pay in Wales down to £1,255 pa. To cover the portion of the fees you have to pay, you can apply for a fee loan.

Welsh students from lower-income families will be able to apply for a Higher Education Assembly Grant of up to £2,835 to help with maintenance. This is means-tested and, while operating in a similar way to the grant in England it has a much lower family income cut-off threshold.

Household income	Grant
£0 – £18,370	£2,835
£18,370 – £39,300	Partial grant depending on family income
Over £39,300	No grant

You can also apply for a maintenance loan (see page 46). For every £1 of grant received, the amount of maintenance loan will be reduced by £1 up to £1,255. You may also be eligible for a bursary from your university.

Students from outside Wales who study in Wales

Students who come from outside Wales and study at Welsh universities can be asked to pay fees of up to £3,145 and you will have to pay whatever the university asks. You will not be entitled to the fee grant given to Welsh students, but you will be able to apply for a fee loan to cover costs (see page 39). Maintenance grants of up to £2,835 will be available for students from lower-income families, as in England (see page 43 for details). And the cut off-point for family income for receiving a grant is much higher than in Wales, at £60,005. You will also be able to take out a maintenance loan (see page 46). In addition, under the Welsh Bursary Scheme, students who receive the maximum maintenance grant (Assembly Learning Grant in Wales), regardless of where they come from in the UK, will be eligible for a minimum bursary of £310 a year. This is instead of the university bursaries given in England. Welsh universities, as in England, may choose to give higher bursaries (see page 44).

Welsh students studying outside Wales

It looks as if you are going to be rather hard done by unless there is a sudden change of mind. If you normally live in Wales but are studying outside Wales, you will not be entitled to a fee grant and will have to pay the fees demanded by the university of your choice – up to £3,145 pa. You will be entitled to take out a loan to cover fees (see page 39) and a maintenance loan (see page 46). You may be entitled to an Assembly Learning Grant of up to £2,835, as given to Welsh students studying in Wales – see above. This is given on a sliding scale depending on family income with an income cut-off point of £39,300 (NOT £60,005 as in England, unless there is a sudden change of mind). You may also be entitled to a bursary from your university (see page 44).

Northern Ireland – what's the deal?

Northern Ireland generally follows the same system as in England (see Chapter 2), but there are a few differences. While the basic grant is higher than in England, the family income cut-off point for receiving a grant is much lower at £39,305 as in Wales.

Maintenance grants and loans – assuming student is living away from home and not studying in London			
Income	Grant	Maintenance loan	Total
£18,360	£3,335	£2,865	£6,200
£20,000	£2,975	£2,952	£5,927
£25,000	£1,878	£3,216	£5,094
£27,810	£1,260	£3,365	£4,625
£30,000	£1,030	£3,595	£4,625
£35,000	£504	£4,121	£4,625
£39,305	£50	£4,575	£4,625

1. The maintenance grant is £500 higher than in England at £3,335. It is non-repayable and, of course, means-tested. But, as you will see from the chart above, the amount of loan that students from lower-income families are able to take out is also reduced.

2. Cut-off point for grant is when family income reaches £39,305.

3. If you are planning to study at a publicly funded college in the Republic of Ireland you will not have to pay tuition fees. However, the college will make a registration charge of €825 (2007/8 figures).

4. Extra help if in a sticky situation: Support Funds are available through your university in Northern Ireland. These operate in a similar way to the Access to Learning Fund in the UK. See page 63 for details.

Where is the best place to live and to study?

Check our comparative funding table – see overleaf.

Students from abroad – what will it cost, who will pay?

EU students

EU students will be treated on a similar basis to UK counterparts regarding fees.

- If studying in England or Northern Ireland you will be expected to pay up to £3,145 pa towards your fees.
- If studying in Wales you will pay £1,255 pa and will receive a fee grant of £1,890 to pay for the rest of your fees (see page 79).
- If studying in Scotland you pay no fees.

Confused by who gets what? This table may help.

Student support	English students in England	Welsh students in Wales	English students in Wales	Welsh students in England/NI	NI students, everywhere except Scotland	Scots in Scotland	Rest UK in Scotland	Scots in England/Wales/NI
Fees	Up to £3,145 pa	£1,255 (rest of fee £1,890 pa covered by fee grant)	£3,145 pa	Up to £3,145 pa	Up to £3,145 pa	None	£1,775 pa	Up to £3,145 pa
Fee Loan	Up to £3,145 pa	£1,255 pa	£3,145 pa	Up to £3,145 pa	Up to £3,145 pa	None	£1,775 pa	Up to £3,145 pa
Maintenance grant	Up to £2,835 pa	Up to £2,835 pa	Up to £2,835 pa	Up to £2,835 pa	Up to £3,335 pa	Up to £2,575 pa	Up to £2,835 pa (up to £3,335 pa if from NI)	Up to £2,095 pa
Full grant – Earning up to	£25,000	£18,370	£25,000	£18,370	£18,360	£18,825	Eng £25,000 Wales £18,379 NI £18,360	£18,825
Earnings threshold for grant	£60,005	£39,300	£60,005	£39,300	£39,305	£33,330	Eng £60,005 Wales £39,300 NI £39,305 pa	£33,330
Max Maintenance Loan–London	£6,475 pa	N/A	N/A	£6,475 pa	£6,475 pa	N/A	N/A	£890–£5,565 pa
Elsewhere	£4,625 pa	£4,625 pa	£4,625 pa	£4,625 pa	£4,625 pa	£890–£4,510 pa	£4,625 pa	£890–£4,510 pa
Live Home	£3,580 pa	£3,580 pa	£3,580 pa	£3,580 pa	£3,580 pa	£590–£3,570 pa	£3,580 pa	£590–£3,570 pa
Extra Maintenance Loan	NO	NO	NO	NO	NO	£590	NO	£590
Uni bursary if receiving grant	Min £310 pa (av. on full grant £1,000)	Min £310 pa if on full grant	Min £310 pa if receiving full grant	Min £310 pa (av. on full grant £1,000)	Min £310 pa (av. on full grant £1,000)	NO	NO	Min £310 (av. on full grant £1,000)
Family contribution	Up to 25% of loan, max £1,618 pa	Up to 25% of loan, max £1,156 pa	Up to 25% loan, max £1,156 pa	Up to 25% loan, max £1,618 pa	Up to 25% loan, max £1,618 pa	Max £3,530 pa (£2,910 pa if student living at home)	Max £1,156 pa (up to 25% of loan)	Max £4,560 pa

All EU students will be able to take out a loan to cover their fees and then pay them off gradually once they graduate.

EU students are not entitled to apply for a maintenance loan or a maintenance bursary and will not receive maintenance grant.

I am French so studying in England is really expensive as there is not much help available. I will have to borrow money from my bank in France because I'm worrying about money. But at least I should have a job when I graduate, and the experiences I'm living are priceless!

1st year Natural Sciences student, Durham

Please give EU students loans and sponsorship – we need help too!

Christopher, Physics student, Oxford

It's a fact!

More EU students than ever (18,089) started degree courses in our universities in 2007: up 17.9% on the previous year. And the number of students from non-EU countries was up 4.4% to 28,225.

(UCAS figures)

It's a fact!

The proportion of graduates recruited from ethnic minorities by UK employers rose to 26.7% in 2007. Main reasons given for marketing UK vacancies overseas were: capturing the very best talent (75.5%), being global employers (73.4%), strong work ethic and desire to succeed (24.5%), lack of UK candidates with the right qualifications (22.4%), can't find enough UK graduates with the right skills (16.3%).

AGR Graduate Recruitment Survey 2008 Winter Review

Non-EU 'overseas' students

Even though most UK students pay fees, the full cost of a course is subsidised by the government. Students from countries outside the EU will be charged the full cost of the course and can legally be charged higher tuition fees than UK students – so for a first-degree course you can think in terms of:

- Classroom taught: £8,600 pa
- Science/lab-based course: £9,900 pa
- Clinical course: £21,500 pa.

(Figures are averages for the year 2007–2008.)

You will not be eligible for a fee loan, a maintenance loan or grant or any help with funding. Some universities do give bursaries to overseas students, and some charities have special funds for overseas students. See Chapter 8, page 171.

Fee rates for postgraduates can be higher (see page 179). Most universities and colleges do have a designated overseas adviser whom you could ask for help.

For details on living in the UK try the educational enquiry service at the British Council Information Centre (tel: 0161 957 7755; email: general.enquiries@britishcouncil.org; or write to the British Council at Bridgewater House, 58 Whitworth Street, Manchester M1 6BB) or contact UKCOSA (website: www.ukcosa.org.uk; Advisory Service tel: 020 7107 9922 – open 1pm–4pm Monday–Friday). Their Council for International Education handles around 10,000 enquiries from students a year. Otherwise, try the British Council, High Commission or Embassy in your own country.

It's a fact

Higher education in England for students from the former colonies of Britain and three other European countries – Denmark, the Netherlands and France – has suddenly become a lot cheaper. Since autumn 2007 university students from places like the Falkland Islands, Bermuda, Anguilla and 18 other territories will pay the same fees as students in England – generally £3,145 pa. For a full list of countries affected contact 0870 000 2288 or info@dfes.gsi.gov.uk.

Refugees and asylum seekers – what help is there?

Very little!

If you have the right qualifications, and can afford it, you are free to apply to any UK university. But any funding, and how much you must pay, will depend on your immigration status and how long you have been in the UK. Most refugees and asylum seekers do not qualify for funding and are considered 'overseas' students, which means they may well be charged the overseas fee rate. (See page 83 – 'Non-EU 'overseas' students'). Also see ruling for students from former British colonies. If you're living and studying in Scotland your situation may be slightly different to that in the rest of the UK.

★ Countries sending students to study in the UK

Country	2007	2006	Change
China	5,058	4,502	+12.4%
Cyprus	2,593	2,022	+28.2%
Ireland	2,572	2,675	−3.9%
France	2,559	2,388	+7.2%
Hong Kong	2,546	2,360	+7.9%
Germany	2,226	2,077	+7.2%
Poland	1,973	1,555	+26.9%
Malaysia	1,942	1,698	+14.4%
Nigeria	1,913	2,078	−9.9%
Greece	1,632	1,521	+7.3%

(UCAS application figures for 2007)

If you have already lived in the UK for three years, funding concessions are occasionally available, but don't expect it.

However, if you are granted full refugee status, you will be eligible for the same funding as UK students – see Chapter 2. If you have already started your degree studies and your immigration status changes it is important to tell your university as soon as possible. You must apply for any support within four months.

So where can refugees and asylum seekers not entitled to funding find help?

- Some universities offer bursaries to students from overseas – see *University Scholarships, Awards and Bursaries*, published by Trotman. Check also individual university websites and prospectuses.
- There are many trusts and charities in this country that have funds to help students from overseas – see Chapter 8.
- Scholarship search databases can be found on www.educationuk.org and www.hotcourses.com.
- For more information check out the following websites: www.egas-online.org.uk/fwa/datapage.asp; www.ukcosa.org.uk; www.refugeecouncil.org.uk; www.britishcouncil.org.uk; www.education-action.org.uk.

You think you've got it hard. As an overseas student I get no government support and I'm working my ass off to support myself.

Connie, a Physics student at Imperial College London, who earns £84 a week during term time and £175 a week during vacations as a Sales Assistant

Further information for international students

EU students

- For information on tuition fees for European Union students, plus other information, contact: EU Customer Services Team, Room 38, Mowden Hall, Darlington, Co. Durham DL3 9BG. Tel: 0141 243 3570 (10am–4pm). Email: EUTeam@slc.co.uk. Website: www.direct.gov.uk/.
- UK Socrates-Erasmus. Address: Rothford, Giles Lane, Canterbury, Kent CT2 7LR. Tel: 01227 762712. Fax: 01227 762711. Email: info@erasmus.ac.uk. Website: www.erasmus.ac.uk.
- Leonardo da Vinci: check with your university or college.
- Investing in the Future – Financial Support for EU Students, from Publications Department. Tel: 0845 602 2260.

Students from abroad studying in the UK

- *Studying and Living in the UK* is a British Council publication which provides detailed information about life in the UK for international students. It should answer many of your general questions on subjects like accommodation, living costs, study options, cultural issues and much more. Download from http://www.educationuk.org/downloads/study_live_uk.pdf.

See also:

- ⊙ Education UK (the British Council's one-stop-shop website for information on UK education) http://www.educationuk.org.
- ⊙ UKCISA (the Council for International Student Affairs) http://www.ukcisa.org.uk.
- ⊙ VisitBritain (the official website for tourism in Britain) http://www.visitbritain.com.
- ⊙ I-UK (an essential guide to the UK) http://www.i-uk.com/.
- ⊙ UCAS Instructions for Completion of the Application Form by International Students. Free from UCAS with your application form.
- ⊙ Useful contact for funding enquiries: British Council Information Centre. Tel: 0161 957 7755. Email: general.enquires@britishcouncil.org. Or access the website (www.educationuk.org) giving full information about courses. Or you can write to the British Council at Bridgewater House, 58 Whitworth Street, Manchester M1 6BB.
- ⊙ *A Guide to Studying and Living in Britain*: full of practical advice. Published by How to Books. Available from Trotman, tel: 0870 900 2665, or visit the website www.trotman.co.uk/bookshop.

Refugees and asylum seekers

Check out the following websites:

- ⊙ www.info-for-asylumseekers.org.uk
- ⊙ www.egas-online.org.uk/fwa/datapage.asp
- ⊙ www.ukcosa.org.uk
- ⊙ www.refugeecouncil.org.uk.
- ⊙ www.educationaction.org
- ⊙ www.hotcourses.com
- ⊙ www.educationuk.org

Courses With a Difference

Sandwich/industrial placements

Will I have to pay fees during my industrial placement?

Yes. Whether it is a thick or thin sandwich placement, all students will have to pay fees. Those who spend an entire year of a course on a industrial/sandwich placement at home or abroad will pay reduced fees. Top-up-fee students will find that universities can set their own figure with a maximum of £1,572 – 50% of the current fee. But why, you might ask, do you have to pay fees when you are not enjoying the advantage of university? This is said to be a contribution towards the cost to the institution of administrative and pastoral arrangements relating to the placement. If the placement is for less than a full year, full fees will be charged, up to £3,145 pa. You may apply for a fee loan (see page 39) and also for a maintenance loan (see page 46). If you are on a full year's industrial training you will only be eligible for the reduced rate of loan – see rates below.

	Full year
London	£3,180
Elsewhere in UK	£2,265
Parental home	£1,700
Overseas	£2,710

I'm a part-time student – will I get any help?

Yes, up to £1,435 pa.

Part-time students doing 50% or more of a full-time course can apply for an income-assessed fee grant towards fees of up to £1,180 and a course grant to help with travel and books of up to £255. Both are means-tested.

Course	England & N. Ireland Fee grant	England & N. Ireland Course grant (max. available)	Wales Fee grant	Wales Course grant (max. available)	Scotland Fee grant
50–59% of the full-time course	£785	£255	£620	£1,050	Up to £500
60–74% of the full-time course	£945	£255	£745	£1,050	Up to £500
75%+ of the full-time course	£1,180	£255	£930	£1,050	Up to £500

There are around 500,000 part-timers in higher education in England, and the government expects around 85,000 to benefit from this financial package.

I'm going to take a foundation course – will I get funding?

Some courses include a preliminary or foundation year. These are designed to prepare students for study in their chosen subject if their qualifications or experience are not sufficient to start a degree-level course of study. The same support is available to students on a foundation year as for undergraduates if, and this is crucial, the following conditions are met:

- The foundation year is an integral part of the course
- The course as a whole is eligible for student support
- You enrol for the whole course and not just the foundation year.

For full details of funding, see page 53 (England), page 76 (Scotland), page 79 (Wales), and page 80 (Northern Ireland).

It's a fact!

The number of students who started foundation degrees in 2007 was up by a massive 23.8%, to 18,194 from 14,691 in 2006. Most popular courses were still: Design Studies, Computer Science and Sports Science (UCAS figures).

Some universities charge lower fees for foundation courses.

I'm taking a second undergraduate degree at Oxbridge – is there any help?

If you are thinking about studying a second undergraduate degree at either Oxford or Cambridge in one of the disciplines listed below you could be eligible for a College Fee Loan (CFL). You will need to hold a UK honours degree from a publicly funded institution to be eligible. A CFL information leaflet and application form is available from your college.

Eligible courses:

- Medicine (undergraduate and four-year graduate accelerated)
- Dentistry
- Veterinary Science
- Architecture
- Landscape Architecture
- Landscape Design
- Landscape Management
- Town Planning or Town and Country Planning
- Social Work
- Course for which graduates are eligible for a healthcare bursary.

I'm going to do a distance learning course, is there any help?

Yes, if you are on a 'designated' full-time distance learning course you can apply for a fee grant of up to £1,180 a year and a course grant of up to £255 a year. If you are disabled you may also quality for allowances for disabled students (see page 94).

Attending a private higher education institution

Students attending a private higher education institution that has been designated by the DIUS should be able to take out a loan to cover fees of up to £3,145. It may not be enough to completely cover your fees, as these can be higher than in other types of university. You may also be able to take out a maintenance loan and could be eligible for a maintenance grant. The course could cover any topic – Theology and Complementary Medicine for example. See also the Dance and Drama entry on page 93.

Healthcare courses

What's the package for those taking nursing and midwifery courses?

You will not have to pay fees and will receive a non-repayable, non-means-tested bursary, provided you have been accepted for an NHS-funded place. If you receive a bursary you will not be able to apply for a student loan.

Bursary rates for nursing and midwifery DipHE

Based on 45 weeks' attendance

England and Wales from April 2007

- Studying in London: £7,443
- Elsewhere: £6,372
- Living in parental home: £6,372.

Scotland from August 2007: £6,255

Northern Ireland from September 2007: £5,770

I'm taking an allied health professional course – what support is there for me?

The UK health authorities pay the fees of full- and part-time pre-registration students on courses in: Audiology, Chiropody, Dental Hygiene, Dental Therapy, Dietetics, Occupational Therapy, Orthoptics, Physiotherapy, Prosthetics, Radiography, and Speech and Language Therapy. A maintenance bursary is available, but means-tested on family income. It is, however, a bursary and not a loan, so what you get is non-repayable. You will also be able to apply for a lower-rate student loan to make up the balance of your living costs, and you may be eligible for help from the Access to Learning Fund (see Chapter 3, page 63).

Bursary and loan rates

	Bursary rates			Reduced loan rates for 2008–09	
	England/ Wales 2007–08	Scotland 2008–09	N. Ireland 2007–08	England/Wales/ N. Ireland	Scotland
London	£3,225	£2,945	£2,765	£3,180	£2,730
Living away from home	£2,672	£2,395	£2,245	£2,267	£2,210
Living in parents' home	£2,231	£1,820	£1,830	£1,700	£1,695

Extra allowances may be available for extra weeks of study, and also for older students, overseas students, single parents, those who have dependants, or students who incur clinical placement costs.

Medical and dental students – is there any extra help?

Medical and dental students who are on standard five- or six-year courses will be treated as any other student in that area for the first four years of their course and will have to pay the fees required.

Those from outside Scotland who are studying in Scotland will be charged standard fees of £2,825 pa. Scottish students studying in Scotland will not be charged fees. See page 79 for fees in Wales. In your fifth and any subsequent years, funding will be provided by the NHS, which means your tuition fees will be paid and you will be eligible to apply for a means-tested NHS bursary and a reduced maintenance loan from the Student Loans Company (see details under allied health professions above).

If you live in England and want to study in Scotland, Wales or Northern Ireland the NHS Student Grants Unit will assess and pay your bursary.

If you live in Scotland, Wales or Northern Ireland and want to study in England you should consult the relevant national authorities.

Graduates taking the four-year accelerated course in medicine for graduates should see Chapter 9, page 197.

A medical student's story

'When you get to your first year of clinics (fourth year) you are still expected to survive on not much more than undergraduates (i.e. the student loan). However, your days and weeks are longer, there are weekend/night shifts, and it's a 48-week year – so not much time to work. All through uni I had relied on a holiday job to keep me afloat. Now it was not so easy. I was maxed out on an already over-extended overdraft and the bank were threatening to charge me, while my landlord wanted the rent. All I needed was £100 to pull me back from the brink. I applied to my university, but the dean of students could not be contacted and the finance office said I would have to wait seven days even for an appointment to be considered for "emergency" funds. So what did I do? Borrowed from a friend.'

4th year medical student, UCL

NHS bursaries

- England: NHS Student Grants Unit, 22 Plymouth Road, Blackpool FY3 7JS. Tel: 01253 655655. Courses helpline for England: 0845 606 0655. Website: www.nhspa.gov.uk/sgu.
- Wales: NHS Student Awards Unit, 2nd floor, Golate House, 101 St Mary's Street, Cardiff CF10 1DX. Tel: 029 2026 1495. Helpline 8045 606 0655.
- Scotland: Student Awards Agency for Scotland, 3 Redheughs Rigg, South Gyle, Edinburgh EH12 9HH. Tel: 0131 476 8227.
- Northern Ireland: Department of Health, Social Services and Public Safety, Human Resources Directorate, D1.4, Castle Buildings, Stormont, Belfast BT4 3SL. Tel: 028 9052 0699.

Specialist courses

What's the deal for trainee teachers?

If you already have a degree and are considering a postgraduate course of initial teacher training (ITT) turn to Chapter 9, page 194, for details of the incentive package that is being offered. You could be in for a nice surprise.

There are no special incentives for undergraduates any more. Undergraduate trainee teachers receive the same funding as other students – sorry!

Trainee teachers in Wales

In addition to the normal funding for undergraduates, in Wales there's a special deal called the Secondary Undergraduate Placement Grant, which is available on an annual basis to support you during school-based teacher training. £1,000 will be paid to undergraduate students who are on a secondary initial teacher training course specialising in one of the secondary priority subjects (which are: design and technology, information technology, maths, modern languages, music, RE, science and Welsh).

This information applies to 2008–2009 and is subject to change in future years. Enquiries about this grant should be directed to the ITT provider with which you wish to study.

Small hardship grants are also available for those who get into unforeseen difficulties that might prevent them completing their course. Postgraduates: see Chapter 9 page 178 for more funding information.

Special bursaries for physics students

To increase the number of students studying physics, especially amongst those who would not traditionally choose it as a subject to study, the Institute of Physics offers 300 new bursaries a year. Each student would normally receive £1,000 pa for the duration of their course (i.e. £3,000 for a BSc and £4,000 for an MPhys/MSci). The bursaries are not scholarships and are not necessarily aimed at high-flyers and not all physics students will receive one. To find out more see Chapter 8 page 169.

I'm taking a degree in Social Work – can I get a bursary?

The Social Work Bursary

The Social Work Bursary is available to students ordinarily resident in England studying on an approved undergraduate course (full or part time).

The bursary is non-income assessed which means that earnings, savings and other sources of income are not taken into consideration. It includes a basic grant, a fixed contribution towards practice learning opportunity related expenses and tuition fees. Financial awards are dependent on individual circumstances.

Undergraduates – What you will get (figures are for 2007–2008, based on a 52 week period)

Full-time students subject to top-up fees

London based HEI	up to £4,975
Elsewhere based HEI	up to £4,575

Part-time students

London based HEI	up to £2,487.50
Elsewhere based HEI	up to £2,287.50

Graduates: see page 182

For full details on eligibility criteria, and funding availability visit www.ppa.org.uk/swb or email your enquiry to swb@ppa.nhs.uk. Alternatively, call the Bursaries customer service team on 0845 610 1122.

I want to study Dance and Drama – will I get funding?

A majority of accredited Dance and Drama courses at private HE institutions offer some form of funding to help with fees and living expenses.

If you are offered a state-funded place on a higher education course you should be eligible for the same funding as students on degree courses. RADA, the Guildhall School of Music and Drama, the Central School of Speech and Drama, Bristol Old Vic Theatre School, Rose Bruford College and many other institutions fall into that category. (See Chapter 2.)

If you are offered a place as a private student by your college and it is not state funded you will have to pay the full cost of the private tuition fee. For those who do not receive an award, a three-year course (including living costs) could set you back £50,000. However, you should still contact your LA (or the SLC) for details of how to apply for help as a private student on a designated course, as some funding might be available. While higher education courses in Dance or Drama no longer offer Dance and Drama Awards (having introduced the 'state-funded places' scheme), awards are given by some 20 performing arts schools. Competition for all these awards is very fierce – not all students who achieve a place will receive an award.

Not all accredited courses attract government funding, so if funding is essential, check the status of a course before you start applying. The booklet *A Guide to Vocational Training in Dance and Drama* is full of useful information, including a full guide to funding. Phone 0845 602 2260 or see ww.direct.gov.uk/studentsupport/dancedrama.

Additional help for specialist groups

I'm a mature student/independent/married; is there any special funding or advice for me?

An independent student is someone who no longer lives with their parents, has been working for at least three years, or is over 25. As an independent student you are entitled to the general funding package for students (see Chapter 2 or the beginning of this chapter if you're based in Scotland, Wales or Northern Ireland). Independent English students can earn up to £25,000 before losing any of their funding entitlement. For students from Northern Ireland the figures is £18,360, and in Wales £18,370. If you are married, or living with someone in a stable relationship, your partner's income may well be means-tested if you apply for a maintenance loan/grant. There is no age limit on taking out a fee loan, and the cut-off point for taking a maintenance loan is now 60 years.

It's a fact!

The number of mature students starting a degree in UK universities in 2007 was 37,663, up 4.5% on last year.

(UCAS figures)

If I become a student will I still receive benefits such as income support?

In order that Income Support or Housing Benefit can be paid, students receive a non-repayable Special Support Grant. This works in a similar way to the maintenance grant (see Chapter 2, page 43) – it is given to low-income families. If you receive the special support grant you will not be eligible for the maintenance grant.

I have children to support – are there any other allowances, grants and bursaries I could apply for?

- A non-repayable special support grant of up to £2,835 a year is available for new full-time students who are eligible for benefits such as income support or housing benefit while they are studying. Main beneficiaries are likely to be lone parents, other student parents and students with disabilities. The grant is based on household income and does not have to be paid back. If you're eligible for the special support grant you will not be eligible for the maintenance grant. This will not affect any university bursary you are offered.
- The Parents' Learning Allowance: up to £1,470 pa for help with course-related costs for students with dependent children. Income is assessed.
- Childcare Grant: up to £148.75 a week for one child and £255 for two or more. Amount given based on 85% of actual childcare costs. Paid in three instalments by the Student Loans Company but does not have to be repaid.
- Child Tax Credit: available to students with dependent children and paid by the Inland Revenue. Students receiving the maximum amount will be entitled to free school meals for their children. The amount you get will depend on circumstances. Call 0845 300 3900 for more details or visit www.inlandrevenue. gov.uk/taxcredits and check out how much you could get.
- Adult Dependants' Grant: up to £2,575 pa for full-time students with adult dependants. Paid in three instalments.
- Access to Learning Fund: see page 63. Universities generally look very favourably on mature students when allocating access funds.

SCOTLAND – please note

Help for parents in Scotland and the amounts available vary from those listed here.

I'm disabled and I want to go into higher education – can I get extra help?

There are a number of ways you can get extra help, depending on your disability. If you follow up every lead offered here, it's going to take time, but the results could be well worth while.

What's the starting point for somebody who's disabled?

First choose your course, then choose the university or college where you would like to study. Next check out the college facilities, and their ability to cope with your specific disability, by:

1. Writing for details of facilities
2. Visiting suitable institutions
3. Having a 'special needs' interview with the institution.

Then fill in your UCAS application.

When should I start getting organised?

It's a good idea to start getting organised in the summer term of your first A level year, as you may have to revise your choice of institution several times.

What financial help can I expect from my local authority?

Like most students on full-time higher education courses in this country, as a disabled student you would be eligible for the full financial support package for students described in the previous chapter.

I am severely disabled – can I get a student loan?

Yes. As an undergraduate you would be eligible for a student loan. In fact, the regulations laid down when the Student Loans Company was set up allow for the loans administrator to delay the start of repayment for people with disabilities, and any disability-related financial entitlements you receive will be disregarded when calculating your repayment amounts. Phone the Student Loans Company helpline free on 0845 607 7577.

Can I apply to the Access to Learning Fund?

Yes. Each institution decides its own criteria for payments – there are no set rules. You might find being disabled gives you more entitlement (see details on page 63).

What extra money is available for disabled students?

There are Disabled Students' Allowances (DSAs) for full- and part-time students, which offer support to those with a disability or specific learning difficulty such as dyslexia.

There are four Disabled Students' Allowances:

1. Up to £20,000 per year for non-medical personal help – e.g. readers, lip-speakers, note-takers. Up to £15,000 if studying part-time.
2. Up to £5,030 for the whole course for specialist course equipment – e.g. computer, word processor, Braille printer, radio microphone, induction loop system.
3. A general Disabled Students' Allowance – up to £1,680 pa (£1,260 for part-time study) for minor items such as tapes, Braille paper, extra use of phone.
4. Extra travel costs incurred as a result of your disability.

Distance learning

Full-time undergraduates who cannot attend their course because of their disability will be eligible for full-time student support in addition to DSAs. (See page 89.)

Can I get help with travel?

The loan for students includes a set amount for transport costs (£295) – as a disabled student you can claim for extra travel expenses incurred over this amount if your disability means, for example, that you are unable to use public transport and must travel by taxi (see point 4 above).

What about Social Security benefits?

Most full-time students are not entitled to benefits such as income support and housing benefit. However, such benefits can be available to students in vulnerable groups such as students with disabilities, but the situation is complicated. The people to put you in the picture are your Jobcentre/JobcentrePlus or Skill: the National Bureau for Students with Disabilities (see below); alternatively phone the Benefits Inquiry line on 0800 882200; minicom users 0800 243355. Opening hours: 8.30am–6.30pm Monday–Friday; 9am–1pm Saturday.

Can I get a Disability Living Allowance?

Yes. This allowance is available to you as a student. It provides funds on a weekly basis for those who need help with mobility – e.g. the cost of operating a wheelchair or the hire or purchase of a car. It also covers those who need care and assistance with any physical difficulties such as washing or eating, or continual supervision. The allowance will not affect your Disabled Students' Allowances in any way. See previous question for people to contact.

Further information for specialist groups

Mature students

- *Returning to Education: A Practical Handbook for Adult Learners.* Published by How to Books. Available from Trotman, tel: 0870 900 2665 or visit www.trotman.co.uk/bookshop.
- *Mature Students' Directory.* Published by Trotman; to order, tel: 0870 900 2665 or visit the website www.trotman.co.uk/bookshop.

Disabled students

- Students' Welfare Officer at your university or college, students' union, local Citizens' Advice Bureau.
- Skill: National Bureau for Students with Disabilities. It runs a special information and advice service open Tuesday 11.30am–1.30pm and Thursday 1.30pm–3.30pm,

tel: 0800 328 5050, and also publishes a number of useful leaflets (free to students) and books for the disabled. From Chapter House, 18–20 Crucifix Lane, London SE1 3JW. Or available on website. Minicom users: 0800 068 2422. Email: info@skill.org.uk. Website: www.skill.org.uk. Fax: 020 7450 0650.

⦿ Benefits Agency or JobCentre/JobCentrePlus: address should be in your local telephone directory.

⦿ Royal National Institute of Blind People, RNIB Education and Employment Network, 105 Judd St, London WC1H 9NE. Helpline open: Monday–Friday 9am–5pm. Wednesday 9am–4pm. Messages can be left on the answerphone outside these hours. Tel: 0845 766 9999. Email: helpline@rnib.org.uk. Website: www.rnib.org.uk.

⦿ RNID, which stands for the Royal National Institute for Deaf People, 19–23 Featherstone Street, London EC1Y 8SL. Tel: 0808 808 0123. Textphone: 0808 808 9000. Fax: 020 7296 8199. Email: informationline@rnid.org.uk. Website: www.rnid.org.uk.

⦿ *Bridging the Gap: A Guide to the Disabled Students' Allowances*, Students' Support Division 1, Room 215, Mowden Hall, Staindrop Road, Darlington DL3 9BG. Tel: 0800 731 9133. Textphone: 0800 328 8988. Fax: 0845 603 3360. Also available from www.studentfinancedirect.co.uk

⦿ *The Disabled Student's Guide to University*, published by Trotman. To order, tel: 0870 900 2665 or visit www.trotman.co.uk/bookshop.

Studying abroad

I have to spend part of my course studying abroad – will I get extra help?

Yes, but it will be a loan. If you study abroad for at least 50% of an academic quarter (which normally means a term) you are eligible for an overseas rate of loan, which for 2008–2009 is:

⦿ England, Wales and Northern Ireland: max £5,510

⦿ Scotland: highest-cost countries £1,185–£6,550; high-cost countries £1,065–£5,510; all other countries £890–£4,510

Don't forget, unless you are on an Erasmus exhange (see page 98) if you spend a year away in another country you will still have to pay reduced fees. These are set by your university up to a maximum of £1,572 (50% of the normal fee). You will be able to take out a loan to cover these.

Scottish students who normally study in Scotland will pay no fees. Welsh students who normally study in Wales and receive a free grant will find around 60% of the fee demanded is paid.

My course abroad is longer than my course in the UK – can I get more money?

Yes. The rate given is worked out on a year of only 30 weeks and 3 days. If you need to stay longer, you can increase your loan.

The rate for 2008–2009 is up to £112 per week (up to £146 per week in Scotland).

Students who have a compulsory study period abroad can get into serious financial difficulties. Nobody warns you of the cost of this before you choose a course such as European Studies and Modern Languages.
3rd year French and Russian student

It's going to cost me a lot more to fly to Tokyo than to take a train to Leeds – can I get any help with travel?

Yes, but not for the full fare. Your loan already includes some travel element (£295 in England/Wales, N. Ireland), and this will be taken into consideration in calculating how much you receive. It is probably best to let your local authority calculate what you are entitled to. Remember when putting in for costs to give all the facts – the journey from your home to the airport costs something, too. (Arrangements differ in Scotland.)

Is there any other help for students who want to study abroad?

Two organisations have been set up to assist students wanting to study in the EU:

- Erasmus (sometimes known as Socrates-Erasmus), the European Community Action Scheme for the Mobility of University Students, is designed to encourage greater co-operation between universities and other higher educational institutions in Europe. Under this scheme students taking courses, including foreign languages, in other European countries may be given a grant towards extra expenses while studying abroad for a period of 3 to 12 months. These could include travel expenses, language courses, or living and accommodation costs. If you're part of this scheme you should also be exempt from paying the reduced fees that sandwich students taking a year out have to pay. For more details phone 01227 762712, email info@erasmus.ac.uk or visit www.erasmus.ac.uk.

- The Leonardo da Vinci scheme provides opportunities for university students and recent graduates to undertake periods of vocational training of up to 12 months with organisations in other member states; placements are largely technology based. While individual employers will provide any salary, the Leonardo scheme can make a contribution towards language tuition and expenses. For more details phone 020 7289 4157.

Who to contact

Funding from these organisations is arranged mainly through your university or college. They should have full information and should therefore be your first point of call. Otherwise, contact the European Commission (8 Storey's Gate, London SW1P 3AT).

What happens if I get sick while studying abroad?

Don't wait until you get sick: take out health insurance cover before you go. (See information about travel insurance on page 143.) Your local authority will probably reimburse the costs of health insurance, providing they consider it 'economical'. Check out the situation with them first. If you are going abroad as part of your course, seek advice from your university; they will know the score. You may have to pay a social security charge. (See page 101, 'Focus on three popular places for studying abroad'.) Remember, above all, to hold on to your receipts. Without those you are unlikely to get reimbursement from your local authority.

If you have to take out medical insurance, you can also get help to cover the cost of the insurance.

Can I study for my whole degree abroad?

You can, but it's not going to be cheap because you won't be entitled to a student loan unless you are studying at the University of London Institute in Paris. As it is part of the University of London, the Institute's three-year French course can be studied in Paris, but you would be treated as any UK student and would be eligible for UK funding. This means you could be eligible for a maintenance grant, the maintenance loan at the overseas rate (which this year is up to £5,510) and could be offered a university bursary. The downside is you would have to pay UK fees of £3,145 per annum (2008–09 figure). If you go to an EU country and study at a non-UK institution, as a resident of the UK you will be treated like the students in that country and will normally pay no tuition fees. In most European countries higher education institutions do not charge tuition fees; if they do, then they are generally set at a nominal rate.

But a number of universities do have registration fees, and there are additional health and personal insurance costs, students' union fees and other expenses to consider. Many countries have special concessions for their students, e.g. concessionary rates for meals, transport and accommodation. As an EU student you would benefit from these.

The most expensive part of your stay will be maintenance costs, and because you are not taking any part of your course in the UK, you will not be eligible for the student loan.

What will it cost me to live?

Living costs vary depending on where you are studying. As in the UK, capital cities are more expensive places to live than country towns.

When it comes to the price of food in the EU, the UK is among the more expensive places. If you are thinking of studying further afield than Europe, the cost factor is appreciably higher as it is unlikely that you will get your fees covered for a full degree course, and travel will be a major expense.

Will studying abroad be very different?

Every country has its own particular approach to study and its own characteristics. In Europe, for instance, individual universities tend to cater for a greater number of students. Lecture classes and seminars are more crowded and there is a greater dependence on printed course material. There is less contact between tutor and student and the system generally is more impersonal.

Another major difference is the exams. Often there is a greater reliance on oral examinations. In Italy, for example, the majority of the exams are oral. While this tends to give students additional self-confidence and make them more articulate, it is something new to UK students and something they need to get accustomed to.

European students are more inclined to attend their local university, and many live at home. As a result, universities do not provide the wide range of social and recreational facilities you would expect to find at a UK university. Students use the facilities of the local city or town, which can be expensive.

The universities of Europe are often situated in fine old towns and in regions you will want to explore, which again will be a drain on your (limited) resources.

My third year was spent abroad, but I still had to pay half tuition fees – for what? It's outrageous!
4th year Languages student, Durham

Tip from a student

'The fourth year of my degree is in France. Even though I don't need a student loan at the moment, I have taken it out and put it in a high-interest account because I know I will want to travel once I get to Europe.'

1st year Chemistry student, Imperial College, London

It's a fact

Countries that attract the most students from abroad:

USA	22%
UK	11%
Germany	10%
France	9%
Australia	6%
Canada	5%

(OECD Education at a Glance 2006)

Focus on three popular places for studying abroad

(Please note: all figures are approximate.)

France

You need to prove you have sufficient resources to maintain yourself while studying in France. Minimum threshold level is about €5,160, with a minimum of €430 a month, but this will be barely enough to cover your living expenses. What are these likely to be? (Figures for 2007–2008.)

- Annual cost of a course: €150–€900 in a public institution and €3,000–€7,000 in a private university
- Accommodation: €150 per month in the university, €300 per month for a studio in the city
- Food: €230 per month
- Transport: €31 per month
- Course charge: €92 per month
- Telephone: €30 per month.

For the first month it is estimated that you will need around €1,500. This will cover:

- First month's rent: €150–€300
- Deposit for lodgings (2 months): up to €600
- Annual insurance for lodgings: €50
- Social security: €180
- Health insurance: €70–€285 depending on risk taken
- Registration fee €150.

Scholarships: very few available. Try the Entente Cordiale Scholarships for Postgraduates. Contact the French Embassy in London. Helpful website: www.cnous.fr.

Germany

A degree in Germany takes between four and six years so you must anticipate a long stay. Each year is divided into two semesters. The first hurdle is registration: this gives you that all-important student card, which will entitle you to special rates on local transport, reduced rates for cultural events and use of the refectory. Tuition in universities is generally free, but a number of states will be introducing fees of up to €500 per semester. Foreign students need to prove they have sufficient funds for their stay – around €770 per month (€7,020 pa) is about what German students have, but you can get by with less, certainly in the former East Germany. Rents vary – in the larger cities like Frankfurt and Hamburg the average is €310 a month. In smaller places – Dresden, Jena, Chemnitz, for example – the average is around €186 a month. Balance that against the fact that it is easier to find a job in a bigger city.

Though EU students are allowed to work in Germany this is not a good way to fund your studies, as unemployment is high at the moment. Expenses will include:

- Enrolment and administration fee €100 per semester
- Semester ticket: for travel (some universities) €50.

Average monthly expenses:

- Rent (including additional charges): €250
- Food: €160
- Clothing: €60
- Transport (car/public transport): €86
- Health insurance: €60
- Telephone/internet/TV licence: €50
- Work/study materials: €37
- Total: €703.

Scholarships: German institutions do not generally award scholarships and grants. The most extensive scholarship programme is organised by the German Academic Exchange Service (DAAD), but this is only for postgraduates.

United States

Students are responsible for paying both their fees and their living expenses. These vary enormously depending on individual colleges and whether they are state-run or privately run. Tuition fees range from around $1,500 to $35,000, with books and equipment adding sometimes as much as $2,000 pa. On top of that you have living costs, which could add another $4,000–$14,000 to your bill each nine-month academic year. You will also need money for travel from the UK and back, health insurance and personal expenses. Some financial aid is granted: in most institutions it is based on academic merit, though some colleges may give funding based on need. Full scholarships are rare. Because of this, students often have jobs during term time and work their way through college. Students can work on campus for up to 20 hours a week, but this cannot be listed as a source of income for visa applications. Other forms of funding include scholarships for special talents such as athletics. (Contact the Fulbright Commission, 62 Doughty Street, London WC1N 2JZ. Tel: 020 7404 6994. Fax: 020 7404 6874. Email: education@fulbright.co.uk. See also their website: www.fulbright.co.uk.) Special loans are available for all students.

Many universities in the USA are vast and can resemble small cities, with their own post office, grocery stores and shopping centres; they can dominate the local community and its economy. The US does not have a system like UCAS, so all applications must be sent direct to individual colleges. This can be expensive: the application fee (non-refundable) is $30–$100 for each university, and you may be charged for prospectuses and test applications. A College Day Fair is held in London when you can meet over 100 representatives from US universities.

Top US university targets UK students

Think Harvard, one of the America's leading universities, is beyond your financial reach? Think again. Harvard has a policy of giving students from low-income families generous financial assistance. In fact, students whose parents earn less than £31,500 ($60,000) a year will study free and this offer is extended to students from abroad. As in the UK, financial assistance is on a sliding scale so students from families earning up to £52,500 ($80,000) can expect some help. Of course you have got to get in, and the standard is high. In 2006, 275 students from Britain applied and only 34 were successful.

Harvard are keen to attract some of Britain's best and have launched a recruitment drive in some of our state schools.

Further information for students from the UK studying abroad

Study Abroad, UNESCO publication, available from the Stationery Office. TSO, PO Box 29, Norwich NR3 1GN. Tel: 020 7873 0011.

Getting into American Universities, published by Trotman. To order, tel: 0870 900 2665 or visit www.trotman.co.uk/bookshop.

You Want to Study Where?! The pros and cons of studying abroad, published by Trotman. To order, tel: 0870 900 2665 or visit www.trotman.co.uk/bookshop.

UK Socrates-Erasmus. Address: Rothford, Giles Lane, Canterbury, Kent CT2 7LR. Tel: 01227 762712. Fax: 01227 762711. Email: info@erasmus.ac.uk. Website: www.erasmus.ac.uk.

Further information – General

Full information about fees, maintenance grants and loans:

- England: *A Guide to Financial Support for Higher Education Students in 2008/9* (the source for the loan statistics in this chapter), Braille and cassette editions also available. Publications: Tel: 0845 602 2260 (booklet: 0800 731 9133). Helpline: Tel: 0845 602 0583. Website: www.studentfinancedirect.co.uk.

- Scotland: *Student Support in Scotland: A Guide for Undergraduate Students 2008/9*, available from any Scottish university or the Student Awards Agency for Scotland (SAAS), 3 Redheughs Rigg, South Gyle, Edinburgh EH12 9YT. Tel: 0131 476 8212. Email: saas.geu@scotland.gsi.gov.uk. Website: www. student-support-saas.gov.uk.

- Northern Ireland: *Financial Support for Students in Higher Education 2008/9*, Student Support Branch, Department for Employment and Learning (Northern Ireland), Rathgael House, Balloo Road, Bangor, Co. Down BT19 7PR. Tel: 028 9025 7710 (booklet: 0800 731 9133). Website: www.delni.gov.uk/index.htm.

- Wales: *A Guide to Financial Support for Higher Education 2008/9*, National Assembly for Wales, Higher Education Division 2, 3rd floor, Cathays Park, Cardiff CF10 3NQ. Tel: 0845 602 8845. Website: www.studentfinancewales.co.uk, and www.learning.wales.co.uk.

5

Paying your way

This chapter looks at the main reasons why students work, what they can do and what they can expect to earn.

- ⦿ Why do students work? (page 104)
- ⦿ Make money to fund your degree (page 104)
- ⦿ Work experience and internships (page 112)
- ⦿ Industrial placements (page 122)

Why do students work?

There are many reasons why students work, either before or during their study course. In this chapter we investigate some of those reasons and give advice on what sort of work you can expect to find; how to go about getting it; who to contact; and what to read. There is also some helpful information on the travel scene, insurance and holidaying abroad, plus anecdotes from students about their experiences. But when all is said and done, the main reason why students would work is to ...

Make money to fund your degree

If you have read the first three chapters of this book, you will realise that what you are likely to get to finance you through university just isn't enough. A large number of students work, most from sheer financial necessity, and their aim is to earn as much as possible.

- ⦿ 44% of students rely on term-time working to keep them afloat
- ⦿ 82% of A level students expect to have to roll up their sleeves and work to get through uni
- ⦿ 15 hours per week was the average number of hours worked
- ⦿ £84.70 – average weekly student wage

◉ 34% said they thought their studies could be adversely affected because they had skipped lectures to earn money.

(NatWest Student Money Matters Survey 2007)

Should you/can you work during term time?

Most universities and colleges allow students to work during term time; in fact, many universities have set up job shops, so you could say they are actively encouraging it. But most suggest a limit on the number of hours you work during term time – generally 15 hours a week, though some say 10–12 and others 16.

The university students' union is a great source of work, giving job opportunities in students' union shops and bars. How many students actually work during term time varies between universities. Many universities just don't know. However, the following universities suggest:

University	Percentage of students who work
Dundee	20%
London South Bank	25%
Aberdeen, Bath, Glasgow, Sheffield, Surrey	30%
Brighton, Edinburgh, Staffordshire	35%
Coventry, Lincoln, Oxford Brookes, Slade	50%
Aston, Gloucestershire, Middlesex, Portsmouth, Northampton, Sheffield Hallam	60%
Sussex	70%
Hertfordshire	80%
Huddersfield (top of the list)	90%

Going against the trend are Oxford and Cambridge, where many (but not all) colleges actively forbid or strongly discourage students from working during term time, except perhaps if they work in the student bar. Since the Oxbridge term is just eight weeks, and as one lecturer pointed out 'very intensive weeks at that', perhaps the colleges have a point. (For full figures and information on individual universities, see *The Student Book* 2009, published by Trotman.)

The tutor's view

‘ When it comes to work, academic staff attitudes vary from the positive to the negative. Obviously they would like it if students didn't have to work, but are realistic, especially with the introduction of fees. If you want to encourage students from diverse financial backgrounds, then you have got to be prepared to let them work. ’
Co-ordinator of Student WorkPlace, the University of Manchester job shop

The students' view

‘ The necessity of finding part-time work means the quality of your college work suffers. ’
PGCE student, Bangor

‘ Get a job with a good employer – for money, experience, skills and references. ’
Final year Sociology student, Kent

‘ Part-time work teaches you discipline and keeps you from being in the bar every night. ’
3rd year Sociology student, De Montfort

How important is it to get a job? Will it make a difference to my finances?

It certainly will, as the table below shows.

Town/City	Av. weekly rent	Av. total weekly expenditure	Av. weekly earnings	Av. hours worked per week	Extra cash needed per week
Aberdeen	£84	£135	£96.60	16.9	£122.40
Bath	£73	£136	£93	14.6	£116
Belfast	£63	£147	£91	17	£119
Birmingham	£75	£138	£109.80	15.9	£103.20
Brighton	£75	£140	£129.70	18.2	£88.30
Bristol	£74	£130	£105.80	13.6	£98.20
Cambridge	£78	£123	£100.50	18	£100.50
Canterbury	£72	£135	£92.90	15.5	£114.10
Cardiff	£64	£131	£91.70	14.9	£103.30
Coventry	£62	£134	£94.70	15.6	£101.30
Dundee	£73	£134	£113	17	£94
Durham	£83	£99	£81.20	10.8	£100.80
Edinburgh	£81	£121	£88.10	13.9	£113.90
Glasgow	£72	£132	£95.20	15.1	£108.80
Lancaster	£62	£112	£70.70	12.3	£103.30
Leeds	£70	£129	£128	18.7	£71
Leicester	£59	£109	£80.60	12.3	£87.40
Liverpool	£70	£120	£107.40	17.2	£82.60
London	£102	£159	£146.10	19.5	£114.9
Manchester	£73	£130	£97.90	15.8	£105.10
Newcastle	£66	£128	£95.50	15.5	£98.50
Nottingham	£72	£148	£78.40	13.4	£141.60
Oxford	£88	£132	£93.50	14.9	£126.50
Sheffield	£59	£132	£97.70	16.6	£93.30
Southampton	£72	£137	£78.80	13.9	£130.20
St Andrews	£78	£116	£97.30	14.8	£96.70
York	£63	£124	£80.80	14.3	£106.20
All	£73	£130	£98.30	15.6	£104.70

(Taken from the Royal Bank of Scotland Student Living Index 2007)

As you can see, Leeds looks the best place to study – providing, that is, you find a job and don't mind putting in the hours – followed by Liverpool. Belfast, Coventry, Cardiff and York seem very reasonable when it comes to rents. The hardest workers are in London, but then they have to be when you look at their rents. Rates will differ, these are just averages.

But the real question is, will you be able to make up the extra cash needed?

What are university job shops?

Among the most important innovations in recent years are university job shops. They can be found in most universities throughout the UK and more are opening all the time. They all seem to operate on their own individual system but have one aim in common – to find work for students during term time and the holidays. Pay is never less than the minimum wage, which is currently £4.60 for 18–21-year-olds (will increase to £4.77 from 1 October 2008) and £5.52 for those over 22 (will increase to £5.73 from 1 October 2008).

However, our research showed that in 2007, on average, students were earning around £6.73 per hour.

★ Student jobs

Barman/barmaid
Waiter/waitress
Shop assistant
Administration
Promotions
Data entry
Lifeguard/coach
Factory work
Lab assistant
Care assistant

Close-up on three job shops

Job shops come under a variety of names. There is Joblink at Aberdeen, Student Employment Service at Edinburgh, WorkStation at University College London, CUBE at Coventry and PULSE at Liverpool. All seem to have different ways of working.

Cardiff University's Unistaff Jobshop was one of the first Student Employment Services established in the country. It offers both a student employment agency and a JobCentre-style service and keeps registered students updated with new vacancies on a daily basis via email. Around 4,500 students register with the Jobshop every year and it provides a great, flexible service that enables them to balance paid work with their study commitments. All kinds of work are offered, from bar/waiting to clerical/admin, flyering, and library shelving. The Jobshop not only provides the University and Students' Union with casual staff, but also the increasing numbers of local companies who are now taking advantage of the service.

The University of Southampton's Careers Service has a free online vacancy service called e-jobs. Up to 150 new vacancies come in weekly and around 8,800 students use the service. There is a wide range of part-time and casual opportunities listed on the site, as well as internship and placement opportunities. Types of work include retail, promotional & marketing activities, IT, admin support, care, tutoring and catering. Asked if they would accept any kind of job, Angela Faux, who works in the Employer Liaison team at the Careers Service, said: 'We check all vacancies that come in. We have a vacancy code of practice and don't carry commission-only or pyramid-selling vacancies.' Students who have registered apply for jobs direct. Employers can also access the system to advertise jobs. The service is open to all undergraduate and postgraduate students. Just log on to www.soton.ac.uk/careers and register for e-jobs via the blue 'e-jobs' button on the home page. How are unsuitable vacancies kept off the site? Angela has her finger firmly on the delete key and commission-only jobs at the local casino were trashed pretty smartly.

Student WorkPlace is the specialist work experience unit of the University of Manchester Careers Service. It handles all types of student work, including part-time jobs, industrial placements, and vacation work positions. Students can search vacancies online or register to receive appropriate vacancies by email. Around 200 jobs are advertised each month. Manchester students can also find information on over 20 company sponsors and a wide range of national and international work experience schemes. Recent jobs included Audit Assistant, Aircraft Design Placement, Sports Coach, Flash Developer, Mystery Shopper, Kids Party Entertainer, Manga Artist, World Music Freelance Writer, Japanese Voice Over Artist, Legal Assistant and Chinese Speaking Researcher.

Does your university have a job shop?

Check it out as soon as you arrive. Jobs go very quickly. Most students want or need to take jobs during the long summer vacations. Your university job shop or that of a university closer to home may be able to help you here.

Try Slivers-of-Time

- Can't commit to regular hours of working, but need to earn money? Then Slivers-of-Time working could be just for you.

- Slivers-of-Time working is for anyone with spare hours to 'sell' to local employers. Ideal for students, this new way of working takes the idea of casual work a sophisticated step further and will give you immediate cash, a range of skills and a verified CV of successful short bookings.

- Work-seekers are called Sellers because they sell their time and skills and interested companies bid for them in an Ebay-style auction. This is how it works. It's 5pm and you realise you have a couple of hours to spare that evening, say 6pm to 9pm, so you enter that onto the Slivers-of-Time website and wait for a text message from an employer – or employers. If you are a good, reliable worker, you will get a higher rating and more jobs.

- The scheme was successfully piloted in East London in 2006. Since then a number of new areas have come on line. These included Kirklees, Westminster, South Liverpool, Hull, Cambridgeshire, Nottingham, Derby, Maidstone, Sheffield, Leeds, Exeter and Walsall and there are more in the pipeline. If your area doesn't come up on the Slivers-of-Time website, check with the local authority to see if they have a scheme in the pipeline. To find out more and get registered log onto www.sliversoftime.com

Thrift tips

'Potatoes and more potatoes – mixed with cheese, with ham, with butter – at least you're full.'

3rd year Egyptian Archaeology student, UCL

'Forget the gym – walk. You'll be fit and save a fortune.'

1st year Korean Studies student, Sheffield

'Cover your plates with cling film and save on the washing up.'

3rd year Forensic Science student, Wolverhampton

Cathryn's story

As an English student at Sussex University, Cathryn was looking for a well-paid summer vacation job. But what she found was an amazing experience and not what you might expect. She became the carer for a paraplegic. When asked why she wanted the job she answered, 'the money'. And in student terms it was good money: £6 an hour for a 24/7 week, every other week. Surprisingly, that was the right answer. Jacob, the young paraplegic, was just 23 and had recently graduated from Sussex University. He wanted someone who saw caring for him as a job, not a mission. Disabled for two years, having jumped into the wrong end of a swimming pool, he was now paralysed from the shoulders down. There was no time in Jacob's life for self-pity. He had a full social life and was an active member of a Youth Group. So for Cathryn this meant a hectic three months of meetings, social events and driving up and down to London: she even went with him to a summer camp in Wales. By the end, Jacob was a friend rather than a job, and still is. Through him she has met a whole new circle of friends. She earned around £3,500 over the summer and enjoyed every moment of it. She found the job through the Sussex University job shop which, she says, has some fantastic and unusual well-paid jobs on offer. If caring isn't your scene, how does hot air balloon instructor – in France – grab you?

Term-time working can be fun, as Jono, a third-year student studying Innovative Manufacturing and Technology at Loughborough University, discovered when he joined the OTC.

Jono's story

It was 3am, dark, cold and the middle of winter; I was sleeping in a ditch. A hand grabbed my shoulder and shook me violently – it was my turn to go on sentry duty, there was three inches of snow on the ground and we were under fire ...

If you want to earn money and have some fun, join the OTC (it's a kind of cop-out TA for students). There are field weekends once every five weeks, when you are paid over £80 to crawl around in the cold and wet from Friday evening to Sunday with a gun in your hand shooting at the enemy (blanks of course).

All too often you'll be sleeping out in the open. If you're lucky, you can sling a hammock between two trees and kip down, but that's luxury. Snow isn't as bad as rain. One weekend it tipped it down for 48 hours non-stop, and it doesn't matter how waterproof your gear is: after ten hours of throwing yourself on the ground and getting into trees, you are soaked to the bone. That's when you start wondering what on earth you are doing there.

But believe me, it is cracking fun. You feel you've achieved something. It's the camaraderie, the challenge, often the sheer absurdity of it all. There are some fantastic expeditions, like parachute jumping in Cyprus. There was just one drawback – I was on work experience at the time and missed it!

> ### It's a fact
>
> Pay for students in the OTC is currently £36.43 per day for Officer Cadets and £69.21 per day as a Second Lieutenant (TA).

What work are students doing and how did they find it?

Students seeking evening or weekend work during term time will probably find it easier in a large city than in a small town. London students should fare better than most – which is just as well, since they are among the most financially stretched.

You are most likely to find work in bars, restaurants or general catering, dispatch-riding (must have your own wheels and a fearless mentality!), pizza delivery, office or domestic cleaning, childminding, market research, modelling, offices (temporary), hotels, and of course shops and supermarkets.

Here are a few examples of what students have been doing:

Type of work	How found job	Pay per hour	University
Clapper loader, BBC Drama	Friend	£9	UCL
Nanny	–	£13	Nottingham Trent
Care home worker	Advert	£5.20	Napier
Smoothie bar	Asked	£5.75	UCL
Bike mechanic	Asked	£5.35	Huddersfield
Office Manager, Shakespeare Co.	–	£6	Oxford
Zoo supervisor	Word of mouth	£5.02	Durham
Website designer	Offer to students	£100 per site	Nottingham Trent
Nightclub	Job centre	£5.50	Essex
National Trust admin	Temp agency	£6.50	Lancaster
Interior design	Relation	£5.20	Kingston
Football club turnstile operator	Advert in programme	£7.50	Southampton
Cinema cashier	–	£5.28	Lancaster
Basketball coach	Interview	£10	Wolverhampton
Door supervisor	Rugby team	£8	Luton
Language teacher	Contacts	£12	Sussex
Party planner	–	£5 approx	Hull
Band musician	Created band	£50 (for a set)	Oxford
Piano teacher	–	£6.80 approx	Robert Gordon
Estate agent	Friend	£10	City
Gym instructor	Gym member	£5.57	Wolverhampton
Ironing	Imagination	£5 approx	De Montfort
Internet shopper	Job shop	£5.50–£11	Hertfordshire

Advice note

Don't leave it too late! If you want to work over the Christmas holidays, start planning early, even before you go up to uni – competition is high.

Further information

Who to contact

- University job shop
- Employment agencies
- Job centres
- Local employers on spec.

What to read

- Local newspaper job ads
- *Summer Jobs Britain* (updated annually)
- *Summer Jobs Abroad.*

Both these books are published by Vacation Work. Tel: 020 8997 9000. See also www.trotman.co.uk.

Work experience and internships

What counts as work experience?

'All experience is good and can count as work experience' according to Liz Rhodes of the National Council for Work Experience (NCWE). 'A placement in an industry where you are being considered for a career is of course excellent and a great way for you to find out if it's right for you, but even a job in the local restaurant, shop or office can help build key transferable skills – from dealing with people to prioritising and keeping a cool head in a crisis', she says. Make the most of the opportunities and experiences that come up. You'll be surprised just how much you have learnt and the challenges you've faced, and it could do wonders for your CV. Visit www.work experience.org.uk for more advice on work experience, from different types of programmes to how to go about setting up the placement.

What is really meant by work experience?

In terms of students, work experience is the opportunities offered by different organisations for students to gain specific experience of working in an area that will help them with their degree studies, or with entrance into a career. Of course it helps that students are paid to do this work, so finding a placement during the vacations is a double whammy.

What is an internship?

Work experience by a different name. The word 'internship' came from the USA and was spread by multinational companies throughout Europe, where it is now widely used. In the States some internships are unpaid, so it is always worth checking. Sometimes the phrase 'vacation placement' is used.

Who provides work experience?

Many organisations that are unable to offer sponsorship or industrial placement do offer vacation work experience – banks, insurance companies, accountancy and law firms, for example.

Big companies such as Balfour Beatty, Barclays Capitol, BP, Shell, Microsoft, National Grid etc. take on a number of students for vacation work each year. Many of these companies offer placements abroad. Some of these placements are better than others. The NCWE holds an annual competition to find the company offering the best work placements. There are nine different categories covering different sized organisations, charities and length of placements. The overall winner for 2007–08 was Shetland Seafood Auctions Ltd. Category winners included Virgin Atlantic Airways, IBM Extreme Blue, Controlled Therapeutics (Scotland) Ltd, Yorkshire Forward and Lancaster University Volunteering Unit.

How do you find a vacation placement?

Companies advertise in your university careers advice centre; or try www.work-experience.org, or www.prospects.ac.uk. Expect a fairly intensive interview, as many companies think vacation work might lead to a more lasting relationship, e.g. full-time employment after you graduate, and are looking at you with this in mind.

You may also find openings in areas where sponsorship is out of the question and industrial placements are difficult to find, such as personnel, marketing or publishing. If you are considering the media, advertising or journalism you may well find securing paid work impossible. However, if you are prepared to work unpaid, just for the experience, then you might have better luck. Try some of the local radio stations, the many TV channels and TV production companies, local papers (especially the freebies) and the wide range of different magazines that are published. It will be a high-energy activity securing success, as you will need to write to individual editors giving details of how you could add value to their publication or programme. Ideally select ones you know something about.

Work experience placements are not all one-sided: the employer gets something out of it, too – the chance to look at a possible new employee while providing you with real and interesting experiences and the opportunity to work on 'live' projects as part of a closely integrated and supportive team. But actually getting a work placement is incredibly competitive.

'Vacation placements and workshops are an excellent opportunity for you to learn first-hand what a particular career would involve', says Caroline Beaton, Graduate Resourcing and Development Manager at law firm Clifford Chance. 'Choosing the right career and the right employer are important and often difficult decisions. There will be a whole range of options to consider and you will want to be as well informed as possible. Spending a couple of weeks with a prospective employer gives you a very good idea of what the work would involve and what kind of atmosphere you would be working in. In addition to vacation placements, there are also opportunities to attend workshops which can offer a more compact way of gaining an insight into a career as a lawyer.'

Clifford Chance offers 100 vacation placements of between two and four weeks during the spring or summer break, and currently pays £270 a week. There are also up to 350 places available on either one or two day workshops through the year. As well as gaining an insight into law at Clifford Chance, students also benefit from unlimited use of outstanding facilities, including the staff restaurant, swimming pool and state-of-the-art gymnasium.

Facts and figures on work experience

- ⦿ Three-quarters of employers who recruit graduates offer work experience.
- ⦿ 50% of recruiters said that placement students were a prime source of graduate recruitment.
- ⦿ Average monthly salary during work placements was £1,079.

(IRS Employment Review 2006)

Cash crisis note

Placement opportunities are advertised on www.prospects.ac.uk.

Cash crisis note

Around half a million students look for work placements for the summer vacations. Competition is high. To avoid disappointment start looking as soon as you have your university place. Work experience is becoming an important deciding factor on a student's CV, and an important aid to financial survival. Check out your uni job shop or the website www.prospects.ac.uk.

How will I find a placement?

Big employers

Large companies such as Procter & Gamble offer what they call summer internships to students on a worldwide scale. They see it as a fair means of assessing students' ability and hope eventually to recruit most of their graduates through their internship scheme. ICI is another major company that has a summer internship programme. It offers 8–12-week placements across Europe to undergraduates from all academic years who have demonstrated high achievement and are confident of getting a good degree. It looks for team players with good interpersonal skills and proven leadership ability. Your university careers office should have details of these and other programmes with major companies. Otherwise contact employers directly, or look on the net.

Small employers

Small companies can be contacted directly, or you could try Shell Step. This UK-wide scheme is designed to encourage small- and medium-sized employers to take on undergraduates for an eight-week summer placement to carry out a specific project which will be of benefit to both the employer and the student. Students have the opportunity to use their existing skills and the chance to develop new ones while experiencing life in the workplace. Opportunities are open to second- and penultimate-year undergraduates of any degree discipline.

You'd earn a minimum of £200 per week. This is in the form of a 'training allowance' and is exempt from tax and National Insurance contributions. In 2007, over 600 projects were undertaken across the UK.

Money, of course, is important, but so is getting the right job at the end of your degree course. The competition out there is very strong, even for top graduates, so you need to make your CV stand out. Taking part in a Shell Step work placement in an area relevant to your future career aspirations is certainly one way to achieve this.

For details, visit the Shell Step website, www.shellstep.org.uk, where you'll find more information and an online application form for the summer programme, or contact your University Careers Advisory Service. While Shell Step operates in England, Scotland and Northern Ireland, Wales has its own scheme, Cymru Prosper Wales (CPW), which is similar to Shell Step (tel: 01792 295246; www.cpw.org.uk), or contact your university careers advisers.

What five Shell Step students achieved in 2007

Laurence Hauser, studying Engineering at Durham University, was placed at Powertile Ltd based in Southampton. Powertile is a research and development company that specialises in developing photovoltaic (electricity producing), integrated solar roofing solutions. Laurence's principal task was the development and manufacture of a trial batch of solar tiles within a pre-determined budget, whilst maintaining high levels of quality control. Through his hard work and professional manner, Laurence was able to develop good working relationships with suppliers and helped to improve the accuracy and efficiency of Powertile's current design technique. The 'Solartile' is now ready for large scale manufacture, with some early orders secured.

Karen Blunden, studying Economics, Finance and Management at Queen Mary College, University of London, was placed at Formosa Films in London. Formosa Films specialises in the production of short films and required extensive research into the investment opportunities for their next British feature film. Karen researched the setting up of an Enterprise Investment Scheme (EIS), which encourages investment in small companies. She used the findings to structure a prospectus/offer document which would help Formosa Films acquire around £1.7m for their next film production 'Twenty8K'. Karen's research also highlighted ways to generate investment, including the incorporation of a charity which helps and supports young people from disadvantaged areas across the UK.

Yiannis Maos, studying Media Production at Coventry University, was placed at Rapide Communication Ltd, a mobile communications company based in Coventry. Yiannis' project involved a number of different elements; he had to produce a demo for a business development event, redevelop a website and develop a new text product around the number 66099. Yiannis' work resulted in heightened brand awareness and over 50 new business leads. The new and improved website is now used as an effective marketing tool, increasing sales by 120% compared to previous months. Yiannis also worked with developers to create a new text messaging service, with its first customer being Rangers Football Club.

Iain Whiteside, studying Computer Science and Mathematics at The University of Edinburgh, was placed at Martin Energy Limited (MEL). Based in Edinburgh, MEL was set up to find new ways to provide balancing and reserve services to the National Grid. Iain's placement involved working on a new addition to their core service (Flexitricity) called the Demand Buyback System. Iain had to create a 'model site' for the system and install the system at its first site. Iain's work will help MEL roll out the system across further sites, which could see MEL generate revenue of £1.3m in 24 months.

Michaela Ellison studies English at The University of Reading. Michaela was placed at Surface View, a new division within VGL (a printing specialist) based in Reading. Surface View had been created for the interior design industry, to provide exclusive images as interior wall murals. The main project objective was to generate interest within the design and architectural industries and to ascertain whether Surface View had a tangible and prosperous future ahead. Michaela researched target markets for high quality bespoke wall murals, helped to develop leads, attended client visits and generated sales. Her work showed that Surface View is a viable business division.

What Shell Step 2007 students thought of their Shell Step experience

- 96% thought their employability had improved as a result of participating in Shell Step
- 94% said the Shell Step programme met or exceeded their expectations.

What Shell Step 2007 companies thought of their Shell Step experience

- 95% of SMEs said that as a result of participating in Shell Step their business will provide further opportunities for young undergraduates in the future
- 96% of SMEs said the Shell Step project will have a positive impact upon their business' future performance.

Ethnic minorities

The Windsor Fellowship Undergraduate Programme

Windsor Fellowship is a unique charitable organisation that designs and delivers high-impact personal development and leadership programmes. It works in partnership with leading UK employers and educational institutions to ensure that talent from diverse communities is realised. The Leadership Programme for Undergraduates is a two-year professional and personal development programme for Black and Asian minority ethnic (BAME) undergraduates. It includes residential seminars, outdoor challenges, voluntary work, mentoring and a minimum six-week paid internship with a sponsor, providing a real-life insight into employment with leading organisations. Sponsors can vary by year but have regularly included the Bank of England, GlaxoSmithKline, John Lewis Partnership, Morgan Stanley, Friends of the Earth and several government departments such as the Audit Commission, Home Office and the Department for Work and Pensions. Application forms and further information about this and other programmes can be downloaded from www.windsor-fellowship.org.

The foundation has been laid. I believe I have more edge than my counterparts and this is a fantastic position to be in at the beginning of one's career. Thank you!
Zanele Hlatshwayo

The WF experience has benefited me by making me more confident, giving me direction and skills needed for the working world as well as introducing me to like-minded people who have become my closest friends.
Aarti Patel

Oxford University

Oxford University Careers Service offers much support for those looking for work experience. Its website has an extensive, searchable database with many types of work experience opportunities advertised on it at any one time. Opportunities include summer internships, part-time work, careers-related courses, longer placements, volunteer work and overseas work. This is backed up by a well-resourced Information Room with further details about the organisations concerned, and a wide range of other resources to assist those looking for suitable opportunities. A team of professional careers staff helps with students' work experience queries – ideal for those wanting tips to track down the more elusive work experience opportunities. The service also runs a Work Experience Fair each January, an introductory event called Get Started with Work Experience, for those beginning to look at work experience issues. In addition, the Careers Service delivers advice, guidance and information specific to work experience via its website. Oxford University students and graduates who completed their courses up to four years ago can access all these services by registering online, free, at www.careers.ox.ac.uk.

Most other university careers services offer similar services. Check with your own university careers service to see what is available. See also University Job Shops on page 108.

> ### It's a fact
>
> More and more students are getting top marks. A record number of Higher Education students gained a first-13%, or an upper second degree – 48% of those graduating.
>
> HESA First Release for 2006–07

Further information

Who to contact for work experience

- Local employers
- Major employers
- Course directors
- College notice boards
- Your university careers advisers
- University job shops
- STEP
- Local employment agencies.

Surf the net

There are a number of websites that can help you find work experience. Here are just a few of the best:

- Prospects, www.prospects.ac.uk, the graduate careers website, which has a work bank section.
- National Council for Work Experience (NCWE) – www.work-experience.org – which aims to support and develop quality work experience and encourage employers to offer more opportunities.
- Best part-time jobs: hotrecruit.co.uk; or through UCAS: www.yougofurther.co.uk.
- Just Jobs for Students: www.justjobs4students.co.uk, www.student-part-time-jobs.com, www.activate.co.uk.
- And for something different: www.sliversoftime.com.

Making your work experience work for you

The supply of graduates continues to grow; fortunately the graduate labour market has been buoyant. Whether this will continue is difficult to predict.

The areas with most vacancies are likely to be accountancy, professional services firms, engineering, industrial companies, investment banks and the public sector. Almost a fifth of all vacancies are in buying, selling and retailing. London and the south-east of England are the graduate hot spots.

Fact check

What is likely to make you happy in 10 years' time?

Based on research carried out with 25,000 university applicants:

- ◉ Having a job that is interesting (82%)
- ◉ Spending time with family (68%)
- ◉ Owning a home (46%)
- ◉ Spending time with friends (46%)
- ◉ Being in a long-term relationship (45%)
- ◉ Having a job that contributes to society (40%)
- ◉ Having a job that pays well (39%)

Future Leaders Survey conducted by Forum for the Future
and UCAS and sponsored by Friends Provident

What are employers looking for?

Whatever the state of the employment market and whatever area of work interests you, getting that first foot in the door is incredibly competitive. All employers are seeking the best students, and with increasing numbers of graduates coming out of our universities the pool is getting larger and larger. It is not unusual to have 4,000 applicants chasing 100 places. Despite the number of graduates around, many companies surveyed said they were not able to find graduates with the skills they required to fill all their vacancies. Obviously companies can interview only a small proportion of prospective applicants. So – how do they seek out the best? What are their criteria? And what do you need to have on your CV, in addition to a good degree and possibly work experience, to make you stand out from the crowd and turn an application into an interview? We asked some major employers.

We find that candidates who have some work experience, or who have taken the opportunity to broaden their horizons by working in the community or even travelling, have normally had a greater chance to develop and practise the sort of skills we are looking for.

Graduate Resourcing, Royal Bank of Scotland

Initiative and follow-through; leadership; thinking and problem-solving; communication; ability to work with others; creativity and innovation; and priority setting. We look for evidence of these skills, which together we'll be able to develop further to run the organisation of the future.

Human Resources Manager, Recruitment, Procter & Gamble UK

'We are looking for the next generation of senior managers, the people who will drive our business forward in the future, so the kinds of qualities we are seeking – conceptual and analytical thinking, strong interpersonal skills, ability to influence and motivate others – can't all be demonstrated through a good academic record, important though it is. We want to know about other areas of achievement as well.'
Group Recruitment, ICI

Don't just sit back and think, 'I have a degree – everybody will want me', because the sad fact is they won't. The notion that students can walk into top jobs simply because they have a degree is a fallacy. Not everybody is a blue-chip high-flyer. So, if you want one of those top jobs then you have got to be proactive and start lining up the kind of skills and experiences that employers are looking for now – which is why getting the right work experience is so important.

Skill check

- Motivation and enthusiasm
- Team working
- Oral communication
- Flexibility and adaptability
- Initiative/proactive.

Fact check

- 84% of students we canvassed said they worked because they needed the money.
- 73% of employers we canvassed said they like the graduates they take on to have had previous work experience.

Job check

Always keep your future career in mind when you head for holiday and even term-time jobs. That's the advice of the National Council for Work Experience. Skills learnt from time spent working can make a great contribution to your CV and help convince a future employer that you are better than the competition. Whatever and wherever the job – supermarket, pub, the SU – make the most of the opportunity to enhance your employability.

To help you, here is the NCWE checklist:

- Set some personal objectives for the period of employment before starting a job: what do you want to get out of it, beyond the pay packet?

- Don't be afraid to ask questions and take notes when being briefed by your boss at the outset. Better to ask now and be clear than make mistakes later.
- Keep a note of challenges you overcome each day and any problem-solving required. This demonstrates initiative and prioritising skills.
- Grab any chance to take on more responsibility: undertaking new tasks is a sure way of developing new talents.
- Do the best job you possibly can for self-satisfaction and the possibility of being asked back for the next vacation – maybe even a permanent position in the future.
- Ask for feedback from your boss and the people you work with – there may be room for improvement – and note successes and achievements: these are what you need to put on your CV.
- Make suggestions – just because you're a holiday worker or work experience student doesn't mean you don't have good ideas, and your colleagues will always appreciate seeing things from a new perspective.
- Keep a diary of your thoughts throughout the placement. This will help you to add your achievements to your CV and will show you how far you've come.
- Ask for a reference from your boss; it will stand you in good stead for moving on to a permanent job.
- Work hard, but take the time to get to know your colleagues and enjoy the work atmosphere. After all, you may be spending every day there for a while!

Advice note

'Dress for success' is the advice for job-seeking students from the *Prospect Finalist* publication. Whether attending an interview, recruitment fair or assessment day, creating a favourable impression is important. Getting the right look shows you understand the employer's business.

Stop press!

- www.getalife.org.uk provides up-to-the-minute information on employment issues for students and graduates.
- www.prospects.ac.uk/chat is a communications channel enabling students to put their careers questions to big-name recruiters – opens Tuesdays at 1pm and Wednesdays at 2pm.
- Prospects also has a 24-hour chatroom, where job-seeking students and graduates who wake up in a cold sweat in the middle of the night need not be in anguish alone. See www.prospects.ac.uk/links/gradtalk.
- Get the balance right. Work–life balance rates as the third most important factor (32%) when choosing a job, topped only by salary, and training and development opportunities (45% each) (MORI Survey).
- Work placements do the business: 50% of employers who offer work placements recruit graduates from their work experience pool of talent (IRS Survey, November 2006).

Salary check

Graduate salaries are on the up.

- Graduate level vacancies are expected to rise by a staggering 16.4% on last year.
- Median starting salaries in summer 2008 are expected to climb to £24,000 – an increase of 2.1%.
- Top median starting salaries of £35,500 are likely to be paid in investment banking and fund management in 2008.
- Starting salaries in legal firms are likely to be £35,000 in 2008.
- The public sector has dropped to bottom of the salary league table for graduates.
- 26.7% recruited in 2007 came from minority ethnic backgrounds.
- 43.5% of employers couldn't fill all their vacancies in 2007.

(Association of Graduate Recruiters Winter Review 2008)

What to read

- *Prospects Pocket Directory*: hundreds of jobs for students and graduates – from your university careers service.
- *Hobsons Directory*: careers service or public library. To order, tel: 0870 900 2665 or visit www.trotman.co.uk.

Industrial placements

The idea of the four-year sandwich course that includes an industrial placement was never envisaged as a financial lifesaver, but many students are finding that a year in industry, with a good salary, is helping them to clear their debts while they gain invaluable experience. But with more higher education institutions developing more sandwich courses, finding good industrial placements is becoming increasingly difficult. This is felt mostly where courses are fairly new and the institutions haven't yet built up a good rapport with industrial concerns. When applying to universities, it is worth checking out the extent and quality of the industrial placements offered to students. There are essentially two sorts of sandwich courses: those where you take a year out – usually the third year – to work in industry; and courses in which you do alternate six months at university and six months at work.

In the beginning, industrial placements were mainly for courses in engineering, but increasingly courses in business studies, retail, computer sciences and languages include an industrial placement year. Aberystwyth has taken this a step further with their YES scheme.

What is the YES scheme?

The University of Wales, Aberystwyth has pioneered an initiative to give any student in the university who is not already on a sandwich course the opportunity to take an industrial year out. The scheme is called YES (Year in Employment Scheme), and currently over 40 students at Aberystwyth are saying YES to the opportunity. They come from a range of disciplines: arts, economics and social sciences, information studies, law and the sciences. You can choose a placement that is relevant to your degree subject, such as accounting, marketing, scientific research, events management or environmental conservation work, or use the time to experience work in an area that is totally new to you, such as human resources, retail management, journalism or production management.

You can even work abroad: YES students have recently worked in Europe, Australia, New Zealand, Africa and the USA. Students also work with major employers in the private, public and voluntary sectors such as IBM, KPMG, the Environment Agency, the National Trust and Voluntary Service Overseas. Salaries vary from around £8,000 up to £18,000, although some voluntary placements may only pay expenses. With everybody now having to pay fees, earning money for a year during study is a definite bonus. Aberystwyth is adamant – with some justification – that the skills learnt during the year out have enhanced both degree performance and employment prospects. The latest figures from the university show that students who have undertaken work experience gain employment after graduation quicker than students who have not participated in any form of work experience. Joanne Hiatt, YES Project Officer, believes 'YES provides an opportunity for students to develop their employability skills whilst earning money and having some fun!'

Karen's story

Karen is a final year student at Aberystwyth studying Business Management. This is how she spent her Yes year.

Hi Yes team,

During my year in employment I worked as a trainee manager for Majestic Wines in Milton Keynes. Now it wasn't the typical Monday to Friday office job, this retail management position involved hard work (both physically and mentally) and long hours. Why did I stay in the job if it was such hard work? – The organisation's culture, the friendly banter between your team and the satisfaction gained from knowing you've helped customers to the best of your ability.

Majestic provides extensive training and development programs, with many useful and fun days at Head Office. During the placement Majestic also funds each trainee manager to study and sit the WSET exam; a recognised examination in the wine and spirits industry.

I decided to take a year in employment to develop my very scarce CV at the time, to gain some experience, and let's not lie, having money left over for when I return to university. However, after working with Majestic, I now understand what kind of working environment suits me and I know exactly what career path I aim to lead.

Along with developing employable skills, I can now understand how a lot of theoretical work in my university studies is practically applied to a working organisation. Overall I have had a thoroughly enjoyable year, met some fantastic people, made some lifelong friends and made an important career decision – ultimate goal wine buyer. I am very excited about going back to Majestic after I graduate.

Cheers

Karen

Pay currently: £16,500 – £18,000 depending on location

When is the best time to do a year in industry?

If you take your year in industry at 20 you are going to earn substantially more than you would at 18, so it could help pay off your debts – you will also know more about your topic so the experience can be more valuable. But if you take a year out before you start at university, the money you save will help to ease your finances once you start managing on student funding, and the experience will help with your studies.

Another point to consider: most universities charge fees during a year out in industry, and though these are much reduced – around 50% of the current fee – if your industrial placement is taken as a gap year either before or after university you won't have to pay this.

Could an industrial placement lead to sponsorship/employment?

Sometimes a year in industry is an integral part of a sponsorship scheme (see Chapter 7 for full details). If it is not, a successful period of work experience can result in your employer offering to sponsor you for the rest or the whole of your degree. With some three-quarters of employers who recruit new graduates providing work experience, there is no doubt the student who has spent a successful placement with an employer is in a good position regarding future employment. An industrial placement provides the opportunity for you to get to know your employer and your employer to get to know you. It will help you to develop work-related skills that employers value.

The Year in Industry

If you are looking for paid work experience in industry, which could really help your future career and possibly lead to university sponsorship, the Year in Industry (YINI) are the people to contact. The Year in Industry is a nationwide programme run by the education charity EDT. The organisation has extensive contacts with UK companies interested in taking on high-calibre students in the year between school/college and university, and also undergraduates during their course.

A year in industry enables students to have a real taste of industry, and experience challenging, interesting, paid work, often undertaking activities that assist in driving businesses forward.

Placements are paid, so students get the chance to gain valuable work experience while saving up cash to help you through university or travel the world and broaden horizons even further. It is also a great opportunity to increase the chance of university sponsorship: many companies go on to sponsor students through university or offer paid summer vacation work and/or jobs on graduation.

The scheme offers a unique type of year out. It is an opportunity for students to confirm their career choice and gain valuable work experience, as well as earning and saving money. Over 250 UK companies take part each year and the Year in Industry has placed over 10,000 students since the scheme began in 1987.

The Year in Industry is a national scheme providing a high-quality package for students with a wide range of organisations. Placements are available for students interested in all branches of engineering, scientific research, IT, e-commerce, business, marketing, finance, logistics and much more. For a list of participating companies, check out www.yini.org.uk.

Applications for placements should be made as soon as possible. The earlier students apply, the more opportunities are available.

Placements follow the academic year and students earn competitive salaries during their placement. An administration fee of £25 is payable after application and acceptance onto the scheme. For further information, contact: The Year in Industry National Office, University of Southampton, Hampshire SO17 1BJ. Tel: 023 8059 7061. Fax: 023 8059 7570. Email: enquiries@yini.org.uk. Website: www.yini.org.uk.

What YINI students think:

The past year has been a brilliant experience and very beneficial. It has given me the confidence to expand my skills, develop within the workplace and to choose my future career with greater accuracy.

Claire Loram, Teign School, Devon (South West Water, Exeter)

I chose to take a gap year, not only for experience and a bit of money but I also needed a bit of a break from academia … the Year in Industry gave me the opportunity to experience the working world, which has made me a lot more focused as a student. It sounds a bit clichéd but in short the Year in Industry scheme was the best thing I could have done for my year out and I don't regret any part of it.

Helen Dawson spent her gap year working for Goodrich Engine Control Systems and went on to study Mechanical Engineering at Imperial College, London

Further information

Thinking about taking a sandwich course?

Then the internet is the place to look. There are a number of electronic resources that can help in the search for sandwich courses or other work placements:

- Sandwich courses are indicated with '4SW' on the Universities and Colleges Admissions Service (UCAS) site: www.ucas.com.
- ASET (Association for Sandwich Education and Training) is the national body for work-based learning practitioners, an educational charity that promotes best

practice for work placements, as well as providing support and advice for all professionals who work in the field. Contact: ASET, The Work-Based and Placement Learning Association, Department for Innovation, Universities and Skills (DIUS), W11 Moorfoot, Sheffield S1 4PQ. Tel: 0114 221 2902. Fax: 0114 221 2903. Email: aset@aset.demon.co.uk. Website: www.asetonline.org.

- The National Council for Work Experience (NCWE) has useful information on a range of work experience opportunities. Website: www.workexperience.org. If you want advice on work experience they are the people to ask.

- Around 120,000 students were thought to be on sandwich courses in 2005–2006 (HESA student returns).

Who to ask about placements

- If you are not a sponsored student, contact your careers department at university. It will have a list of possible employers who might offer placements.

- Contact employers directly – don't forget the smaller companies, which might have just one placement but don't advertise in case they get deluged.

What to read

- *Engineering Opportunities for Students and Graduates,* published by Professional Engineering Publishing Ltd, available free from IMechE, c/o Marketing & Communications Department, 1 Birdcage Walk, London SW1H 9JJ. Tel: 020 7222 3337. Email: marketing@imeche.org.uk.

- *Everything You Wanted to Know about Sponsorship, Placements and Graduate Opportunities,* regularly updated and published by Amoeba Publications. Available from Trotman, tel: 0870 900 2665, or visit www.trotman.co.uk/bookshop.

6

Taking a gap year

This chapter will look at all the opportunities open to those who opt to take a gap year before or during university.

- ◉ A gap year to raise money (page 127)
- ◉ A voluntary work gap year (page 130)
- ◉ A gap year for travel abroad (page 137)
- ◉ The student travel scene (page 140)

Taking a gap year after A levels is becoming increasingly popular: each year around 230,000 students are thought to take a year out. After 13 solid years on the academic treadmill many young people just feel that they need a chance to recharge their batteries. Most universities will accept deferred entry; some institutions actively encourage it. But don't assume that deferred entry is an automatic right. You must always ask, and if the course is popular, you may be refused.

Many young people use their gap year to gain a skill or experience in a specific organisation as well as to make money. Often this results in them having a ready-made job to walk into during vacations, once they have started their degree course. Others just want fun and new experiences or the chance to do something to help others. Here we look at three very different kinds of gap year: to raise money, to do voluntary work and to travel.

It's a fact

520,000 UK residents take a gap year each year (not all students) and it's estimated that by 2010 that number will increase to 2 million, with the total expenditure reaching £11 billion (Source: MINTEL). Gaptravelguides.co.uk claims that a staggering 70% of students aim to take a gap year and 75% of people are seriously considering taking a career break as a means of broadening their horizons and experiencing new cultures.

A gap year to raise money

If your aim is to save money, your best bet is to work as close to home as possible, where bed and board are likely to be at a very advantageous rate – if not free – and to avoid travel costs. There are always plenty of jobs going in shops, restaurants and pubs. Go for the multiple outlets, such as Next, Tesco or a pub chain. You will then have street cred, and may be able to find a part-time term-time job in your university town. But since you have a whole year to work and a clutch of A levels to offer, you might be able to find a job with better pay and which stretches your ability more. But be realistic: you are not going to earn great bags of gold. A gap-year student could expect to earn at least the minimum wage, which is £4.60 ph for 18–21-year-olds (increasing to £4.77 from October 2008) and £5.52 ph for those aged 22 and over (increasing to £5.73 from October 2008). But you might be offered more. One student we interviewed was earning £7.50 ph. Save just a quarter of that and you will be thankful for it once you start at uni. The first term is very expensive. Of the students we contacted last year who had taken a gap year, 54% said they had managed to save on average £2,000.

A gap year isn't only about earning money: many students see it as a chance to gain useful experience towards their career, to gain skills or to help others.

What students did in their gap year

Anna spent her year working for a life assurance/insurance company to fund her Politics and International Marketing course at Reading.

Joanne worked for a supermarket driving a fork-lift truck, but managed to get heavily into debt before she even started an Equine Science course at Aberystwyth.

Ruth travelled in Nicaragua for six months, but still managed to save £600 for uni working in a pub. She is studying Latin American Studies at Essex.

Lucky Ryan split his time between working in a ski resort and surfing in Australia before his Engineering course at Cambridge.

Christopher worked in a sausage shop where he learned how to mix up a 'mean banger'. It paid for driving lessons, got him his wheels and gave him a £2,000 bank balance when he started a course in Business Administration at the University of the West of England.

Kerry started her year working in Disneyland near Paris. She then worked at Eurocamp in Italy and Camp America in Northern California. She didn't save a bean but had a great time. She went on to study Maths at Liverpool.

Giles worked as an associate director on a film project before studying Politics at Hull.

Jordan went to China to study martial arts at a school near Si Ping City but saved remarkably little. He is now studying Chinese Language and History at Sheffield.

Conni took a job as a classroom assistant in the dance and drama department of a school and sometimes helped out with PE – useful experience for her degree course in Dance and Sport at Wolverhampton University.

Sophie spent an exciting gap year as a clapper loader for a BBC period drama and travelling to the rainforests in Ecuador before starting a course in Human Sciences at UCL.

Lily worked as a trainee behaviour support worker in schools, which was good experience for her course in Applied Criminology at Huddersfield.

Emma became an HR/training assistant, which was an excellent move. Since starting her degree in Human Relations Management at Huddersfield, she has continued to work for the company part-time.

Globetrotting Laurel undertook volunteer conservation and community work in Kenya and then worked as an office assistant in an American summer camp. She is now studying Zoology at Durham.

Will travelled to France to learn the language. As a result, he now subsidises his studies in Law at Durham running his own business arranging French language programmes in France.

Anna's gap year was a glorious mix of holidaying in Australia and Canada and skiing in Switzerland, and working as a nursery nurse. She is now studying Developmental Biology at UCL.

Sapphire worked hard for 11 months in research at Merck, Neuroscience Research Centre before taking a month off in Kenya. She is now studying Medicine at UCL.

Mark took a Diploma in Art Design Foundation Studies course but still managed to save £1,000 towards his course in Interior Architecture at Nottingham Trent University.

Julia 'A' went to Calcutta with the Baptist Missionary Society, where she worked with street children, and lived with the Mother Teresa nuns. She is now studying Law at Reading.

Julia 'B' took a job in a factory to get enough money to join a volunteer conservation project in Australia. On her return she worked at a scientific research centre to gain experience and save money – around £3,000 – for her degree in Natural Sciences at Durham.

Rory was on duty at the Odeon cinema for six months, then blew everything he'd saved on a fabulous six-month trip to Australia. He is now studying English at Durham.

Students talk in more detail about their gap years on page 134.

Further information

Who to contact

- Year Out Group – see page 130.
- Banks, insurance companies, accountancy firms – many offer work experience; always worth a try.
- Shops, supermarkets, chain stores – try to find an organisation with a number of local outlets, and one that offers a training scheme.
- Teaching – you don't actually need any training to take up a temporary position as assistant teacher or matron in a preparatory school. As an assistant matron you could find yourself darning socks and getting the kids up in the morning. As an assistant teacher you'd probably be involved in organising sport and out-of-school activities, coaching and supervising prep and classes when staff are away. Current rates of pay are in line with the minimum wage with a small amount deducted if food, accommodation, etc. are included. Term ends in July, so you would then have two months' travelling time. For gap year vacancies try

Gabbitas Educational Consultants, Carrington House, 126–130 Regent Street, London W1B 5EE. Tel: 020 7734 0161. Websites: www.gabbitas.co.uk and www.teacher-recruitment.co.uk.

A voluntary work gap year

How would you like to undertake projects in Africa, Mexico or Peru, while having the experience of a lifetime? Go on an Art History Abroad course to Venice, Florence, Bologna? Work and travel in the USA? Help the needy – the homeless, young offenders, children with special needs? Take a Trekforce or Greenforce expedition which offers the chance to help international conservation projects in such far-flung places as Belize and Guyana? Do you see yourself working to save endangered rainforests, wildlife or coral reefs, or perhaps developing some theatre techniques?

Year Out Group

Once you've made the gap year decision, the Year Out Group is a good starting point if you are seeking adventure or a great experience.

The Year Out Group is an association of more than 35 leading year-out organisations that was launched in 2000 to promote the concept and benefits of well-structured year-out programmes, to promote models of good practice and to help young people and their advisers in selecting suitable and worthwhile projects. All the organisations have agreed to adhere to a code of practice and appropriate operating guidelines. Projects last from four weeks to a year and are available in the UK or overseas. For many of them you will have to finance yourself (this is considered part of the challenge) – but others do pay quite well. It is wise to start your planning early and to do it in as much detail as possible. In a full gap year there is time to work to earn money as well as to work on a project that is worthwhile, exciting and which could change your life forever. Each year, Year Out Group produces a booklet called *Planning your Year Out* that provides information on planning a well-structured gap year. The booklet is sent to all schools, colleges and careers offices each autumn and can also be downloaded from their website. To learn more about the members of Year Out Group and the opportunities they offer, read on. You can also contact them directly or via the Year Out Group website, www.yearoutgroup.org, from which you can also request a copy of the booklet.

So what's on offer?

- ⊙ Africa & Asia Venture, which combines teaching and coaching sports, plus community projects, with adventure in Africa, India, Nepal, Thailand or Mexico. Tel: 01380 729009; email: av@aventure.co.uk; website: www.aventure.co.uk
- ⊙ African Conservation Experience – opportunities to work on game and nature reserves in southern Africa. Tel: 0870 241 5816; email: info@ConservationAfrica.net; website: www.ConservationAfrica.net
- ⊙ Art History Abroad courses including a Grand Tour. Tel: 020 7731 2231; email: info@arthistoryabroad.com; website: www.arthistoryabroad.com
- ⊙ Blue Venture – projects and expeditions that enhance global marine conservation and research. Tel: 020 8341 9819; email: enquiries@blueventures.org; website: www.blueventures.org

- BSES Expeditions. Six-week expeditions in a challenging environment, usually between July and September. Tel: 020 7591 3141; email: info@bses.org.uk; website: www.bses.org.uk

- BUNAC work and travel programmes – USA, Canada, Australia, New Zealand. Volunteer programmes in Africa, Asia and Latin America. Tel: 020 7251 3472; email: enquiries@bunac.org.uk; website: www.bunac.org (see also BUNAC, page 138)

- Camp America – join the staff at a summer camp. Tel: 020 7581 7373; email: enquiries@campamerica.co.uk; website: www.campamerica.co.uk

- CESA language courses abroad. Tel: 0120 921 1800; email: info@cesalanguages. com; website: www.cesalanguages.com

- Changing Worlds offers volunteer and paid placements worldwide. Tel: 0188 334 0960; website: www.changingworlds.co.uk

- Coral Cay Conservation – coral reef and rainforest conservation – in the Philippines, Honduras, Fiji, Malaysia, etc. Tel: 0870 750 0668; email: info@ coralcay.org; website: www.coralcay.org

- Crystal International Academy – winter sport instructor courses in Canada and elsewhere: dive and flying courses. Tel: 0870 060 1381; website: www. international-academy.com; email: info@theinternationalacademy.com

- Flying Fish – full range of courses to help you upgrade your water sport and winter sport qualifications. Tel: 0871 250 2500; email: mail@flyingfishonline. com; website: www.flyingfishonline.com

- Frontier Conservation – conservation projects worldwide. Tel: 020 7613 2422; website: www.frontier.ac.uk

- GAP Activity Projects worldwide – assist in schools, hospitals, on conservation projects and outdoor projects in 34 countries. Tel: 0118 959 4914; email: volunteer@gap.org.uk; website: www.gap.org.uk

- GAP SPORTS – international volunteer placements, sports qualification courses in South Africa, Costa Rica, Ghana and Canada. Tel: 0870 9797; email: info@gapsports.com; website: www.gapsports.com

- Global Vision International; Conservation and humanitarian projects in over 30 countries. Tel:0870 608 8898; email: info@gvi.co.uk; website: www.gvi.co.uk

- Greenforce – join a conservation project and help scientific understanding. Tel: 020 7470 8888; website: www.greenforce.org

- i to i – work worldwide in media, health, building, teaching, conservation, community work. Tel: 0870 333 2332; fax: 0113 242 2171; email: info@i-to-i.com; website: www.i-to-i.com

- Madventurer – volunteer projects as part of a team or as an individual in Africa and elsewhere. Tel: 0845 121 1996; email: team@madventurer.com; website: www.madventurer.com

- NonStopAdventure – winter sport instructor courses in Canada. Water sport experiences from UK. Tel: 0870 241 8070; email: info@nonstopadventure.com; website: www.nonstopadventure.com

- Outreach International – volunteer projects with local communities in Mexico, Costa Rica, Sri Lanka, Cambodia and Ecuador. Tel: 01458 274957; email: gap@outreachinternational.co.uk; website: www.outreachinternational.co.uk

- Oyster Worldwide. Paid and voluntary work in Canada, Tanzania, Nepal, Chile, Brazil and Romania. Tel: 01892 770771; website: www.oysterworldwide.com
- Peak Leaders – winter sport instructor courses and more in Canada and elsewhere. Tel: 01337 860879; email: info@peakleaders.co.uk; website: www.peakleaders.co.uk
- Personal Overseas Development. Volunteer projects in Nepal, Peru, Tanzania, Thailand. Tel: 01242 250 901; website: www.thepodsite.co.uk.
- Projects Abroad – Projects in Africa, Latin America, Asia, Eastern Europe. Tel: 01903 708300; fax: 01903 785779; email: info@projects-abroad.co.uk; website: www.projects-abroad.co.uk
- Project Trust – worthwhile volunteer placements in 26 different countries. Tel: 01879 230444; website: www.projecttrust.org.uk; apply online info@projecttrust.org.uk
- Quest Overseas – projects and expeditions in South America and Africa. Tel: 01444 474 744; email: emailus@questoverseas.com; website: www.questoverseas.com
- Raleigh International – challenging community and environmental projects overseas. Tel: 020 7371 8585; email: info@raleigh.org.uk; website: www.raleighinternational.org
- Real Gap Experience. A variety of programmes in over 30 countries. Tel: 01892 516164; email: info@realgap.co.uk; website: realgap.co.uk
- Tante Marie School of Cooking – specially designed courses to simply survive or to enable you to work your way round the world. Tel: 01483 726957; email: info@tantemarie.co.uk; website: www.tantemarie.co.uk.
- The Leap – volunteer and paid work placements in Africa, Asia, South America and Australia. Tel: 01672 519922; email: info@theleap.co.uk; website: www.theleap.co.uk
- The Year in Industry – places potential graduates in leading industrial companies in the UK. Tel: 0870 360 1329; email: enquiries@yini.org.uk
- Travellers – voluntary teaching, work experience and conservation projects on many continents. Tel: 01903 502595; email: info@travellersworldwide.com; website: www.travellersworldwide.com
- Trekforce Worldwide – project based expeditions and volunteer placements in Central and South America. Tel: 0845 241 3085; email: info@trekforceworldwide.com; website: www.trekforceworldwide.com
- VentureCo – expeditions offering language training, conservation and community projects in challenging environments. Tel: 01926 411122; email: mail@ventureco-worldwide.com; website: www.ventureco-worldwide.com
- Worldwide Experience – conservation and community projects in southern Africa and elsewhere. Tel: 01483 860560; e-mail: info@worldwideexperience.com; website: www.worldwideexperience.com. Provides valuable advice on planning
- Year Out Drama – develop your theatre skills while working with professionals. Tel: 01789 266245; fax: 01789 267524; email: yearoutdrama@stratford.ac.uk; website: www.yearoutdrama.com
- Year Out Group – the association that has brought together all the leading year-out organisations mentioned here. Provides valuable advice on planning your gap year. Tel: 01380 816696; email: info@yearoutgroup.org; website: www.yearoutgroup.org.

Voluntary work abroad in developing countries is not as easy to find as it once was, especially if you have no recognised skill, and many organisations seek people over 21. Some projects will pay maintenance costs, and sometimes give pocket money, but it is not unusual for volunteers to be asked to pay their own fares.

Conservation work is much easier to find, both in the UK and abroad. Most of it is completely voluntary and unpaid. You might even be asked to contribute to your food and accommodation. You could become involved in projects for the National Trust, the Royal Society for the Protection of Birds, on the restoration of cathedrals, working with disabled people and underprivileged children, painting, decorating – it's amazing what some students turn their hands to.

While the financial returns on both voluntary and conservation work are likely to be zero, in terms of your CV it could be of considerable value. Employers are impressed by the altruistic and enterprising qualities needed for voluntary work.

You could also try:

Long-term volunteering

The National Trust

If you are looking to fill a gap year, change career or gain work experience, and have six months or more to spare, then you could join the National Trust's full-time volunteering programme. As a full-time volunteer you could get involved in many different activities at Trust properties throughout England, Wales and Northern Ireland. You could work alongside a warden or gardener, assist house staff with aspects of running and preserving historic buildings and help with learning and events coordination. On the job training is provided and accommodation may be available; some placements are available through the New Deal scheme. There's no pay, but out-of-pocket expenses are covered. For an information pack contact the central volunteering team on 01793 817632, visit the National Trust website at www.nationaltrust.org.uk/volunteering or email volunteers@nationaltrust.org.uk.

You can also volunteer for National Trust Working Holidays. Fruit picking and costume conservation are just two of the more unusual opportunities on offer. The Trust runs more than 400 conservation working holidays a year throughout England, Wales and Northern Ireland for as little as £70 for a week's full board and lodging (from £40 for a weekend). They take place at beautiful Trust locations and are open to volunteers aged 16 upwards. For a current brochure write to Working Holidays, Sapphire House, Roundtree Way, Norwich NR7 8SQ, phone the brochure line on 0870 429 2429, email working.holidays@nationaltrust.org.uk or see their website: www.nationaltrust.org.uk/workingholidays.

Archaeological digs

It won't earn you a fortune – more likely nothing (subsistence pay is rarely given) – but it can be fascinating work. See the special section included in every issue of *British Archaeology*, published six times a year by the Council for British Archaeology, St Mary's House, 66 Bootham, York YO30 9BZ, tel: 01904 671417. Supplement gives full details of current UK digs. For subscription rates (including student reductions) and forms see the CBA website at http://www.britarch.ac.uk/shop/index.html. But the magazine should be available in public libraries and selected retail outlets. For full details of membership and details of digs in your area see the CBA website http://www.britarch.ac.uk/briefing/field.asp.

Alternatively, contact the County Archaeologist for your district, details available from http://www.torc.org.uk/orgsearch.asp, under local government archaeologists. For archaeological digs abroad phone the Institute of Archaeology to contact Archaeology Abroad on 020 7504 4750.

BTCV

BTCV runs around 252 conservation holidays worldwide throughout the year. Prices start at about £60 for a weekend in the UK. Projects include pond maintenance, tree planting, step building, hedge laying, scrub clearance, dry stone walling and community development. Contact BTCV, Sedum House, Mallard Way, Doncaster DN4 8DB. Tel: 01302 388 883; email: information@btcv.org.uk. You can browse and book online at www.btcv.org/shop.

In the case studies below, four students talk about their gap year and the skills they gained.

Sophie's year

'I started my year as a clapper loader on the BBC drama *Casanova*. A friend, who is a film cameraman, was working on the drama and needed an assistant. Take 1 Scene 1 – my role was to operate the clapperboard and then load and re-load the camera with film. It was hard work – a six-day week of 50–60 hours. Often we were on the road by 4.30am to ensure we were at the next location before the day's filming began. We (cast and crew) even spent two weeks filming in Croatia. But what an experience! I was rubbing shoulders with the stars – David Tennant (the current Dr Who), Matt Lucas (of *Little Britain*) and Peter O'Toole – and earning fantastic money – £485 pw for 10 weeks' work. I also worked on a couple of music videos – nobody famous yet!

'Then it was straight off to the Amazon for another amazing experience. I joined a team working with the Kichwa tribe in Ecuador to save the rainforest. To explain: lying between two national parks in Ecuador is a corridor of pristine virgin rainforest beneath which is thought to be a large reserve of oil and gas. The aim was to keep the oilmen out by establishing that this was an area inhabited by rare species. We travelled – mostly by canoe – to a remote area 200 nautical miles into the rainforest. There we met and lived with the tribespeople. Living was very rudimentary, a thatched shack raised from the ground to keep dry. I ate snake and stingray – not recommended – and you never went anywhere alone or without a whistle and compass. Step a few metres off a path and you were lost. We discovered a rare baby howler monkey, some extremely rare species of birds and trees. I can't profess to be an ardent eco-warrior, to be honest I went for the experience, but what we achieved was very rewarding.'

Sophie is now studying Human Sciences at UCL.

Skills gained:

- ◉ living the dream
- ◉ being away from restrictions
- ◉ learning to cope/addressing fear whatever the drama, e.g. a cockroach in your bed
- ◉ knowing yourself.

Celia's year

'My two elder sisters had spent their gap years in Tanzania, and my younger sister was also planning a year in Africa, so I decided I wanted to do something completely different. I started by travelling to Spain, to Hacienda Dos Olivos, where I worked as a groom in exchange for dressage classes – six lessons a week for eight weeks. If you love horses, and I do, it was the greatest opportunity, though incredibly hard work.

'Unfortunately, most of us were English, so I didn't get a chance to speak Spanish which I really needed to do, as I had arranged to join a project organised by Changing Worlds [now Oyster Worldwide] in Chile. I was to teach English to children and adults of all ages in a small town called Chile Chico in Patagonia close to the border with Argentina – not easy with only rusty GCSE Spanish.

'I lived with a family whose own children had left for university, so they treated me like a daughter. I do not think I was a brilliant teacher, but I loved the country and learnt a lot of Spanish. What was surprising is that two gap year students I met in this remote town are now studying here at Durham. I am now taking Spanish as one of the modules in my social sciences degree and as part of my studies I will return to Chile Chico next year.'

Skills gained:

- speaking Spanish
- self-confidence
- ability to adapt to different cultures.

Will's year

Will worked like crazy as a manual labourer for the first four months of his year to earn enough money to take a French language course in Grenoble – which he did, and learned to ski at the same time.

However, getting his course sorted out proved difficult. The company he found on the internet to organise his trip let him down in many ways. And that set him thinking – 'I'm sure I could do it better.'

Back in the UK and studying Law at Durham, he decided to have a go at setting up a web-based company of his own that would send people on French language courses to Grenoble.

This was completely new territory for Will. He had never run a company before. With the help of Neil, an Economics graduate of Sheffield University, and another friend based in Grenoble, he set up and registered his company, calling it Apprendre. He negotiated with the course providers, and developed a website to advertise the programmes offered.

Now in its second year, Apprendre is already making a profit. 'And we have had no complaints from the students we have sent to Grenoble so far,' he says. 'In fact, we have had people book a second course.' Take a look for yourself on www.apprendre.co.uk. As Will points out: 'The more hits we get the higher up the Google listing we go.' Said like a true marketer.

Skills learnt:

- setting up a business
- dealing with people
- marketing
- negotiating.

Hannah's year

'Meet your class – your biology lesson will last three hours.' This is how Hannah, then aged 18, started her teaching assignment in Botswana. She was on her own. No warning. No time for preparation. No time to think. Her students were aged 18–35 and eager to learn. She had studied Biology for A level, but she soon found teaching it was very different.

So started six incredible months living in a tiny village. She had a small room built in the bush with just one electric ring to cook on, and a separate toilet and shower even further into the bush, which she shared with hornets, baby snakes, spiders and a poisonous toad. 'You couldn't help but enjoy yourself. Botswana people are so friendly and generous – always giving. And the pace of life is incredibly relaxed. Their favourite phrase was "No worries".'

Hannah had decided she wanted to do something worthwhile as well as exciting during her gap year, so she started her search by looking at charities on the internet. A small organisation called Project Trust based on the Island of Coll in the Hebrides caught her eye and she applied. 'Just getting to Coll was a test of ingenuity,' says Hannah. 'Two missed connections, a night on a ferry and a £200 speedy taxi drive across Scotland, financed by Virgin Trains, were just part of the adventure. After that, tests such as making a model of the Eiffel tower or giving an impromptu talk on a random topic seemed like nothing at all.' To go on the trip she had to raise £3,500, which she did by organising raffles, contacting likely companies, even charging her friends to come to a big party.

After six months in Botswana, Hannah moved on to Johannesburg to work in a children's home. Johannesburg was a Mecca for gap-year students and time off was spent travelling round South Africa, often 16 of them at a time, which she found incredible fun. Hannah is now studying Law at Anglia Ruskin University.

Skills gained:

- dealing with the unexpected
- organising projects
- speaking up when things aren't working out
- handling difficult situations.

Ten tips for a gap year

1. Decide what you want to do with your year – work, travel, both, make a plan and stick to it
2. If you have a university place ask for deferment, otherwise secure your place before going travelling
3. Work locally and live at home, you'll save more
4. Make sure you travel with a reputable organisation – the Year Out Group (see page 130) is a good start
5. Work out the cost before you go – with some voluntary projects it's you who pays. Factor in socialising, food, clothes, topping up your iPod when budgeting
6. Check health regulations and take out health insurance. Get necessary vaccinations. Do you need a work permit and visas?
7. Make sure you have a return ticket or enough money to get home

8. Arrange accommodation before you go
9. Limit luggage to the amount you can carry yourself
10. Don't run up credit card/bank debts: you'll do plenty of that once at Uni.

Further information

What to read

- *A Year Out in the UK or Overseas: Student Guidelines,* try www.yearoutgroup.org
- *Taking a Year Off,* Margaret Flynn, published by Trotman. To order, tel: 0870 900 2665 or visit www.trotman.co.uk/bookshop
- *A Year Off ... A Year On?*, published by Lifetime Careers. Available from Trotman, tel: 0870 900 2665 or visit www.trotman.co.uk/bookshop
- *Opportunities in the Gap Year,* published by the Independent Schools Careers Organisation. Available from Trotman, tel: 0870 900 2665 or visit www.trotman.co.uk/bookshop
- *The Gap-Year Guidebook,* published by John Catt Educational Ltd. Available from Trotman, tel: 0870 900 2665 or visit www.trotman.co.uk/bookshop
- *Before You Go: The ultimate guide to planning your gap year,* Tom Griffiths, published by Bloomsbury Publishing plc. Available from Trotman, tel: 0870 900 2665 or visit www.trotman.co.uk/bookshop
- *Working Holidays Abroad* – try grape picking, yacht crewing, driving, tour guiding, beekeeping – there's information on 101,000 jobs in 70 different countries. Available from the Central Bureau, Seymour Mews House, Seymour Mews, London W1H 9PE
- *Making the Most of Your Gap Year,* published by Trotman. To order, tel: 0870 900 2665 or visit www.trotman.co.uk/bookshop
- *Taking a Gap Year,* Susan Griffith, published by Trotman. To order, tel: 0870 900 2665 or visit www.trotman.co.uk/bookshop.

A gap year for travel abroad

What employer is going to give you time off to travel the world? None. You will never, ever get a chance like this again. So if you have a yen to travel, make the most of your time, and budget wisely. Many gap-year students, especially those who take their gap year after their studies, do it to travel. Some work before they go and see it as a great holiday. Others work their way around from country to country.

When you start to investigate the student travel scene, you'll discover that there's plenty of help available. The path to the Far East, the kibbutz or Camp America is well worn. There is a plethora of publications and organisations, cheap travel firms, ticket concessions – even government advice – handed out to get you safely there and back. If that makes it all sound rather overplayed, pioneers can be accommodated. Backpacking and inter-railing are always journeys into the unknown. Things rarely turn out exactly as you had envisaged. That's the excitement. As for working your passage, most students do a wide range of jobs in a variety of countries before they get back home again. Skiing instructor, courier, au pair, grape picker, summer camp assistant – *Students' Money Matters* has found them all.

Further information

Who to contact

The Year Out Group (see page 130) has more than 30 organisations eagerly looking for willing students in order to help fulfil their travel dreams.

- ⊙ AIESEC runs an International Exchange Programme – the Work Abroad Programme – which provides the opportunity for undergraduates and recently qualified graduates to work for companies and other organisations throughout the world. Placements can last from 2 months to 18 months. Typical placements are for marketing and business studies (Management Placement), IT and engineering (Technical Placement), teaching (Education Placement) and voluntary and NGO work (Development Placement). AIESEC operates in 100 countries and is represented in 23 universities across the UK. Check out its website, www.aiesec.co.uk, or contact AIESEC United Kingdom, 29–31 Cowper Street, London EC2A 4AT. Tel: 020 7549 1800.

- ⊙ Au pair/nanny: try adverts in the *Lady* magazine and *The Times*; also see the *Au Pair and Nanny's Guide to Working Abroad*, published by Vacation Work, available from Trotman, tel: 0870 900 2665; or visit www.trotman.co.uk/bookshop.

- ⊙ BUNAC – to meet the cash crisis facing many students, BUNAC (British Universities North America Club) organise various paid work and volunteer programmes for students and young people interested in working in the USA, Canada, Ghana, New Zealand, South Africa, Australia, Costa Rica, Cambodia, China and Peru (see information on the Year Out Group on page 130). It offers financial help through its BUNAC loan plan for Work America schemes. Those working on the Summer Camp USA and KAMP programmes will find that their air fares are paid in addition to all food and accommodation. Every year, BUNAC awards three scholarships of up to £1,000 each to help applicants cover the costs of taking part in a BUNAC work-abroad programme to the USA or Canada. To enter the Green Cheese Scholarships, all you need to do is submit a humorous piece of original creative writing based on a travel-related topic. You're free to write about anything at all – whether it's a trip to the other side of the world or a journey you made closer to home. Entries should be no more than 1,500 words. Contact your university/college or BUNAC, 16 Bowling Green Lane, London EC1R 0QH. Tel: 020 7251 3472. Fax: 020 7251 0215. Email: enquiries@bunac.org.uk. Website: www.bunac.org.

Try the internet: enter 'student gap year' in your favourite search engine and you'll have an amazing choice – Ultimate Gap Year, Mad Gap Years, 100s of gap year ideas, Global Gap Xperiences, Mad adventures and the Gap Year Directory – which tells you what to do, where to go, and has a range of special travel offers and much more besides.

Advice note

While hunting out an amazing adventure, bear in mind that one day you will need to impress a future employer, and what you decide to do now could give you the skills needed to secure a career. That trek through the jungle when a wild beast slunk off with the rations might provide the ideal answer to the question, 'Have you ever been faced with a challenge when your swift actions saved the day?' Even losing your tickets need not be a complete disaster and dismissed as incompetence, but turned into a useful episode of resourcefulness. Get the picture – always keep your CV in mind.

What to read

All these titles are published by Vacation Work and are available from Trotman, tel: 0870 900 2665; or visit www.trotman.co.uk/bookshop.

- *Summer Jobs USA, Summer Jobs Abroad*
- *Live and Work in France, ... in Spain and Portugal, ... in Italy, ... in Germany, ... in Belgium, the Netherlands and Luxembourg* – a series of books giving details of temporary and permanent work in various countries
- *Working Your Way Around the World* – offers authoritative advice on how to find work as you travel, with hundreds of first-hand accounts. Find out how to become a barmaid, kiwi-fruit packer, ski guide or jackaroo
- *Working in Ski Resorts* – details on a variety of jobs from au pair to disc jockey and snow cleaner
- *Teaching English Abroad* – guide to short- and long-term opportunities for both the trained and untrained. Eastern Europe, Greece, Turkey, Japan – the choice is vast and varied
- *Directory of Jobs & Careers Abroad*
- *International Voluntary Work* – gives details of over 500 organisations that recruit all types of volunteers for projects in all parts of the world. It's the A–Z of voluntary work, published by Vacation Work and available from Trotman, tel: 0870 900 2665; or visit www.trotman.co.uk/bookshop.

If you can't afford the books suggested in this chapter, look in your local library. Nearly all the books mentioned here should be found in the reference section of your local public library, and if they are not your library might well order them for you. A group of you might think it worthwhile buying some of the publications mentioned.

Students have the time and the opportunity to travel and experience the 'ideal' of freedom. You won't get that chance again.

Loughborough University student, back from Africa

Thrift tips

'It is much more economical to pay rent with bills included. It may look more expensive initially, but works out cheaper in the long run.'

3rd year Performing Arts student, Derby

'Work in a fast-food take-away and eat your favourite junk food for free.'

4th year English student, Cheltenham

'Choose flatmates the same size – it extends your wardrobe.'

1st year Animal Management student, Bradford

The student travel scene

It's all very well to whet your appetite for travel, but how are you going to manage to get to that exotic destination? This section looks briefly at the student travel scene.

As a student, can I get cheap travel abroad?

Yes: there are a number of travel organisations that operate special schemes for students. In fact, you will find they are vying for the privilege to send you off on your travels, often dropping the price in the process. If you decide to take the cheapest, make sure it is a reputable organisation, with ABTA (Association of British Travel Agents) membership. It's better to be safe than stranded.

How do I go about getting cheap travel?

If you are already a student, your college Student Travel Office is the best place to start. There you'll find experts who will understand your particular needs and financial restraints, and are ready to give you advice. If you are taking a gap year, or your college has no travel office, then one of the biggest names in the student travel business is STA Travel.

Whether you're planning a weekend away, a ski-trip at Christmas or you get itchy feet every time you think about the long summer holiday ahead, STA Travel can help you to make the most of your time away with tons of travel inspiration and amazing student deals.

STA Travel's well-travelled consultants have all taken time out and are perfect to give advice, tips and deals for you to get the most out of your time away from home. You can also visit www.statravel.co.uk to be inspired about planning your perfect trip. You'll find a round the world trip planner – the easiest way to decide your ideal route around the globe and check out all the best flights for your chosen destinations. You can keep your family and friends up to date by building your own travel journal, as well as find out about other peoples' travel experiences and see blogs, photos and videos of people on their travels. You can also download live travel talks directly to your mp3 player and STA Travel's expert speakers will encourage you to plan your adventures to all parts of the world ... plus loads more.

With 48 branches in universities and on high streets throughout the UK, over 400 branches worldwide and travel help available in over 85 countries, STA Travel offer essential back up for students and travellers on the move.

In addition to flexible, low cost flights STA Travel offer a great choice of adventure trips, conservation and volunteer projects, accommodation, language courses, travel insurance, visas, package holidays, city breaks, hop-on-hop-off bus passes and loads more.

Thomas Grist of STA Travel says:

'Whether you want to coach rugby in Fiji, take an African safari, inter-rail around Europe or simply need a cheap flight home, STA Travel can help you get there.'

On-campus STA Travel offices are at: Bath University; Belfast University; Birmingham University; Durham University; University of Kent; University of London Union; Imperial College, London; Leeds University Union; London School of Economics; Manchester University; Nottingham Trent University; Sheffield University; and Warwick University. High street branches near universities include: Aberdeen, Belfast, Birmingham, Bournemouth, Brighton, Bristol, Cambridge, Cardiff, Dundee, Edinburgh, Exeter, Glasgow, Leicester, Leeds, Liverpool, London, Manchester, Newcastle, Norwich, Nottingham, Oxford, Portsmouth, Preston, Reading, Sheffield and Southampton. National telesales: 0871 230 8569; website: www.statravel.co.uk.

Also big on the student travel scene are the International Student Travel Confederation ISTC with 500 offices in 116 countries (including 33 in the UK) and some 10 million students and youth travellers on the move. Their website is a must for any would-be adventurer: www.isic.org. Make sure you have an ISIC card: it gives you the entrée to an amazing range of around the world opportunities. See details of the ISIC card below.

Advice note

The web is a great source for cheap travel and excellent deals for students, but make sure you are dealing with a reputable firm.

Never pay full fare on bus, coach, train or plane. Take advantage of rail and coach cards, bucket shops selling bargain tickets, classified ads, chartered flights, stand-by fares, advance bookings and deals offered by student travel companies. Some of the budget airlines are giving the most fantastic deals.

What should I join before setting off?

There are five cards that all travel-hungry students should look into:

⊙ ISIC: £9.

The International Student Identity Card (ISIC) offers you thousands of discounts in the UK and around the world. From high street fashion stores, to hotels and hostels, weekend breaks, flights, buses, trains, restaurants, guidebooks, nights out, attractions, museums, galleries, CDs and books – ISIC will help to keep you entertained year round.

Plus you get free access to ISIConnect services, low-cost international calls, free email address, travel safe and voicemail. ISIC is available to any student who is studying for more than 15 hours a week, and you can get yours from the ISIC website www.isic.org, any branch of STA Travel, via their call centre on 0871 230 8569, or on the website at www.statravel.co.uk. Don't leave home without one.

⊙ IYTC Youth Card: £7.

If you are not a full-time student but are aged 26 or under, the International Youth Travel Card (IYTC) is for you. You'll get tons of the fantastic discounts available through ISIC.

⊙ YHA: £9.95.

YHA (England and Wales) Ltd offers access to domestic and international Youth Hostels. Changes made to membership rules a couple of years ago mean that you don't even have to be a member to use their youth hostels. Non-members just pay a £3 a night supplement, or £1.50 per night for under 18s. However, you do need a membership card to use hostels in other countries. An annual card is now down to £9.95. A two-year card costs £16.50 and a three-year card £20.95 (if you are under 26). There are more than 5,000 Youth Hostels across 64 countries. They all have assured standards for hygiene and safety. An annual card for those over 26 costs £15.95, but couples can buy a joint annual card for £22.95. To join call 0870 770 8868 or visit www.yha.org.uk. Address: YHA England and Wales, Trevelyan House, Dimple Road, Matlock, Derbyshire DE4 3YH.

⊙ Young Person's Railcard: £24.

This entitles all young people aged 16–25 to a third off most rail fares in the UK. Did you know that it also covers the London all-zone One-Day Travel Card? See leaflet for travel restrictions and useful discounts. (Mature students of 26 and over in full-time education also included.)

⊙ Student Coachcard: £10.

This entitles all students aged 17 and over to a third off National Express and Scottish Citylink fares; also some continental and Irish services – check with your local coach station or Victoria Coach Station, London, or phone National Express Call Centre on 08705 808080.

Cards to carry checklist	
Young Person's Railcard	£24
Coachcard	£10
ISIC	£9
IYTC under-26 card	£7
YHA card	£9.95

What is InterRail?

InterRail gives you the flexibility to see Europe the way you want to – you can go where you like, when you like. Your InterRail pass gives you unlimited travel on the extensive network that covers over 30 European countries. Choose a one country pass from £24 or a global pass from £117. It is available to European citizens and anyone who has been resident here for six months. Available from STA Travel (pop into a branch, call 0871 230 8569 or click www.statravel.co.uk).

Further information

Who else could I consult?

The National Tourist Office or Board. Many countries have a national tourist office or board in this country. Most are based in London. London telephone directories can usually be found in the reference section of your local library.

What to read

The 'Rough Guide' series and the 'Lonely Planet' series cover almost every country and provide a useful insight into an area. Cost varies according to the country covered; try your local library.

As a student, do I need insurance?

Yes! Don't leave home without it. Travel Insurance is often the last thing you think about, but the first thing you'll need if things go wrong. Enjoy your trip safe in the knowledge that you are covered for the unexpected with travel insurance from just 32p per day.* STA Travel offers 3 levels of cover to suit every trip. Whether you prefer bungee jumping, white water rafting or snowboarding, STA Travel has a policy to suit you and your luggage.

*32p per day assumes an individual under 35 years of age with European Budget cover for a period of 24 months.

Some work camps and voluntary agencies arrange insurance for those taking part in projects. Check this out, and check what it covers. There are certain reciprocal arrangements for medical treatment in some EU countries. These also need to be checked out. (Bear in mind: this doesn't mean that all medical expenses will be covered, and your property won't be covered if it's stolen.) Get the Department for Work and Pensions leaflet SA 28/30.

How much will it cost? What should it cover?

Every trip and every traveller is different: STA Travel offers three different types of cover – Backpack, Standard and Premier – to help you find the most appropriate cover for your needs. Pop into your local branch, call 0871 230 8569 or visit www.statravel.co.uk for a quote.

Some banks offer travel insurance and you may get a good discount as part of the student package – see Chapter 10.

Endsleigh's travel products are also designed to reflect the lifestyles of their customers and suit all types of holidays and travel experiences. They offer a choice of cover options including basic, essential and comprehensive benefits in the UK, Europe or worldwide

Contact STA Travel on 0871 230 8569 or www.statravel.co.uk, or visit one of their branches. Or call Endsleigh Insurance on 0800 028 3571 to be connected to your local branch. Alternatively visit one of their 130 branches, many of which are on university campuses, or click on www.endsleigh.co.uk.

Thrift tips from Oxbridge

'Enter competitions you see. Sell things you don't need. Use tea bags twice'

Economics student

'Ebay.co.uk is fantastic for selling anything'

Veterinary Medicine student

'Get involved in student marketing, medical testing,
police ID parades – means a little cash to make life easier'

Chemistry student

'Mystery shopping! www.gapbuster.com: quick good money'

English and Drama student

Advice note

Find out about any rail passes offered by individual European countries. STA Travel should be able to help you out – 0871 230 8569 or www.statravel.co.uk.

⭐ **Most popular full time first-degree courses**

	Number of students studying subject
Business & Administrative Studies	152,635
Subjects allied to Medicine (figur does not include Medicine and Dentistry: 42,950 students)	148,870
Creative Arts & Design	125,420
Biological Sciences	108,830
Social Studies	107,275
Engineering & Technology	77,120
Languages	76,500
Computer Sciences	59,090
Law	52,960
Historical & Philosophical Studies	52,385
Most exclusive: Veterinary Science	3,855

(Figures provided by HESA from 2006/2007 student returns)

7

Sponsorship

A guide to getting sponsorship, and what to expect from it

Probably the best and most comprehensive way of raising extra finance to help you through higher education is sponsorship. It gives you money during term time and work during the vacations.

In this chapter we turn the spotlight on sponsorship, on the changes to the sponsorship market that have been taking place recently, and on some of the companies most likely to give it.

Sponsors and sponsorship

What is sponsorship?

You've heard of big companies sponsoring events such as the London Marathon, the FA Cup and cricket test matches. It means that they back the event with money. In the same way, an organisation could sponsor you through university.

Fast facts on sponsorship	
Who gives it?	Major companies
When?	For a full course
	After first year of study
	After industrial placement
	For final study year
To whom?	Degree and HND students
Most sponsored subject	Engineering
Most likely sponsors	Manufacturing and production companies
What it's worth	£1,000–£2,000 pa bursary
	£800–£1,650 per-month work periods
Other plus points	Work experience – industrial placement, additional skills
Will it secure a job?	Helpful, but no guarantee

Who gives sponsorship?

- Employers – mainly large companies, banks, accountancy firms etc. (see also the Power Academy, page 148).
- The three Armed Forces (see page 159).
- Ministry of Defence – Defence Engineering and Science Group www.desg.mod.uk (see page 151)
- Professional bodies, e.g. the Institution of Mechanical Engineers (IMechE) (see page 162).
- Universities, on behalf of employers.

Sponsorship of university students has been going on for many years. It was originally started to attract more young people into engineering. Even today engineering is the major area where sponsorship can be found.

Why do companies give sponsorship?

We canvassed some 150 employers. The reasons most often given were: to have access to high-quality students before they graduate, with the hope of future employment; to assess students over a longer period as potential employees; to develop a student's skills and have an input into their training; to publicise the company as a potential employer among other students. Or, in their own words:

Opportunity to see trainees in work situations before graduation.

Input of fresh ideas into the company.

Gives students a chance to look at us and us a chance to look at them before job offer made.

How does sponsorship work?

There are no hard-and-fast rules – every company devises its own scheme. In principle it works like this.

As a sponsored student you would get training, work experience and financial help while at college – to varying extents, depending on the company scheme. You might be asked to work for a whole year in the company either before or during your course; you might be expected to work only during the summer vacations.

In return, the sponsor gets the opportunity to develop close ties with 'a potentially good employee' and to influence your development. There is generally no commitment on either side to employment after the sponsorship. However, since the company has invested a considerable amount of money in you as a student it is unlikely not to offer you a job.

Check out the Power Academy

The Power Academy is an engineering scholarship fund launched in 2004 for students studying an IET-accredited (Institute of Engineering and Technology) degree course at a partner university. It is backed by the Institution of Engineering and Technology, six universities and 17 companies in the power industry. There are over 55 scholarships available in 2008 to students studying at the University of Cardiff, Imperial College London, the University of Strathclyde, University of Manchester, University of Southampton and Queen's University, Belfast, for the full length of their course.

The sponsorship offers:

- £2,200 annual bursary
- payment towards university fees
- £220 book allowance
- summer vacation work
- free membership of the IET
- annual seminar for all PA-sponsored students.

Why such generosity? The Power Academy was set up because there is a shortage of good power graduates coming out of our universities, and the industry could be facing a crisis. It is anticipated that 25% of the power industry's current engineering workforce will retire over the next 15 years, and there are not enough good people around to fill the vacancies. So it looks as if there could be some good jobs available in the future.

The companies involved include CE Electric, Central Networks, EDF Energy, National Grid, Scottish and Southern Energy, Scottish Power, United Utilities, Western Power Distribution, EA Technology, Siemens, ABB, AREVA T&D, Atkins Power, Jersey Electricity, Rolls-Royce, UKAEA and Viridian.

To find out more, log on to www.theiet.org/poweracademy. See also Dave's story opposite.

Dave's sponsorship

'Two weeks after starting my degree course at Manchester, the University Industrial Liaison Manager burst into one of our lectures to announce that the Power Academy was looking to sponsor students – were we interested? You bet we were!

'You had to apply online, picking three companies you were interested in, and if successful you went for a day's interviewing and team building exercises. I got through all that, but fell at the final interview stage.

'The next year I applied again. The procedure was the same, but I picked my three companies with more care. The result: I got two offers of sponsorship. I chose Siemens because they were into the design of power equipment and that was the area I wanted to move into.

'I accepted the offer just before Christmas: by January the £2,000 bursary was in my bank account. I also received a £200 book/software allowance. They would have paid my fees, but the local authority was already doing that.

'That Easter, I knew I had to earn some money, so I contacted Siemens and they gave me an admin job for a week so I earned another £471. It wasn't engineering but it did give me a chance to get a feel for the company and see what projects were on offer for the summer vacation.

'I worked for three months during the summer designing a substation test rig and earned £3,063. I was working on my own and allowed to get on with the job. It was a fantastic experience and I had a great time. There were seven other sponsored students on site and we often met up after work.

'Back at uni I was sent another £2,000 bursary and £200 book/software allowance and was given the offer of a job at Siemens when I graduated. Added to that, I was awarded a Whitworth Scholarship worth a further £4,000.'

Dave is now a graduate Whitworth Scholar having graduated last July and is working at Siemens, his sponsor.

(See Paul's story, 'How I got a Whitworth Scholarship', page 170.)

What Dave received:

Year 2	
Bursary 2006	£2,000
Book/software allowance	£200
Earnings at Easter, 1 week 2006	£471
Earnings summer, 3 months 2006	£3,063
Year 3	
Bursary 2007	£2,000
Book/software allowance	£200
Whitworth Scholarship	£4,000
Total:	£11,934

What would sponsorship mean to me?

There are many types of sponsorship. Generally, a sponsorship will include a bursary given while you are studying, and paid work experience, which is usually at the going rate for somebody of your age. In financial terms, it would probably mean that you would be around £40–£70 a week better off than your contemporaries during term time, with guaranteed work for at least eight weeks during the summer. But it's not just about money – the work experience and training are valuable assets, too.

The question of cash

Looking at it purely in cash terms:

- ⦿ £1,000 – £2,000 annual bursary

Given during academic study. For manufacturing and production students this could be higher. The Armed Forces give higher rates still, but they have a different kind of arrangement.

- ⦿ Salary £800 – £1,650 monthly

This is what you could expect to earn when working for your sponsor. However, salaries are generally age-related, so a third-year student would earn appreciably more than a pre-university student.

Employers' additional costs

From the employer's point of view the costs don't stop there. Generally a sponsorship includes training, which may well mean several weeks at their training centre. Some companies provide a personal tutor for students. There are also courses and meetings to arrange work experience. All this takes time, and time costs money. Every time somebody stops to tell you how to do something, it's work time lost to the employer.

Will my sponsorship bursary affect what I get as my financial support package?

Any scholarship or sponsorship you receive should not be included when calculating how much loan, grant and uni bursary you can have. Money earned during vacations is also not included. So for a normal sponsorship the answer is probably no.

Ministry of Defence DESG undergraduate sponsorship scheme

- ⊙ The aim of the DESG Student Sponsorship Scheme is to help you explore the variety of careers available in the Ministry of Defence while gaining valuable work experience.

- ⊙ There is no commitment to work for the MoD on graduation, but obviously they hope that you will.

- ⊙ A bursary of £1,500 pa will be given while studying.

- ⊙ Ten weeks' guaranteed work experience at a MoD establishment in the UK is given during summer vacations; pay based on an annual salary of £14,025.

- ⊙ Work placements are designed to give valuable experience to engineers and scientists, so expect a challenging project that will make a real difference to the team you are working with.

- ⊙ All students will be assigned a mentor who will help you select summer placements and provide advice on professional development.

- ⊙ The scheme is open to those studying an approved engineering or science degree in a UK university and who are likely to achieve a 2:2 degree or better. (See website for subject list.)

- ⊙ Check www.desg.mod.uk/downloads/desg_sponsorship_factsheet.pdf for more details and www.desg.mod.uk for online application form.

Application for sponsorship

How do I get sponsored?

1. You apply to a company that offers sponsorships. These are generally offered to students doing specific subjects.
2. You are offered sponsorship after a period of work experience.
3. Your university has contacts with employers.

What subjects are most likely to attract sponsorship?

Engineering outstrips any other subject, with the largest number of sponsorships being found in the manufacturing and production sector. However, there are good opportunities for civil engineers in the construction industry.

Many employers look for subjects with a close link to their own business activities. Good examples would be Food Science, Quantity Surveying and Polymer Technology. So if you feel you are studying a degree relevant to a company's business it is worth a try.

Any discipline: a few organisations, especially in the financial sector, will sponsor people on any degree course, but you have to have an interest in finance.

When could I get sponsorship?

- After A-levels or BTEC for a full degree or HND course.
- After a gap year spent with a company, between A-levels and higher education.
- After your first year of study.
- After a successful period of work experience or an industrial placement year.
- For your final year of study.

While sponsorships are still given to A level students for their full three to four years of academic study, more and more companies are choosing to sponsor students later in their degree course, when a commitment to the subject has been established. Work placements and sponsorships are now considered to be one of the best graduate recruitment tools by large employers.

The University Schools Liaison Officer of IMechE says:

> *The sponsorship market has changed. Companies have certainly cut back on numbers and many offer only a final-year sponsorship, but I think it has reached its trough. Many of the smaller organisations that only want one or two sponsorship students are now going straight to the universities of their choice and asking for who they want. This is largely to avoid having to deal with the thousands of applications which advertising in our publication would engender. There are some good sponsorships around which are well worth going after.*

What to expect when applying for sponsorship

The application form

These are more likely to be online than paper forms and you need to think carefully when filling them in, because you only get one chance. Mess it up, and your application will go no further.

Employers are – quite naturally – looking for the brightest and best students to sponsor; they want to have the pick of the potential high-flyers at an early stage. If you are applying for sponsorship before you start university, you may only have GCSE results, possibly some AS level results and a headteacher's report to show what you are capable of. This can be tough on those who wake up academically after GCSE or who really excel only in their one chosen subject. But good employers are more aware than you might expect; selection is not on academic qualifications alone. Sponsors are looking for signs of those additional qualities needed to succeed in your chosen career: leadership potential, the ability to grasp ideas quickly and to work in a team. They want ambitious, innovative, get-up-and-go people who can think for themselves and get things done. So if your GCSE grades slipped a bit – or, as one student we interviewed put it, 'you look like Mr Average on paper' – think through what else you have been doing. Playing in the football or hockey team; helping out at the local club;

hiking across Europe; getting a pop group together – it could help to redress the balance. Remember: the application form is the first weeding-out process, and you are up against stiff competition. This is no time for false modesty – you've got to sell yourself for all you're worth.

The interview

Interviews vary enormously. Some companies give a full-scale assessment with psychometric testing, tricky questioning and watching how you respond to certain situations. Others are much more laid-back and go for a straight interview. Whatever the process, if you are an A level student it will probably be something quite new to you. Don't worry. The company will be fully aware of this and will not ask you to do something you are not capable of. Remember, too, that your competitors will be in much the same position.

Still, don't expect an easy time at an interview.

How I got my sponsorship

Alex is 20 and a third-year student at Manchester University. This is her story.

'Out of the blue a letter arrived from Manchester University saying Procter & Gamble were offering sponsorships and would I like to apply? Would I! I had applied to Manchester University to study Chemical Engineering with Chemistry; I had a provisional place, but A levels were still several months away. If I was interested, I had to apply direct to P&G – online.

'Having filled in my application form, I was then asked to complete a "personality test", again online.

'Next I went to Manchester to take yet another test, this time "critical thinking". This was in two parts – an English section and a lateral thinking section. I was told it was the same test given to graduates wanting to join the company. It was not exactly difficult, but certainly challenging. I think if you didn't have an engineer's mind you might struggle. We were told the results right away.

'Two weeks later I was back in Manchester for an interview. I was very nervous and a bit scared. By now I had learnt this was a new sponsorship programme being set up and that there were just two or possibly three sponsorships available – 25 students had applied. My chances of success were slim.

'I had never done anything like this before. It was a one-to-one interview with the head of the sponsorship programme. Most of the questions were based on how you would cope in difficult situations and leading a team – and they wanted examples. Fortunately I had been on the Duke of Edinburgh's Award Scheme, so I had plenty of examples of leadership. But it was tough. You had to think on your feet, and concentrate hard.'

Alex was successful. In her first year she received a bursary during her academic year and then worked for P&G at a plant in Essex for around 11 weeks during the summer. She was engaged on the environmental side and undertook her own project. Having paid for her accommodation in Essex, she used the money she earned, about £4,200, to pay off her university debts of around £2,000. Of her work experience she says: 'It was brilliant, the P&G people were very welcoming and supportive. I learnt a lot about day-to-day life and issues of working in a process plant as well as developing my technical knowledge. I also made some good friends.'

$\ominus$

Last summer Alex worked at P&G's Manchester plant so could stay in the house where she currently lives. She undertook two projects: one involved looking at new equipment, and the other gave her experience in day-to-day production on the plant. The highlight of her internship was a business trip with another employee to Poland where she had a fantastic few days in Warsaw. The internship lasted ten weeks and she earned £1,650 a month. She used the money to have a good time, go on holiday and pay off her overdraft. Next summer she has been given the option by P&G to have the summer off and not do an internship.

What Alex receives:

1st year	Bursary of £1,500 pa (she used this to cover her fees and books)
	Ten weeks' guaranteed work experience during the summer (she did 11 weeks). Pay of £1,650 a month – £4,200 in total
	Entrée to the P&G staff shop – 'Anyone fancy a Pringle'?
2nd year	Bursary of £1,500 pa
	Ten weeks' guaranteed work during the summer at £1,650 a month
3rd year	Bursary of £2,000 pa
	Ten weeks' guaranteed work during summer at £1,650 a month

Estimated total: £17,375

Work experience

Students gain amazing experience during placements, but make sure it is the right experience for you. It is important not to be so mesmerised by the bursary money that you don't consider what the company offering sponsorship does and whether it can provide experience that will help your career. The downside to a sponsorship is that during your degree all your work experience will be in one company and, because of this, it can shape the direction of your future career. When you go for your interview ask about the experience and training you can expect and the skills you will acquire.

Thrift tips

'Get a bike.'

1st year Social and Political Sciences student, Cambridge

'Swap socialising for work so you don't drink.'

2nd year Politics/Philosophy student, Durham

'Make roll-ups out of cigarette butts.'

2nd year English student, Sussex

Terms and conditions

How much time do I have to spend with my sponsor?

Some sponsors demand you spend a year working with them either during your course or for a gap year before university. Others give you the choice. Most stipulate summer vacation work of six to eight weeks. Students often ask for more and may do Easter vacation work as well. Engineering firms are generally more demanding and the sponsorship is more likely to be geared to a sandwich course, so you could be looking at a full year in industry plus two summer vacation placements.

Planned vacation work

Some companies will hold special vacation-planning sessions. These are usually during the Easter vacation and can last anything up to a week. During these sessions you would plan with your sponsor how you want to spend your summer vacation time.

Comment: sponsors occasionally allow their sponsored students to gain experience in other companies during vacations, as they feel that it will help to broaden their mind and knowledge. But most are loath to do so, for obvious reasons.

Am I obliged to join my sponsor after graduating? Are they obliged to employ me?

No, you are not obliged to join your sponsoring company after graduating, unless it says so in your contract. Equally, they are not obliged to offer you a job. But there is no doubt that companies are taking a tougher stand these days, and seeking value for money from their sponsorships. For example:

- Some companies will stop your bursary payment for the final year if you don't agree to join them after graduating.
- A few companies demand reimbursement of their sponsorship money if you don't join them. You would have been informed of this before you agreed to a sponsorship.
- Some companies only give sponsorship for the final year after a job offer has been accepted.

Comment: The Armed Forces are slightly different from other employers; they have always included service as part of their sponsorship schemes.

Fact file

50% of employers recruit from students who undertake work experience with them.

75% of employers offer work experience/sponsorship as part of their recruitment strategy.

(IRS Employment Review, November 2006)

Can my sponsor terminate my sponsorship?

Sponsorship is a legal contract. Look at the terms carefully. Most agreements will have a clause that allows the employer to withdraw if your academic performance is unsatisfactory. There may be other clauses you should watch out for.

What exactly is meant by academic performance?

If you fail the odd exam, you're probably all right, but if your end-of-year results are so bad that you have to repeat the year, you may find that your sponsor is no longer interested.

Other aspects to consider

How do I choose a sponsor?

'Be practical – go for the cash' was one student's advice on selecting a sponsor. Certainly cash is something to bear in mind, but there are many other factors to consider:

- ◉ Compare salaries for work experience and bursaries: the plus on one might rule out the minus on the other.
- ◉ Check out the training engineers: is the training accredited by the appropriate institution? and the experience – is it a well-organised programme of development or are you just another pair of hands?
- ◉ Talk to students on the scheme; find out about projects undertaken; how many sponsored students joined the company as graduates?
- ◉ Where would you be located? Do they provide accommodation if away from home? Are there opportunities to gain experience abroad?
- ◉ Finally, ask yourself: is this the kind of company where you would want to make your career?

Advice note

- ◉ Make sure any literature you are reading on sponsorship is up to date – school and college careers libraries are notorious for displaying last year's information.
- ◉ Look at your contract in detail and, above all, check the small print.
- ◉ Question your sponsor; they will respect you for that.

When should I apply for sponsorship?

- ◉ **Full degree course sponsorship:** some companies offer sponsorship for your full degree course. Applications for these schemes should be made early in your final school year, and at least by the time you send in your UCAS form.

- **Second-year degree course sponsorship:** some sponsors like to see commitment to your course before offering sponsorship. Applications should be made early in your first year at university. Ask your department head for likely sponsors.
- **Final-year degree course sponsorship:** increasingly, employers are offering sponsorship to students for just the final year of their degree course. Often this will be offered after a successful industrial placement year or summer vacation period. Employers offering sponsorship at this stage will expect students to agree to join them after graduation.

Jono's sponsorship

I went to Loughborough to study Mechanical Engineering, but a week after getting there I was asked if I would like to be a guinea pig. They were starting up a completely new course called Innovative Manufacturing and Technology. If I took the course I would get sponsorship – a bursary of £500 a year for the first two years and then £1,000 for the next two years. It wasn't the money that decided me: the course is really interesting; I liked the idea of doing something so new. There are only three students on the course. Another feature of the course is that the sponsorship comes from a mix of companies, so you receive a wide range of work experience and work in a number of different companies such as Perkins, Bentley, IMI Morgan, Caterpillar – all good names.

What's the competition for sponsorship?

Phenomenal. All sponsors say that applications outstrip sponsorships available, and it is getting worse – so get in early. The earlier you apply, the better. Applications for full course sponsorship should have been made by the time you send in your UCAS form.

What is a sponsor looking for?

A straw poll of sponsors suggested that sponsors favour students with:

- good A level (or equivalent) grades
- maturity
- potential
- ambition
- evident team skills
- sense of humour
- hard-working attitude
- ability to get a good second-class degree
- interest in their degree topic
- ability to assimilate information and learn quickly
- a spark that sets you apart from the rest
- business awareness
- interpersonal skills.

Fact check

- Median starting salary paid to graduates in 2007 was £23,500 pa. Anticipated figure for 2008 is £24,000 (AGR Graduate Recruitment Winter Review 2008).
- 319,260 first-degree students – a record number – graduated from higher education institutions in the UK in 2007 (HESA release 2008).
- Having difficulty getting sponsorship? Four-fifths of graduate employers said that sponsorship schemes were too costly to justify their use to their organisations (IRS Employment Review, November 2006).
- Typical sponsors are large firms with 1,000–9,000 employees.
- Approximately 120,000 students in the UK are enrolled on sandwich courses (ASET figures).

Which comes first – UCAS or sponsorship?

They both come at once, which makes for complications. However, both sides are aware of this, so a system has been worked out.

First you should discover whether a sponsor you are interested in requires you to gain a place on a particular course – if so, you should name that course on your UCAS form.

However, it could happen that an employer you had not originally been very interested in offers you a sponsorship with the proviso that you gain a place on a course not named in your selection on your application form. While UCAS does not generally allow students to make alterations to their original application, in the case of sponsorship they usually relax this rule.

What about deferred entry?

Another complication is whether you want deferred entry or not. If you get sponsorship, your sponsor may require you to do a pre-degree year in industry, but at application time you may not know this. If in doubt, apply for the current year. It is always easier to ask a university to defer your entry rather than bring it forward. On some courses, especially popular courses such as Law, deferment may be more difficult to arrange.

Will my university find me sponsorship?

If you are accepted on to a course either conditionally or unconditionally, it is always a good idea to ask the course director if they know of any sponsoring companies. Often they will have a list. Some students will find that they are automatically offered sponsors to apply to, and on some courses that are actually sponsored by employers, the sponsors are involved in the selection procedure. College prospectuses may give you some guidance. A number of universities advertise sponsored courses in *Engineering Opportunities for School Leavers, Students and Graduates* – for details see 'What to read' at the end of this chapter.

Not all sponsors advertise

If you look down the list of sponsors in most sponsorship books, you will be surprised how many large companies appear not to offer sponsorship or work experience, yet in fact they do. Many companies just don't have to bother to advertise – the requests flood in anyway. Others will have special relationships with selected schools or universities. So, just because a company doesn't advertise sponsorship, that shouldn't stop you from asking.

Don't forget the smaller companies

If you're thinking in terms of your CV, it must be admitted that a well-known name will carry more weight than a smaller company. But with a smaller, little-known company there is less competition. Perhaps more important, you are likely to be treated as an individual. You may well be the only sponsored student they have and you can develop your own training and experience package. Of course, if they have no experience of sponsored students, they may not know what you are capable of and what experience you should be getting. So you could find you have to stand up for yourself.

Is it best to apply to local companies?

It is always best to apply to a company that interests you. Nevertheless, some companies do prefer to take on local people. From their point of view, there is no accommodation problem when it comes to work experience, and statistics show that many students want to return to their own home town to work when they complete their studies. So the company is more likely to keep the sponsored student as an employee.

Will sponsorship be good for my CV?

Yes, but with reservations: 73% of the companies we asked said sponsorship was a plus point. The others felt that it made little difference. A careers adviser at Bath University said that, while sponsorship on your CV shows that you have been 'selected', it was the work experience that would be seen as the important element on a CV.

Of course, employers will probably ask why you didn't join the company that sponsored you, so you will need to have a well-phrased answer. Most employers realise that a decision made at the age of 18 may not look so right when you are 22. It's always worth remembering that your would-be new employer may write to your sponsor for a reference, so it's important to leave your sponsoring company on good terms.

Should I try the Armed Forces?

The three Armed Forces offer very generous sponsorships, which can cover fees and full living costs. But their Cadetship and Bursary schemes are not open-ended. There is a service commitment involved and those taking them up should think very carefully about what they are getting involved in. Full details are available from:

- Army Officer Entry, Freepost LON15 445, Bristol BS38 7UE. Tel: 08457 300111. Websites: www.army.mod.uk/servingsoldier/condofserv/mm/index.html (for students looking for support while at university); www.army.mod.uk/careers/officer (for students looking for an army career); www.armyjobs.co.uk (for army jobs).
- Royal Air Force, Officer Careers, Freepost 4335, Bristol BS1 3YX. Tel: 0845 605 6555; website: www.rafcareers.com.
- Royal Navy and Royal Marines Careers Service, Dept BR211, FREEPOST GL672, Cirencester GL7 1BR. Tel: 0845 607 5555; website: www.royalnavy.mod.uk.

Will I pay tax on my bursary?

You do not have to pay tax on a bursary. But if your annual earned income is above the tax threshold – currently £6,035 – you would have to pay tax. So in theory a year's placement would not be tax-free. However, since your year's work probably falls into two tax years you may find you pay very little or none at all.

Advice note

Were you unlucky in securing sponsorship? Try the back-door entry. When you're looking for a summer vacation job, seek out companies that you feel could be interested in sponsoring your particular skills. You may be lucky, and there's no harm in asking.

Can I get sponsorship once I've started my degree?

Yes. As we said in the 'When should I apply for sponsorship?' section, more and more companies are giving sponsorship just for the final year or from the second year of a course. These sponsorships often develop from a successful period of work experience during the summer vacations, or through an industrial placement during a sandwich course.

Should sponsorship determine which course I choose?

In theory, no. First you should decide on the course that best suits you. You're going to spend at least three solid years – and possibly more – studying, so make sure you're going to enjoy it, otherwise the results could be at best disappointing and at worst disastrous.

I'm a sponsored student, but find I don't like the course I'm studying. What can I do?

This happens. You choose a course in something that you may never have studied before, and after a term or so you discover that you and the subject just don't get along together. A sponsorship is not a life sentence, and neither is a degree course. Talk first to your college tutor. It may be just one aspect of the course you don't like. Then talk to your sponsor. You will probably be able to change your degree course, but it may be more difficult – or impossible – for your sponsor to put you on an appropriate sponsorship scheme. Don't despair. Whatever you do, be frank about your change of heart – and the sooner the better, before too much time and money are wasted.

To sum up

What do I gain from being sponsored?

- Money – probably an annual bursary plus good rates of pay when working.
- Training – most sponsorships will involve some form of training.
- Meaningful work experience.
- Guaranteed employment for the summer in an area that will assist you with your studies.
- Chance of future employment – but no guarantee.
- Help with final-year project work – possibly.
- Opportunity to gain first-hand knowledge of the working environment where you might possibly start your career.
- Understanding of what it means to work in industry.
- Chance to gain new skills.
- Plus-point to put in your CV.

What do I lose?

- Your holiday time is not your own. So, for example, you would not be able to spend the whole summer abroad going Inter-Railing.
- You have the chance to see only one industry/company during work experience.
- You make a career choice at 18 that may not be what you want at 21.
- You may be obliged to work for a company whether you want to or not, because of a payback clause.
- You may be asked to work in locations that are not very appealing and possibly a long way from home.

Further information

Who to contact

- The Year in Industry (see page 124).
- Local employers that interest you – many employers prefer to sponsor local students.
- Don't forget the smaller companies. Some may never have thought of offering work experience before, so it can be a matter of making yourself sound a good bet.

- ◉ Your course director.
- ◉ Your university or college may well have a list of sponsors who are interested in sponsoring students on your particular course. Some universities advertise in the books listed below.
- ◉ Black and Asian high-flyers can also try the Windsor Fellowship Undergraduate personal and professional development programmes, which include summer work placements and community work. Application forms and further information can be downloaded from www.windsorfellowship.org/leadership.

What to read

- ◉ *Everything You Wanted to Know about Sponsorship, Placements and Graduate Opportunities*, regularly updated and published by Amoeba Publications. Available from Trotman, tel: 0870 900 2665, or visit www.trotman.co.uk/bookshop.

- ◉ *Engineering Opportunities for School Leavers, Students and Graduates*, published by the Institution of Mechanical Engineers on behalf of the engineering profession. It lists sponsors and universities with sponsored courses, companies offering industrial placements and internships and is available free from IMechE c/o Marketing & Communications Department, 1 Birdcage Walk, London SW1H 9JJ. Tel: 020 7222 3337, email: education@imeche.org.uk.

- ◉ *University Scholarships, Awards and Bursaries*, published by Trotman. To order, tel: 0870 900 2665 or visit www. trotman.co.uk/bookshop.

- ◉ Scour the web.

★ Social spending universities	
Going out + Alcohol	*Weekly spend*
Belfast	£56.7
Leeds	£50.4
Brighton	£49
Nottingham	£46.4
Southampton	£46.2
Oxford	£45.8
Manchester	£45.3
Newcastle	£45.3
Leicester	£44.9
Cardiff	£44.6
(RBS Student Living Index 2007)	

8

Other sources to tap

Scholarships, charitable awards, trusts, competitions

The topics covered in this chapter are:

- Other sources of finance: a reality or a vain hope? (page 163)
- What is a scholarship? (page 164)
- Finding out about scholarships and charitable awards (page 165)
- Professional institutions (page 168)
- Charities and trusts (page 171)
- Competitions (page 174)
- Further information (page 177)

In this chapter we investigate all the other legitimate sources of finance you could tap to raise extra cash, and how to set about approaching them. They include trusts, charitable awards, scholarships, grants, bursaries (from sources other than your local authority or university) and competitions.

Other sources of finance: a reality or a vain hope?

You are right to be a little sceptical. If there were a prodigious number of organisations all eager to hand out money to students, you wouldn't have seen so many student demonstrations called to highlight their financial plight. But there are a surprising number of educational charities, trust funds and foundations, professional bodies, and benevolent funds available in this country offering financial help to students.

This may take the form of a scholarship or charitable award. One directory of grant-making trusts we consulted listed over 1500 organisations under the broad heading of Education. But before you get too excited and think you've found the route to a crock of gold, be aware that when you start sifting through the many restrictions which trusts generally have to abide by, you soon realise there are relatively few – if any – that could meet your exact needs.

What is a scholarship?

Scholarships differ from sponsorships in that they provide money while you study, but without the industrial training. They can, of course, be for a specific purpose, such as travel, to fund some special area of research or possibly to study abroad. They are usually, though not always, given by an institution – this could be your university, a professional institute or a charitable trust – rather than by individual companies.

Competition is keen. Awards can be made on grounds of academic achievement or need. Whatever the criteria, they are not going to come your way without considerable effort and often disappointment, so be prepared. Nobody gives money away easily.

How does a scholarship differ from a bursary?

It doesn't, really. Look up 'scholarship' in the dictionary and you'll find the definition is: 'award of money towards education'. Look up 'bursary' and it says, 'scholarship or grant awarded to students'. Sometimes a bursary is awarded if you meet certain criteria – for example, bursaries are given to low-income students under the funding arrangements – for English students see Chapter 2, for all other students including nurses/midwives see Chapter 4. To win a scholarship there is more likely to be an element of achievement (for example academic, musical or sporting).

Fast facts on alternative sources of finance	
Who gives bursaries and scholarships?	Charitable trusts, universities and colleges, professional bodies and institutions
How much?	From £12 to £4,000 and everything in between
What is the success rate?	Low

What is a charitable award?

The difference between a scholarship and a charitable award is, again, very indistinct, and you could say there is no difference at all, as charitable awards can often be scholarships. Charitable awards are always paid out by a charitable organisation, which must abide by the terms and conditions of the original endowment. So, however good and reasonable your case may be, if the money has to be paid out to a student from Gloucester studying Chemistry, it is no good being an Arts student from Leeds. To claim an award, both you and your financial predicament must fit the charity's help profile.

What kind of awards are available?

Often the payments are small – to buy books or equipment – but they can be quite substantial and cover fees or maintenance. So it could be from a few hundred pounds to a few thousand. They can be one-off payments, or given each year for the duration of your course.

Who gives scholarships and charitable awards?

Universities, schools, trust funds, professional institutions.

Finding out about scholarships and charitable awards

Can my school help me?

Yes. Most schools will have a list of local charities that offer help to students. The fact that you have been to the school could be a condition of receiving a grant. Also try your primary school. It is a good idea to find out if such scholarships, grants and charitable awards are available before you send off your UCAS application, as these sometimes stipulate a certain higher education establishment.

Can my local authority help?

Your local authority should have details of any local charities offering help to students in higher education. Try also:

- The Welsh Assembly, which offers bursaries to Welsh-born students attending Welsh universities.
- The Carnegie Trust for the Universities of Scotland, which provides financial assistance to students of Scottish birth or who have at least one parent born in Scotland or who have completed at least three years' secondary education in Scotland, and who want to attend Scottish universities to study for a first degree. They also offer vacation scholarships to enable undergraduates at Scottish universities to undertake a research project during the long vacation. Scholarships are also given to graduates from Scottish universities with a first-class honours degree for three years' postgraduate research at a university in the UK, usually in Scotland. Contact Carnegie Trust for the Universities of Scotland, Andrew Carnegie House, Pittencrief Street, Dunfermline, Fife KY12 8AW. Tel: 01383 724990. Fax: 01383 749799. Email: jgray@carnegie-trust.org. Website: www.carnegie-trust.org.

- The Students' Award Agency for Scotland maintains a Register of Educational Endowments on Scottish trusts, many of which are local and open only to Scottish-born students wanting to attend Scottish universities and colleges. The agency will search the register on behalf of any student who submits an enquiry form. Forms are available from the Students' Award Branch, Gyleview House, 3 Redheughs Rigg, Edinburgh EH12 9HH. Tel: 0845 111 1711. Email: saas. geu@scotland.gsi.gov.uk. Or you can contact them through their website: www.saas.gov.uk.
- See also 'What to read', page 177, for directories and registers on trusts.

Check out your parents' employers!

Or at least get your parents to. A surprising number of companies and large employers have special trusts set up to help with the education of their employees' or past employees' children. Typical examples:

- The National Police Fund, which helps the children of people who are serving in or have served in the police force.
- The Royal Medical Benevolent Fund, which helps the children of medical graduates, and the Dain Fund Charities Committee (contact the BMA), which helps the children of registered members of the medical profession.
- The Royal Pinner School Foundation, which helps the children of sales representatives.

Do universities and colleges give scholarships?

Some higher education institutions are endowed by generous benefactors and can award scholarships and bursaries to selected students who meet the required criteria. Usually an institution will have a very mixed bag of awards, which bears very little relation to its academic strengths and interests. Most establishments don't give many awards, and competition in the past has been keen. But with the advent of top-up fees, universities are having to provide bursaries for students to offset the high cost of university education (see page 44). Many of the university scholarships on offer have a subject or location condition attached, which does considerably limit those eligible to apply.

University Scholarships, Awards and Bursaries (published by Trotman) supplies full information on the bursaries universities give, especially to students from low-income families, and lists over 100 institutions offering scholarships or awards. These are largely for people studying specific subjects, or are travel awards. Subjects vary from the more usual (engineering, history, geography, languages, law and the sciences) to the distinctly unusual, such as cultural criticism studies, paper science, rural studies, retail studies, leisure, town planning, textiles – and a whole lot in between.

Sports scholarships and bursaries are increasingly commonly available. These cover areas such as rugby, cricket, netball and even golf. A sports scholarship is a boon for any student who plays in a national team and needs to take time out and coaching to train for an international/world cup series. You can be studying any subject to get a sports scholarship.

A number of universities and colleges give music or choral awards. Many of these are old foundations, and the award may include a commitment to take part in services in the college chapel or local church or cathedral. Then there are awards with geographical restrictions. For example, students at Bangor University might get an award of £300 if they live in Criccieth or, better still, £1,500 if they were born in one of the counties of Anglesey, Conwy or Gwynedd; and Exeter University students whose parents have resided in Devon for at least three years could be in line for a scholarship ranging from £12 to £80 pa.

Your university may also give travel awards to undertake special projects during the vacation, for certain subjects. Ask your university for details of possible awards, check their prospectus/website (see also *University Scholarships, Awards and Bursaries,* published by Trotman). For English Universities try http://bursarymap.direct.gov.uk.

Are there awards for foreign students?

Yes. Overseas students are eligible to apply for many of the awards offered by universities. In some universities there are awards specifically for foreign students. For example, Engineering and Applied Science at Aston (£1,500–£3,000), Law scholarships at City University (£1,500) and ten £1,000 scholarships for students from Japan, Malaysia, Singapore, Thailand and the USA at Edinburgh. For further information contact the British Council or British Embassy in your own country, the British Council here in the UK (www.britishcouncil.org) or the university where you will be studying.

How much would a college scholarship be worth?

Awards vary tremendously: some are given annually for the length of the course, others are a one-off payment. The highest award we found for undergraduates was £5,000 while the lowest found, at Exeter, was £12 – this is because the foundation was made in the nineteenth century, when £12 was a lot of money, and its status cannot be changed.

Thrift tips

'Student tutoring for GCSEs and A levels pays extremely well.'
3rd year Medicine student, Oxford

'Borrow from your parents: they are interest-free loans.'
3rd year Applied Psychology student, Liverpool John Moores

'Get the free overdraft and put it in a high-interest account, bond or ISA.'
Business Studies student, Staffordshire

How would I go about getting a college scholarship?

Scholarship distribution methods differ from institution to institution and, of course, according to the terms of the foundation. Aberystwyth, for example, holds formal examinations during February. These can be taken at the student's own school or college. It gives some 300 Entrance Scholarships and Merit Awards each year worth between £1,000 and £1,200 a year. Music bursaries (£400) are also available to experienced players of orchestral instruments who can make an active contribution to the university's wide range of orchestras and bands. Closing date for applications for these are mid-April.

The ancient Scottish universities all offer a range of bursaries. Those at Glasgow are awarded once students have begun their courses. However, at Aberdeen, Edinburgh and St Andrews, bursaries are available to entrants. Traditionally awards were made on the basis of exam performance, but at Aberdeen and Edinburgh, in particular, the bursary schemes have developed to include a significant number of awards, which take into account applicants' financial and personal circumstances. Application forms are available from the universities concerned; increasingly, bursary information and application forms can be found on university websites. Most of these scholarships are worth £1,000 for each year of degree study (in total, £4,000 for a Scottish Honours degree or £5,000 for a degree in Clinical Medicine).

First look in the college prospectus or its website – it should either list the awards given, or give you an address to write to for details. This should be done early in the autumn term of your final school year and before or about the time you are filling in your UCAS form. Obviously at this stage you do not know which university you are likely to go to, and any exam can be held early in the academic year, before you have made your final decision.

Fact file

Remember, these scholarships and bursaries are not necessarily for students from low-income families and are totally different from those offered by universities now that top-up fees have been introduced.

Professional institutions

Do professional institutions give scholarships?

Some do, some don't. The engineering institutions are among the most generous. Awards are made to students studying accredited degree courses.

Institution of Engineering and Technology, Michael Faraday House, Six Hills Way, Stevenage, Hertfordshire SG1 2AY. Email: awards@theiet.org. Through its scholarships and awards the IET promotes engineering as a career, rewards achievement and assists with postgraduate research. In 2008, the IET will award 82 scholarships of £1,000 to £3,000 per annum for the duration of an IET-accredited MEng degree course, including 50 IET FUSE (Funding Undergraduates to Study Engineering) Scholarships, available for high-ability students in need of financial assistance. There are also eight grants of £1,000 (one year only) available for final-year undergraduate students. For postgraduates there are 13 scholarships ranging from £1,250 to £10,000 pa, including the prestigious Leslie H. Paddle Scholarship, and 15 travel awards ranging from £500 to £1,000. To find out more, go to www.theiet.org/ambition. See also information on sponsorship through the Power Academy, page 148.

Institution of Civil Engineers, One Great George Street, Westminster, London SW1P 3AA. Tel: 020 7665 2193; email: quest.awards@ice.org.uk; website: www.ice.org.uk/quest. The Queen's Jubilee Scholarship Trust (QUEST) aims to award around 100 scholarships each year to students aiming to achieve Chartered, Incorporated or Technician Membership of ICE through embarking on a JBM-accredited course at university. The awards are up to the value of £3,000 per year for the duration of the course, to a maximum total value of £12,000 for one undergraduate course of study. Most QUEST awards are now provided in partnership with top engineering and construction companies that provide summer work placements and possible graduate employment. Students are also provided with mentors, who can give them a head start on the path to becoming professionally qualified.

Institution of Mechanical Engineers, Prizes and Awards Department, ASK House, Northgate Avenue, Bury St Edmunds, Suffolk IP32 6BB. Tel: 01284 717887 or 717882. The Institution gives 35 undergraduate scholarship awards of £1,000 pa for a maximum of four years (students must be or become an affiliate member of the Institution and have a place on an IMechE-accredited degree course); 3 Postgraduate Research Scholarships valued at £6,500 pa, 3 Postgraduate Masters Scholarships valued at £6,500; 20 awards of up to £750 for students studying or taking a work placement overseas; three awards of up to £1,000 for overseas voluntary or project work; ten hardship awards of up to £1,000 for students on IMechE-accredited degree courses; around 20 postgraduate awards of up to £1,000 for advanced study, research programmes, hardship or overseas projects; and additional funds available for original research in the science or practice of mechanical engineering. They also give up to ten Whitworth Scholarships for undergraduate degree-level courses (including MEng and MSc) valued at £4,500 pa (full-time study) and £3,000 pa (part-time study). These scholarships are for outstanding engineers who have served at least a two-year 'hands-on' engineering apprenticeship before commencing their undergraduate studies. They also offer Whitworth Senior Scholarships of £7,500, awarded to postgraduate students who go on to study for a PhD or EngD. Whitworth Scholarships are open to engineers of any discipline, not just mechanical engineers. Applicants must be British, Commonwealth or European Union citizens normally resident in the UK for at least three years prior to commencing their degree-level course.

Institute of Marine Engineering, Science and Technology (IMarEST), 80 Coleman Street, London EC2R 5BJ. Tel: 020 7382 2600. Up to seven scholarships of £1,000 are awarded each year to undergraduate students attending approved accredited courses leading to registration for Chartered status – Chartered Engineer (CEng), Chartered Marine Scientist (CMarSci) or Chartered Marine Technologist (CMarTech) – who demonstrate a commitment to maritime engineering, marine science or marine technology by spending at least two years in the industry or in study. The institute also offers awards to postgraduates through the Stanley Gray Fellowship scheme and prizes to students through various industry schemes. More information at www.imarest.org.

Institute of Physics, 76 Portland Place, London W1B 1NT; tel: 020 7470 4800; email: physics@iop.org; website: www.iop.org. The Institute of Physics provides around 300 bursaries to undergraduate students who intend to study physics at university. The aim is to encourage more students to study physics, especially those who would not traditionally choose the subject. The bursaries are worth £3,000 over the duration of a bachelor's degree and £4,000 over the duration of an MPhys/MSci degree. To be eligible you must be a UK or Irish national entering an accredited degree programme. These are not scholarships and aren't aimed at high-flyers. University physics departments administer the scheme on behalf of the Institute and will select the students who receive bursaries according to certain criteria such as financial hardship, students from schools with poor records for university attendance, mature students with families etc. Academic performance will only be used as a criterion when the number of deserving candidates outstrips the number of awards available. Bursaries will also be given to part-time students on a pro rata basis. To find out more, talk to the university where you are to study.

How I got a Whitworth Scholarship

Paul Tuohy left school at 16 with a clutch of 11 GCSEs and then started to study for his A levels. But illness meant that he would have to repeat a year and he decided to begin a Modern Apprenticeship instead. Having scored excellent marks for a BTEC ONC and HNC through day-release, he wanted to continue studying. This is his story.

'I liked to learn something new, I had the study bug; so when the personnel officer at the company where I was working said the firm would sponsor me if I wanted to take a degree part-time, I jumped at the chance. However, there was one proviso: I needed the permission of my boss, the Chief Engineer. It seemed like just a formality, but to my horror he said categorically "No!". I could not believe it. Nor could anyone else. A few months later I left the company.

'To be honest, he probably did me a favour. I decided to study for a degree anyway, but to do it full time. It was to be a BEng (Hons) in Mechatronics with Industrial Experience. Fortunately I lived in Manchester and the course being offered at Manchester University was much better than the part-time course I had considered. Even though I had no A levels, the university said they would give me a chance. "You may struggle with the maths," they said, and they were right, but other topics came more easily and I was prepared to work hard.

'I was used to having plenty of money to spend – I'd been on a salary of over £20,000 – and wondered how I would cope as a student. I had some money saved. I took out a student loan. My parents said I could live at home free while I studied and I bought a bicycle to save on travel fares.

'In my first semester my results averaged 76%. In my second semester I did even better, and with an average of 81% was awarded the Mechatronic Student of the Year Prize. It was then that our Industrial Liaison Manager, Eddie Welch, suggested I should apply for a Sir Joseph Whitworth Scholarship given by the Institution of Mechanical Engineers (IMechE).

'There were around 40 applicants that year and only ten scholarships to be awarded. Having filled in an application form, I attended an interview with a panel of some five lecturers and engineers down at the IMechE in London. It was tough. Two days later they phoned to say I had been awarded a scholarship valued at £3,000 a year. That certainly helped with my finances.

'The next year I spent in industry, at Rolls Royce. When I returned to uni for my final year I received another award under the Whitworth Scholarship scheme – this time £4,000.'

Paul graduated with a first class honours degree in Mechatronic Engineering. As a Whitworth Scholar he can put the prestigious letters BEng WhSch after his name.

He is now doing a PhD at Manchester, in the development of a new type of marine propulsion engine in collaboration with Rolls Royce and receives a £12,300 stipend to live on. In addition he has been awarded a Whitworth Senior Scholarship which this year amounts to £7,500.

Charities and trusts

Which charities and trusts give help to students?

You may be surprised to learn that it would take a book several times the size of this one to list them all. For example, the *Educational Grants Directory* (see the book list at the end of this chapter) lists more than 1,200 charities that between them give away more than £40 million a year – and this is by no means an exhaustive list.

But before you get too excited, most charities have restrictions on how much they can give away, to whom and for what reasons. Also, most charities and trusts will only consider you after you have exhausted all the more conventional avenues such as loans and Access funds.

Trusts and charities fall largely into four major groups:

- **Need** – charities for the disabled fall into this group. Well-known names such as the Royal National Institute for the Blind (RNIB) and the RNID – Royal Association in Aid of Deaf People would come into this category, along with less familiar organisations such as the Shaftesbury Society and Scope.

- **Subject** – into this category fall charities that will give help to students studying certain subjects. For example, the Company of Actuaries Charitable Trust Fund helps those studying to be actuaries; the Chartered Surveyors Company Charitable Trust and Mr Sidney A. Smith's Fund help those studying Surveying; the Honourable Society of Gray's Inn is just one of a number of charities helping those studying Law; and there are quite a few charitable organisations set up to help those studying Medicine – for example the Charity of Miss Alice Gertrude Hewitt, which helps some 40 students aged under 25.

- **Parents' occupation** – this can be a great source of additional income. If one of your parents is an airline pilot, artist, banker, barrister, in the clergy, coalminer, gardener, in the precious metals industry – you name it, there could be some help. Some trusts stipulate that your parent should be dead, but not all.

- **Geographical location** – where you study and also where you live can really make a difference. Take, for example, the lucky students living in the parishes of Patrington and Rimswell in East Yorkshire, in Oadby in the Midlands or in Yeovil in Somerset – they could be in line for help towards books, fees, living expenses or travel abroad. There are literally hundreds of these trusts covering many areas of the country. It has to be said that pay-outs can be small – under £100 – but they can be substantially more – say £1,000.

My income was extremely low, so I applied for as many bursaries (in and outside college) as possible. The effort paid off: I got a bursary from college for around £2,000 and another from a company trust of £1,000.
1st year Law student, Cambridge

What sort of help do trusts give?

Help with fees, maintenance, books, equipment, travel either to and from your college or abroad, special sports activities, child-minding and special projects. They all vary in what they will offer, and to whom.

Advice note

Before making an application to a charity, it is important to be clear in your own mind exactly what kind of student they are likely to help, and what kind of financial assistance you are after, otherwise you could be wasting both your time and theirs.

Is there anybody who could advise me on applying to charitable trusts?

EGAS, which stands for the Education Grants Advisory Service, is an independent organisation that will advise students (aged over 16) on organisations to contact. You will need to fill in their questionnaire and they will then dip into their extensive database of charities and trusts and see which are the most likely bodies to help you. The criteria for eligibility are set by the individual trusts and charities or by the people who bequeathed the legacy, not EGAS, and these are extremely diverse. Trusts can seldom help in an immediate financial crisis. The more time you have to raise the funds, the more likely you are to succeed. To find out more and carry out your own search of trusts, the quickest route is to visit the EGAS website: www.egas-online. org.uk/fwa/trustsearch.htm. Otherwise you can phone the EGAS helpline on 020 7254 6251, open Tuesday, Wednesday and Thursday 2–4pm. Or write to EGAS, 501–505 Kingsland Road, London E8 4AU, including a large stamped addressed envelope if requesting a questionnaire.

Can EGAS help overseas students and those wanting to study abroad?

It is very difficult to find trusts willing to fund overseas students who are already studying in the UK, and EGAS cannot assist students wishing to study outside the UK. However, there are trusts that give funding for travel, and these should be contacted directly. See the booklist at the end of this chapter for help if you would like to winkle them out.

What are my chances of hitting the jackpot?

Your chances are slim, though the odds are certainly better than the likelihood of winning the national lottery. Competition is fierce. Last year EGAS received around 5,300 written applications, and its website received over 148,000 visitors with some 27,000 people completing a search.

EGAS does not itself provide support but it is part of the Family Welfare Association (FWA), which does offer support to students from disadvantaged backgrounds. Last year FWA gave around 1,550 grants totalling around £285,370 to HE and FE students. However, any funding it does offer is usually small, around £150, for something specific like books, equipment or travel. It handles about 100 grant applications a month and most grants are given to help students in their final year. Typical examples of why money might be given are:

- For books or equipment
- If a parent is suddenly made redundant and can't continue to finance your college course fees
- To a student who has been paying their way through part-time work but feels they need to give up their job to concentrate on that final two-month push.

But EGAS warns that at peak times it can have a backlog of up to six weeks, so students should plan in advance if they are hoping to raise funds through educational trusts.

The EGAS website also includes a Guide to Student Funding, which has information on HE and FE funding throughout the UK, and the implications of student funding on benefits.

Last word

Be realistic when contacting EGAS. Don't expect miracles – they can rarely be worked.

When should I contact a trust?

Most trusts have an application deadline. This is usually given along with the general information in the trusts and grants directories. Check out each entry carefully; they are all different. Trusts are not the answer for a fast financial fix. Like all bodies, they tend to move exceedingly slowly. Your case will be scrutinised along with many others, so it could be months before you get an answer.

Could I get through higher education funded only by a charitable trust?

It could be done, but don't depend on it. Many charities won't consider you until you have tried all the usual channels available to students, and they do tend to give help towards the end of a course, rather than at the beginning.

If I get help from a charity, will it affect my loan and fees?

It shouldn't. Charitable awards, scholarships and sponsorships are not generally taken into consideration when calculating your grant and loan package.

Can I apply to more than one charity?

Yes, but blanket saturation is not advisable. Limit your applications to organisations that are really likely to give you funds.

How do I go about applying to a charity?

There are no set rules. What one charitable trust wants, another doesn't. Here is a general procedure to follow:

- Put together a list of suitable charities by consulting either EGAS or the directories in the library.
- Find out exactly what each charity is offering and whether you meet their criteria. Check if there is a final entry date for applications.
- Write a brief note to selected charities, explaining your need and asking for an application form.
- Fill in the application form. Make sure answers are clear, concise and truthful. You may be questioned on them later. Bear the trust's criteria in mind.
- Photocopy the completed form before you send it back.
- Wait patiently. These things can take many weeks to process.

Do students actually get help?

'As an Engineering student I needed a computer, but couldn't afford one. Were there any charities that could help? I searched around, and discovered the Earl's Colne Educational Trust, which assisted students living within ten miles of Earl's Colne in Essex. I lived in Halstead, just within the limits – it was worth a try. I wrote to them explaining my needs; they sent me a form; I filled it in; I waited; I went for an interview. The result: £500 – easy money. It cost just two sides of A4!'
Jonathan, when studying Electronic Engineering at Loughborough University

Competitions
Are they worth it?

The world is full of competition addicts. There are magazines devoted solely to the topic, steering readers to the next give-away bonanza. Whole families eat crazy diets just to get the labels off the right tins and jars. People do win – holidays in exotic places, new cars, toasters, DVD players, washing machines and cuddly toys. It's always worth having a go, if it only means the cost of a stamp and perhaps writing a catchy slogan. However, competitions cannot be seen as a serious means of raising finance. A little icing on the cake is the best you can hope for, and even that is a long shot.

But don't dismiss them altogether. If it's a competition aimed specifically at students, it very often involves writing an essay. Students, being the overworked (or lazy?) lot they are, tend to give them a miss, so the number of entries can be low. All the more reason to give it a try.

Win £700

All you have to do is write a 900-word essay about your industrial placement and you could win £700. The winner this year is Clare Dinham from the University of Surrey. She wrote about her placement at a psychiatric in-patient unit for children in London. The runner up was Joshila Oree from Brunel University who wins £200 for her essay on working as an electronics engineer with 3M in Bracknell. Next time it could be you. The competition is run by ASET, the Association for Sandwich Education and Training. Entries should be in by the beginning of December, and the results are announced in February.

On the other hand, you might find it more fun, though not so lucrative, to enter ASET's bloggers competition, called Student Stars. For this you have to produce a blog at various stages during your placement year. Successful blogs will be put on the ASET website and in their newsletter and could win you £200. To find out more about both competitions, log onto the ASET website: www.asetonline.org, email aset@aset. demon.co.uk or phone 0114 221 2902.

Best of luck!

Some years ago the chartered accountancy firm KPMG ran such a competition, and seven lucky undergraduates won the chance to work for six weeks for the firm in such exotic places as São Paulo, Toronto, Cologne, Melbourne, Sydney, Harare and Tai Pei, earn a good salary and to travel. Not bad for a few hours' work on a 1,500-word essay.

Every year BUNAC (the British Universities North America Club) awards three scholarships of up to £1,000 each to help applicants cover the costs of taking part in a BUNAC work-abroad programme to the USA or Canada. They're called the Green Cheese Scholarships, and all you need do to enter is write a humorous essay based on a travel-related topic. It can be about anywhere: an exotic trip to the other side of the world, or something less adventurous. Entries should be no more than 1,500 words. For further details see www.bunac.org.

If it's a competition set by your university with prizes for excellence, in a subject area you know well, you're in with a real chance, and winning could be a useful addition to your CV.

Take for example the Student Skills competition run at the University of Wales, Aberystwyth. This is a unique event that sets out to help students recognise the employability skills they are developing whilst at university. The final runs alongside the university Careers Information Fair, and teams from most departments get involved. Each team designs and runs a stand at the fair. They also make a group presentation, which is assessed by a panel of national judges. The prize for the winning team is £1,000. There are two other prizes of £500 each for the best stand and presentation. All students who take part will receive a £20 book token and will gain from the experience – the exposure to employers – and have a lot of fun. Each team is twinned with an employer; this is to help them identify what skills employers are looking for. International Politics was twinned with Reuters of London and spent four days with the company; Environment Science went to visit the Environmental Consultancy RPS Group; and Law went to Wragge and Co., a large law firm.

Lotteries

Then, of course, there's the lottery. Not strictly a competition, but an option. This book is not in the business of advocating gambling, and at £1 a go, or at least £104 a year, depending on how addictive it becomes, is it worth it? The odds on winning the jackpot are 14 million to one, and if you did win, what would happen to your studies?

Finally, students have been writing in with news of competitions on the web and in the media. Here are a couple of their stories:

> *Enter internet competitions using uni computers, since the web is free. I did and won a round-the-world trip, a TV, a video, a computer and £1,000 in cash.*
>
> 3rd year Economics student at York University

> *Whatever the prize, have a go. You can always sell it. I won a scooter worth £1,000 in a radio competition. It was a life-saver. I sold it immediately, and was able to solve my financial problems, which were dire. I still have a student loan, of course, but no overdraft.*
>
> 2nd year student, Lancaster

The litmus test with any competition has to be: 'Is it worth it?' Look at the hassle involved, the cost, the time factor, the number of cans of baked beans or cat food you have got to get through and, above all, the odds – and then make your decision. The drawback with any competition is that the winner takes all, and the also-rans get nothing. Still, it doesn't hurt to keep your eyes open.

Cash crisis note

Try www.prizefinder.com, www.studentstuff.com or type 'competitions' into your search engine. This will give you information on all the competitions that are available on the web at the moment – best of luck!

Further information

Where to look

- On your college noticeboard
- In the careers office
- National newspapers
- Student newspapers
- The web.

Who to contact

- EGAS helpline: tel: 020 7254 6251; website: www.egas-online.org.uk/fwa/trustsearch.htm
- Scholarship Search UK: www.scholarship-search.org.uk.

What to read

- *The Grants Register* lists over 3,500 awards. Published by Macmillan. Tel: 01256 329242. Email: macdir@macmillan.co.uk. Very expensive (£185 for the new 2008 edition) – try your local library.
- *Directory of Grant-Making Trusts*, published by the Charities Aid Foundation. Available from Trotman, tel: 0870 900 2665, or visit www.trotman.co.uk/bookshop.
- *Educational Grants Directory*, published by the Directory of Social Change. Available from Trotman, tel: 0870 900 2665, or visit www.trotman.co.uk/bookshop.

★ Most voluble students	
Weekly spend on telephone	
Canterbury	£15.50
Belfast	£13.80
Leicester	£13.70
Birmingham	£13.60
London, Bristol	£13.10
Coventry	£12.20
Southampton	£12.10
Dundee	£12
St Andrews	£11.60
Newcastle	£11.50

- *University Scholarships, Awards and Bursaries,* published by Trotman. To order, tel: 0870 900 2665 or visit www.trotman.co.uk/bookshop.

9

Postgraduate study

Where to find funding

The main topics covered in this chapter are:

The number of postgraduate students in the UK keeps increasing. In the last ten years the number of students on postgraduate courses has almost doubled. How are they managing to pay for their studies? Has funding kept pace with the demand? In this chapter we look at the main sources of finance for postgraduates.

Is it worth obtaining a postgraduate qualification?

Yes, if it's a subject you are particularly interested in or if it is a vocational course, and certainly if you are seeking a post in academia or a research-based organisation. But further qualifications are not going to guarantee you a better-paid job.

News update

The online postgraduate applications system enables postgraduate students in the UK and overseas to apply electronically to HE institutions. Access is via www.prospects. ac.uk, which hosts the national postgraduate database, or through a participating institution's website.

How many postgraduates are there?

There are around 559,390 students on postgraduate courses in the UK (HESA figures 2006–07).

Fact file: bigger earners

Holders of postgraduate degrees earn more than their graduate counterparts: on average £70,000–£80,000 over a lifetime; less if you hold a postgraduate certificate – £30,000 – £40,000 (Report published by Universities UK 2007).

The AGR Winter Graduate Recruitment Review 2008 reports that just under two thirds of employers, who responded to the survey, offered higher salaries for postgraduate qualifications. Median amounts: PhD £6,450 extra; MA, MSc etc. £3,506 extra; MBA £12,000 extra.

How much will it cost?

Tuition fees

UK residents and EU nationals:

- Fees: £3,300–£7,000 (Research councils fee level) most likely average figure. Certain courses may cost more. Part-time students: about half the full-time rate.
- Law: Graduate Diploma in Law/CPE course £2,500–£7,000. LPC course £5,200–£9,000 and possibly more.
- MBA general range: £9,900–£15,000 (£11,000 average, but could be more than double that at top schools).

Students from abroad – average for 2007–2008		
	Taught	Research
Classroom	£8,700	£8,700
Laboratory/workshop	£10,900	£10,700
Clinical	£21,600	£21,600

Maintenance

The results of our research given in Chapter 1 will give you some idea of how much it is going to cost you to live. Just for basic costs that's around £200 a week. The NUS reckon it would be much higher – £12,129 would be needed if living in London and £10,050 everywhere else, but that is just for a 39-week academic year and was based on NUS figures for 2007–08. And, remember, none of these figures include fees.

Cash crisis note

London is a lot more expensive than you think: just a two-zone day pass on the Tube is over a fiver; and landlords can ask for up to two months' rent as a deposit.

Sources of funding
Will I get funding?

Don't bank on it. Competition for funding for postgraduates is phenomenal. There is no all-embracing funding system as for first degrees, and students generally have to search around to get help. It is much easier to get a place on a course than it is to get the money to pay for it. Many postgraduates have to finance themselves with loans etc., which is probably why part-time study for postgraduates is increasing in popularity. If you are offered funding, make sure it covers both tuition fees and maintenance.

What are the possible sources of funding?

1. **Government funding** from research councils – these are by far the largest sources of funding in the UK. Some 7,000 new awards are made each year. Each 'awarding body' funds different courses and there is little overlap, so it is important to identify the appropriate body for your needs (see page 182; for Scotland and Northern Ireland see also pages 191–2).

2. **Erasmus** (often known as Socrates-Erasmus) is a programme developed by the European Commission to provide funds for the mobility of students and staff in universities throughout the EU member states and the countries of the European Free Trade Association (EFTA). See page 94 for full details and information on Erasmus and other similar programmes, such as the Leonardo da Vinci scheme.

3. **Employers** will occasionally sponsor employees through courses, especially MBAs.

4. **Companies** may sponsor students on a research project. This could be as the result of a work experience association during a first degree, or in co-operation with one of the research councils.

5. **Trusts and charities** are more likely to award small amounts of money rather than full financial support, but certainly worth considering (see Chapter 8). Your

Local Authority Awards Officer would have details of any local charities. Otherwise contact EGAS (see page 40 for details) or look in the published charities and grant-making trusts' directories and registers. Apply early: processing can be inordinately slow.

6. **Local authorities**. Except in the case of teacher training, local authorities are not required by law to fund postgraduates. Funding is discretionary, is given mainly for vocational courses that lead to certificates or diplomas, is means-tested and is subject to differing criteria between authorities. Likely subjects are accountancy, journalism, law, music, secretarial work, youth work and computing. If you are tapping your local authority it is essential to apply early as their funds are limited, and you'll need to present a good case for yourself. But because there are no set rules for funding, it is always worth a try.

7. **Universities' own postgraduate studentship awards**. Many institutions have a small number of studentships available for specific courses. Aberystwyth, for example, gives around 12 awards each year to UK/EU students for research degrees. Awards generally cover fees and maintenance. Closing dates vary. For the Aberystwyth competition it's 1 March. Check your university of choice for details.

8. **University departments**. They may have nothing, and probably won't advertise. But if they particularly want you, or there's something they are interested in doing, they may have sources they can tap. You could find that they stipulate you have to take on some tutorial work or assist the department. Tip from Aberystwyth: 'We say to graduates it's always worth a try; all it needs is the right phone call just at the right time.'

9. **Research Assistantships** are salaried posts in academic departments, which provide the opportunity to study for a higher degree. Salaries vary and opportunities can become available throughout the year. Watch the relevant press for adverts – the *Guardian*, *The Times*, *New Scientist*, *Nature*, *Prospects*, the Web, etc.

10. **Loans from banks** – see later in this chapter, pages 202–4.

Can I get a student loan?

Only if you are taking a Postgraduate Certificate in Education (PGCE). Even though it's generally only a one-year course, you will be classed as a first- rather than a final-year student, so you can take out the maximum loan offered. You can also take out a loan to cover fees. (See page 195 for full details of special funding arrangements for PGCE.) Or you could try a bank loan (see page 217).

Cash crisis note

From a student who knows:

'You always need double the money you think you need when you are moving to a new location to study. There are always hidden costs.'

Award-making bodies

These are the main sources of government funding for postgraduates. There are eight major award-making bodies in the UK. Each one operates independently and the awards they offer are all slightly different, as are their regulations. The information given here should therefore be seen as a general guide to what you could expect to get. All the award-making bodies issue information about their own awards, which you can get by writing to them or phoning them (addresses are given later in this chapter) or by looking on the internet. The areas of study covered by individual research councils can change, so make sure any information you get is up to date.

What kind of government award could I get?

Basically there are four kinds of awards for postgraduate students:

- **Research Studentships**, which are generally a three-year award leading to a doctorate (PhD or DPhil).
- **Collaborative Research Studentships**, when the research project is part-funded by an outside industrial organisation and may well give the student some experience outside the academic environment. The collaborating company generally gives the student extra cash on top of the studentship award. The awarding body may also give an additional award on top of the basic studentship. This is certainly so with CASE awards (Co-operative Awards in Science and Engineering).
- **Advanced Course Studentships**, which are given for taught courses which must be of at least six months' duration, but are generally for one or possibly two years, often leading to a master's (MSc, MA) or other qualification.
- **Bursaries,** which are allocated by the Central Social Care Council for courses in social work; the amounts offered are much lower.

Not all awarding bodies give all types of award. And some give additional awards and fellowships.

Is the award means-tested?

Only maintenance grants for training in social work are means-tested.

What could an award cover?

- Payment of approved fees to the institution
- Maintenance allowance
- Dependants' and other allowances
- Assistance with additional travel and subsistence expenses for something like fieldwork.

Do I have to get a 2:1 to take a postgraduate course?

Each course will set its own requirements. If you are thinking of specialising in your degree subject, a first or 2:1 is probably what you will need. For a vocational course, you'll need to show real commitment and interest in the subject. If, however, you are seeking funding from a government funding council, they will generally demand:

- A first or upper second class honours degree, or a lower second with a further qualification such as an MA for a Research Studentship.
- At least a lower second class honours degree for a taught/one-year course. (This does not apply to social work courses.)

How do I go about getting funding?

Start with your university careers office where you want to study. Most are clued up when it comes to tapping the scarce resources available to postgraduates. They may even publish a special leaflet on sources of funding for postgraduate study. Many of the publications listed at the end of this chapter, which we suggest you consult, should also be in the university careers library. Talk also to the tutors in your department, especially if you want to undertake a research degree, as they will know what projects are likely to gain funding. Consult university prospectuses.

When should I approach the award-making bodies?

If you want general information on their award scheme – any time. It is important to read thoroughly the individual information produced by the different award-making bodies, as closing dates, methods of application and what is on offer will vary. In most cases, application for awards is done through the institution you hope to join. Check information for procedure.

How do I apply for funding?

In the case of most research councils (BBSRC, EPSRC, ESRC, MRC, NERC, STFC), funding to students is funnelled through university departments and courses. They select the students for their courses/projects and submit their names to the awarding body. Application forms are obtained from the department for your intended studies, and must be returned to them well in advance of 31 July when the department will submit it to the appropriate awarding council.

In the case of the Arts and Humanities Research Council (AHRC), awards are allocated by competition. Having secured an offer of a place on a course, students apply for an award through their referees and the institution at which they will be studying. Applications must be with the appropriate awarding body by the beginning of May, so make sure your application is with your course 'organisers' long before then.

A fresh approach to flexible work

Need to earn while you study? FreshMinds could be the answer.

FreshMinds is an award-winning research and recruitment consultancy that allows some of the brightest brains in the UK to flex their intellectual muscles while working at big-name clients in every sector from banking to government. Among our pool of Minds are top graduates, postgraduates and business analysts drawn from the world's leading universities, business schools and companies.

If you're in between periods of study or looking for a job, FreshMinds can help you find the perfect way to while away the time and bring home some much needed money. Research ranges from information and data gathering to more complex analysis, including market research, company profiling and competitor benchmarking. Depending on where the wind takes you, you could be working in the heart of FreshMinds' Holborn office or on placements with clients for anything from three days to six months.

FreshMinds only works with the best – graduates who not only have a 2:1 degree or better from a top university, but who have revelled in excelling among their peers. If you are a glowing example of a fresh, young Mind take a look at www.freshminds.co.uk or give us a ring on 020 7692 4300 to find out more.

Will it make a difference where I choose to study?

Yes. Not all courses or departments attract funding. It is important to find out the situation when you apply. And just because a course is eligible for studentships, and you have a place on that course, it still doesn't mean you will necessarily get one. It is very competitive. And remember, if you don't get funding it could mean you have to pay not only your own maintenance but also your course fees. In that case, a university close to your own home might be the answer, or studying part-time (day release, evening courses or distance learning).

When and how can I find out what projects have funding?

From April onwards your university should have a list of university departments that have been given funding by the awarding bodies. Under the scheme, universities are committed to attracting the very best students for the awards, so must advertise for candidates outside as well as within their own university. Typical media: *New Scientist*, *Nature*, the *Guardian* or university magazines, depending on the topic.

If you want a list of which courses and projects throughout the country have received funding, contact the appropriate awarding body after 1 April. Information may also be on their websites.

Can I approach more than one awarding body?

No. There is generally no overlap between the awarding research councils: they each have their own designated topics that they fund. So it is important to identify which body to apply to, as you can only apply to one. In the case of the Arts and Humanities Research Council there does appear to be some overlap between its three different arms. However, a course that attracts bursaries from one will not generally gain funding from other state sources.

The award-making bodies

Subjects given for each body have been selected to give a broad view of topics covered, and are by no means exhaustive. Candidates should check with the appropriate organisation, or on the appropriate website.

Quick check				
Awards		**In London**	**Elsewhere**	**Any location**
BBSRC		£14,940	£12,940	Vet £19,970
ESRC		£14,940	£12,940	
MRC		£15,100	£12,940	
STFC		£14,940	£12,940	
AHRC	Research Master's	£11,040	£9,040	
	Professional Master's	£10,420	£8,420	
	Doctoral Award	£14,940	£12,940	
EPSRC	PhD studies			£12,900
	Engineering Doctorate			£14,400
NERC	PhD studies			£12,940
	Advanced course	£10,280	£8,280	
GSCC				Not supplied

Arts and Humanities Research Council (AHRC)

Awards are available for master's courses and doctoral study across eight subject panels as follows:

- ⊙ Classics, Ancient History and Archaeology
- ⊙ English Language and Literature
- ⊙ Medieval and Modern History
- ⊙ Modern Languages and Linguistics
- ⊙ Librarianship, Information and Museum Studies
- ⊙ Music and Performing Arts
- ⊙ Philosophy, Religious Studies and Law
- ⊙ Visual Arts and Media: practice, history, theory.

Research Master's Preparation Scheme

Type of award: Support for students undertaking master's courses that focus on advanced study and research training, which provides a foundation for further research at doctoral level. Awards will normally be for one year's full-time study or two years' part-time study

Amount: Studying in London: £11,040
Elsewhere: £9,040
Part-time study: £4,520 (London £5,520)
Tuition fees: £3,300 full-time/£1,665 part-time

Professional Preparation Master's Scheme

Type of award: Support for master's or postgraduate diploma courses that focus on developing high-level skills and competencies for professional practice. Awards will normally be for one year's full-time study and two years' part-time study

Amount: Studying in London: £10,420
Elsewhere: £8,420
Part-time study: £4,210 (London £5,210)
Tuition fees: £3,300 full-time/£1,665 part-time

Doctoral Scheme

Type of award: Support for up to three years of full-time study or up to five years' part-time study leading to a doctoral degree.

Amount: Studying in London: £14,940
Elsewhere: £12,940
Part-time study: £7,760 (London £8,960)
Tuition fees: £3,300 full-time/£1,665 part-time

Address: Postgraduate Awards Division
                        Arts and Humanities Research Council
                        Whitefriars
                        Lewins Mead
                        Bristol BS1 2AE
                        Tel: 0117 987 6543
                        Fax: 0117 987 6544
                        Email: pgenquiries@ahrc.ac.uk
                        Website: www.ahrc.ac.uk

Biotechnology and Biological Sciences Research Council (BBSRC)

Subject areas: Biological Sciences and associated technologies (agriculture and
                        food sciences, animal sciences, biochemistry and cell biology,
                        biomolecular sciences, engineering and biological systems,
                        genes and development biology, plant and microbial sciences)

Type of award: Research Studentship
                        Master's Studentship

Amount: Study in London: £14,940
                        Elsewhere: £12,940
                        (Doctoral Training Account minimum stipend can be higher.)
                        For students with a recognised veterinary degree: £19,970.
                        Students holding a first degree who wish to intercalate a PhD
                        during their veterinary training receive an annual supplement
                        of £2,000 pa from BBSRC. CASE awards (Co-operative Awards in
                        Science and Engineering) – additional minimum £2,500 by
                        collaborator

Address: Biotechnology and Biological Sciences Research Council
                        Polaris House
                        North Star Avenue
                        Swindon SN2 1UH
                        Tel: 01793 413200
                        Email: postgrad.studentships@bbsrc.ac.uk
                        Website: www.bbsrc.ac.uk

Economic and Social Research Council (ESRC)

Subject areas: Area studies, economics, economic and social history, education,
                        human geography, linguistics, management and business
                        studies (accounting, finance, industrial relations and other
                        specialist management courses), planning, politics and

international relations, science technology and innovation studies, psychology, social anthropology, social policy, socio-legal studies, sociology, statistics, research methods and computing as applied to the social sciences

Type of award:
Annual Studentship Competition (1+3 & +3)
1+3 Quota awards
Joint ESRC/NERC Studentships
Joint ESRC/MRC Studentships
Joint ESRC/Department for Transport Studentships
Joint ESRC/Scottish Executive Studentships
Joint ESRC/Department for National Statistics Studentships
GLC Grants Research Studentships
GLC Grants 1 year master's
Welsh Assembly Research Studentships
CASE Studentships
Centre Linked Studentships
Language Based Area Studies
Project Linked Studentships

Amount:
Studying in London: £14,940
Elsewhere: £12,940 students
(Enhanced stipends given by the Welsh Assembly and Scottish Executive of £2,000, if studying Economics or Quantitative Methods an additional £3,300)

Address:
Economic and Social Research Council
Research, Training & Development Directorate
Polaris House
North Star Avenue
Swindon SN2 1UJ
Tel: 01793 413150
Email: ptd@esrc.ac.uk
Website: www.esrc.ac.uk

Engineering and Physical Sciences Research Council (EPSRC)

Subject areas:
Engineering, chemistry, mathematics, physics, information and computer technologies, materials science and the life sciences interface

Types of support:
EPSRC supports all of its postgraduate training through packages of funding provided to the universities. It is the responsibility of the university to assess student eligibility for and select students to receive funding. Prospective students should contact universities or departments directly

Funding is provided for:	Standard Research Studentships, Industrial CASE Studentships, CASE for New Academic Appointees, Engineering Doctorate (EngD), master's degrees (MSc and MRes)
Amount:	Amounts may vary depending on university but EPSRC requires that PhD students receive a stipend of at least the national minimum rate. PhD Students: £12,900; Research engineers at Engineering Doctorate Centres: £14,400
Address:	Engineering and Physical Sciences Research Council Polaris House North Star Avenue Swindon SN2 1ET Tel: 01793 444000. Website: www.epsrc.ac.uk

General Social Care Council (GSCC)

Subject area:	Social Work
Type of award:	The social work bursary for students on full-time postgraduate courses is available to students normally resident in England studying on an approved full-time postgraduate course. Students must also meet other certain eligibility criteria. The bursary consists of a non-income assessed basic grant including a fixed contribution towards practice learning opportunity related expenses and tuition fee support. It also includes an income assessed maintenance grant and income assessed allowances to assist with certain cost of living, as recipients of the postgraduate bursary will not ordinarily be entitled to local authority funding. Financial awards are dependent on individual circumstances
Address:	Social Work Bursary NHS Business Services Authority Sandyford House Archbold Terrace Newcastle Upon Tyne NE2 1DB Tel: 0845 6101122 Email:swb@ppa.nhs.uk www.ppa.org.uk/swb

Medical Research Council (MRC)

Subject areas:	Medicine (including tropical medicine), areas of biology including molecules and cells, inheritance, reproduction and child health, infections and immunity (including HIV and AIDS), cancer, imaging, neurobiology, cognitive science, clinical neurosciences and mental health, health services research, clinical psychology, epidemiology, medical statistics, quantitative biology
Types of support:	MRC supports much of its postgraduate training through packages of funding provided to the universities as Doctoral Training Accounts. Prospective students should contact universities or heads of departments direct to see if there is funding available
Funding is provided for:	Research PhDs, Research Master's (MRes), Collaborative PhDs, Advanced Course Master's Studentships, Capacity Building Area (Priority Area) Studentships, Industrial Collaborative Studentships, MRC/ESRC Interdisciplinary Studentships
Amount:	May vary depending on university but a PhD student should receive a minimum stipend of:
	Study in London: £15,100
	Elsewhere: £12,940
Address:	Barry Wynne
	Medical Research Council
	20 Park Crescent
	London W1N 4AL
	Tel: 020 7670 5408
	Email: students@headoffice.mrc.ac.uk
	Website: www.mrc.ac.uk

Natural Environment Research Council (NERC)

Subject areas:	Geology, organic pollution, geophysics, physical oceanography, marine ecology, hydrology, freshwater ecology, terrestrial ecology, soil sciences, earth observation and associated science, atmospheric chemistry, science-based archaeology
Type of award:	PhD (3-year Research Studentship): can be a straight research award; a CASE award (Co-operative Award in Science and Engineering); or an OPEN CASE Award (these studentships are awarded to the universities in competition – approx. 25 a year). MSc and MRes (1-year Advanced Course Studentships)
Amount:	PhD stipend: £12,940 pa

Advanced Course stipend: £8,280 (£10,280 in London)
                            Extra PhD allowances: conference allowance, £450
                            Research Support
                            Training Grant (RTSG): £3,000
(CASE awards – minimum of £1,000 pa by collaborator)
London weighting: £2,000 for PhD, MSc and MRes students

Address: Natural Environment Research Council
                           Polaris House
                           North Star Avenue
                           Swindon SN2 1EU
                           Tel: 01793 411500
                           Website: www.nerc.ac.uk

Science and Technology Facilities Council (STFC)

Formerly Particle Physics and Astronomy Research Council (PPARC)

Subject areas: Particle physics, astronomy, astrophysics, solar system
                           science, nuclear physics

Type of award: Research Studentship – 260 allocated

                          Co-operative Award in Science and Engineering
                          (CASE) – 10 allocated

Amount: Studying in London: £14,940 pa
                           Elsewhere: £12,940 pa
                           (CASE award – additional £615 pa given plus minimum
                           of £2,760 pa by collaborating company)

Address: Science and Technology Facilities Council
                           Polaris House
                           North Star Avenue
                           Swindon SN2 1ET
                           Tel: 01793 442000
                           Email: studentships@stfc.ac.uk
                           Website: http://www.stfc.ac.uk/

See box on page 185 for a quick reference guide to postgraduate awards.

Wales

Graduates are eligible for funding from the research councils listed above. Those taking a postgraduate teaching course should turn to page 195.

Scotland

Graduates seeking funding for science-based subjects are eligible for studentship awards from most of the research councils mentioned here. Funding for postgraduate vocational courses mostly at diploma level (usually for one year) may be available through the Postgraduate Student Allowance Scheme (PSAS). Not all postgraduate courses are supported. Students taking PGCE or PGDipCE will be funded in the same way as undergraduates. Tuition fees up to a maximum of £3,315 will be paid for eligible students. All funding is means-tested. Contact SAAS on 0845 111 1711 for general enquiries.

PSAS rates for 2008–09

Location	Grant
London	£4,660
Elsewhere	£3,675
Parents' home	£2,780

Northern Ireland

- Postgraduate students can compete for funding from the award-making bodies already listed.

- The Department for Employment and Learning (DEL) offers two types of award: for research (MPhil, DPhil, PhD) and for approved courses of advanced study (master's) in fields of humanities, science and technology and the social sciences. Awards are not means-tested.

- For studentships to pursue postgraduate study in Northern Ireland (at either Queen's University Belfast or the University of Ulster) apply to the university for an application form. The offer of a place does not mean that funding will be provided.

- The Northern Ireland Department of Agriculture and Rural Development provides funds for study (in Northern Ireland) in agriculture including horticulture, and related sciences such as agricultural economics, engineering science and food science (closing date: last Friday in February).

- Medicine – see the Medical Research Council's details for Great Britain.

- The basic rate of maintenance grant for 2008–2009 is £12,900. Additional allowances may also be paid for dependants and students with special needs.

- CAST awards (Co-operative Awards in Science and Technology) support research projects at Northern Ireland universities for one year or three years in collaboration with industry. Maintenance grant of £12,900 pa is supplemented by a payment from the collaborating body of at least 60% of grant figure.

- Johns Hopkins Fellowship Award – a one-year Fellowship Award covering fees only for the Johns Hopkins University's School of Advanced International Studies in Bologna.

- One student is funded by DEL to take a one-year course in Administration, Economics and Law at the College of Europe, Bruges.

Booklet on awards available from: Department for Employment and Learning Student Support Branch, Adelaide House, Adelaide Street, Belfast BT2 8FD. Tel: 028 9025 7756. Website: www.delni.gov.uk/studentfinance.

Channel Islands/Isle of Man

Apply direct to the appropriate education department.

David's story

How I got £25,600 tax free to study for an EngD.

'I was in my final year at Manchester and thinking of going on to take a PhD when an advert came through for an Engineering Research doctorate working in collaboration with the engineering firm NIS Ltd. The project involved RF imaging for industrial processes, just up my street.

'It was actually for a EngD, which I preferred since it included a management element, and was sponsored by EPSRC who would pay my fees and provide a stipend of £13,800 pa. What's more, by working with a company, I not only received another £3,500 pa, but would gain valuable work experience. Everything was falling into place.

'Then, for the first time, the Whitworth organisation decided to give Whitworth Senior Scholarships to postgraduate engineers doing a PhD or EngD – £7,000 a year for the length of your course – so I applied.

'To be eligible for a Whitworth Scholarship you have to be an "outstanding student" – their words, not mine – who has done a "hands-on" engineering apprenticeship before taking your degree – which I had.

'Whitworth scholarships are open to engineers from any discipline, but as they are awarded through the Institution of Mechanical Engineers, I had no idea that an electrical engineer, like me, was eligible. If I had, I would have applied during my first degree – now that would certainly have helped the finances and debt.'

What David receives :

	1st yr	2nd yr
Stipend from EPSRC	£13,800	£14,100
Allowance from sponsoring company	£3,500	£4,000
Senior Whitworth Scholarship	£7,000	£7,500
Fees	Paid by EPSRC	
Total	£24,300	£25,600 – and all tax free

I want to study abroad – can I get funding?

There are a number of routes you can take:

If you are thinking of undertaking postgraduate studies at the European Union Institute (EUI) in Florence, the College of Europe in Bruges or Warsaw, or the Bologna Centre in Bologna you may be eligible for an award from the Department of Innovation, Universities and Skills in England, the Student Awards Agency for Scotland or the Department of Education and Learning in Northern Ireland.

Socrates-Erasmus, generally known as Erasmus (the European Community Action Scheme for the Mobility of University Students), and Leonardo da Vinci, which covers vocational training (see page 94).

The UNESCO publication *Study Abroad* has 2574 entries and provides information on courses, international scholarships and financial assistance available in countries and territories worldwide. It should be available at your local library or careers office or can be purchased from the Stationery Office. (See booklist at the end of this chapter.)

Hot tips on funding from an Edinburgh postgraduate

- Many departments provide opportunities for undergraduate teaching and demonstrating. Pay varies – it may only be a few pounds a term (e.g. £500 a year) or could amount to several thousand.

- Work as a Research Assistant. Many staff secure a funding award that they must spend on their project, which includes assistants.

- Don't aim to fund tuition and living costs by taking a job. It is possible for master's students to maintain a part-time job – and many do. But it is rare for a full-time PhD student to do so: a PhD is a job in itself. A few hours' work a week can ease the financial burden and provide useful respite from academic work – but only that.

- Try raising funding for individual experiments. Start with your department and funding sources for your individual subject. Success is more likely with experimental degrees than bog standards like French literature.

- Don't underestimate the time your PhD will take. Practically all PhDs overrun. It can easily take four or more years to complete. Research Council funding lasts for three years only and they won't pick you for the fourth year. Budget for this. There is a good chance there'll be good money coming in once you qualify. In the meantime have a contingency plan – it would be dreadful to give up on the last lap.

- Money, or perhaps one should say lack of it, is a major stress factor for many postgraduates. Excellent students quit because they can't afford to be a student any longer. Unrealistic budgeting undoes many: whilst rent and food are generally factored in, things such as holidays, contents insurance etc. are not. These all add up.

What help can I get if I want to train as a teacher?

England

Up to £225 a week just to train. This is the package of incentives available for students beginning a postgraduate course of initial teacher training (ITT) in England.

- Training bursary of £9,000 (non-repayable) for students training to teach the following secondary shortage subjects: maths, science, physics, chemistry, design and technology, ICT, modern languages, music, RE and Welsh.

- Training bursary of £6,000 (non-repayable) for students training to teach all other secondary-phase subjects not listed above.

- Training bursary of £4,000 (non-repayable) for trainee primary phase postgraduate students.
- A non-means-tested loan to cover the cost of fees – up to £3,145*.
- A non-means-tested non-repayable grant of £1,230 may be given to all students.
- An additional means-tested grant of £1,535, which is non-repayable*.
- Student loan based on the full-year allowance for students (up to £6,475 in London and £4,625 elsewhere or £3,580 in parents' home) 25% of which is means-tested (see Chapter 2).
- Postgraduate students taking a subject enhancement course prior to an ITT course leading to qualified teacher status will receive £225 a week and fees will be paid.
- 'Golden hello' paid to secondary-shortage-subject teachers on completion of their induction year: £5,000 to those teaching maths, science, physics and chemistry; £2,500, to those teaching ICT, modern languages, music, RE and Welsh.

The training bursary will be given in nine monthly instalments (18 monthly instalments if you are studying part-time). It is not means-tested and is not a loan. Tax and National Insurance will have to be paid on any golden hello. For more details see www.tda.gov.uk

Wales

The package of incentives on offer in Wales for 2008–2009 ensures that Wales-domiciled students receive a level of support comparable with their English counter-parts. The level of training incentive grant offered in Wales takes account of the fact that Welsh domiciled PGCE students studying in Wales will be entitled to a fee grant of up to £1,890 (depending on the level of course fees), which is not available in England.

Domiciled and training in Wales

- Training grant of £7,200 (non-repayable) for students training to teach secondary priority subjects. (Priority subjects include: design and technology, information technology, maths, modern languages, music, RE, science and Welsh.)
- Training grant of £4,200 (non-repayable) for students on all other secondary postgraduate initial teacher training courses.
- Training grant of £2,200 (non-repayable) for students on primary postgraduate ITT courses.
- Fee grant of up to £1,890 (non-means-tested and paid direct to place of study).
- Fee loan available for balance of fees.
- A means-tested Assembly Learning Grant (ALG) of up to £2,835. The first £1,255 (if studying for 10 weeks or more; the first £625 if studying for 6–10 weeks) for PGCE students is non-means-tested.
- A means-tested student loan for maintenance (see page 46).*
- A teaching grant for eligible trainees who go on to complete at least four months as a qualified teacher in a maintained school in a secondary priority subject, following completion of their induction period: £5,000 for those

*Note: maintenance loan and fee loan to be repaid in line with income after students have left their courses and are earning over £15,000 per annum.

teaching mathematics and science; £2,500 to those teaching other secondary priority subjects.

⊙ There is also the Welsh Medium Incentive Supplement Scheme, under which students studying to teach any subject in Welsh but feeling their language skills are not up to the job can apply for a bursary of £1,500 pa (£1,800 for those on mathematics and science courses) in addition to any other award held. Enquiries about this scheme should be directed to the ITT Provider with which you wish to study.

⊙ Finally, if you really are strapped for cash, there are the Financial Contingency Funds that provide small hardship grants for those who face unexpected difficulties. The student must make application to the ITT Provider.

To find out more about teacher training in Wales, phone 0845 6000 991 (or 0845 600 0992 for a Welsh-speaking consultant) or visit www.tda.gov.uk/recruit.

Welsh domiciled but studying in another part of the UK

If you are domiciled in Wales but choose to study in another part of the UK, i.e. England, Scotland or NI, you should contact Student Finance Wales (details as above) for information on the full range of available student support. Also check your entitlement to any other grants with the ITT provider with which you are hoping to study – you may be in for a surprise.

Teaching in Scotland

There is no training bursary or secondary-shortage-subject scheme in Scotland. Scotland does not suffer from a lack of teachers as in some parts of England. In Scotland local authorities (LAs) are the employers of teachers and there are 32 LAs in Scotland. Some of the more rural LAs suffer from not attracting the numbers of teachers they would like. A pilot scheme was introduced for Scottish trained teachers only who are eligible for the teacher induction scheme. If you tick the box to say you will teach anywhere in Scotland during your induction year, you will be given what's called a 'preference waiver' payment of £6,000. This is given in three instalments – £3,000 in your first August pay packet, another £1,500 in January and a further £1,500 in April. If you are allocated to a Scottish island you may also qualify for the Distant Islands Allowance, which would give you an additional £1,659 pa. The success of the 'preference waiver' scheme is assessed each year. To find out more, phone 0845 345 4745, or visit www.scotland.gov.uk/education/teaching, or www.infoscotland.com/teaching. The preference waiver payment is only available for Scottish trained teachers. If you have trained as a teacher in another part of the UK you will not receive the funding offered.

Teaching in Northern Ireland

While students will receive the same general funding as undergraduates in Northern Ireland (see Chapter 4), no additional incentives are available. However, if you train in England you will receive the incentive package being offered to students there. See page 194.

What do graduates do?

- Highest gain in graduate numbers in architecture and building, psychology, law, sports science and history.
- Highest fall in graduate numbers in IT and computing.
- 2.5 % drop in unemployment for geography graduates, now at lowest level for 17 years.
- Most popular destination for graduates – the health sector (13.3%) followed by management and business and finance.
- 32.9% of physics and 34.4% of chemistry graduates are likely to go on to take higher degrees/training.
- Graduates taking a higher degree – 6.1%.
- Teacher training – 2.8%.
- Sports science graduates at 62.3% showed highest employment rate amongst scientists. One in five were employed in professional coaching/instructing job.
- 71.9% of graduates were working/combining work and study six months after graduating.
- Only 6% of graduates were unemployed – lowest rate since 2,000.

(What Graduates Do, 2008: Higher Education Careers Services Unit (HECSU) survey based on 2006 graduating cohort six months after leaving university)

Further information for trainee teachers

- In England – Teaching Information Line: 0845 6000 991; website: www.tda.gov.uk.
- In Wales – Teaching Information Line: 0845 600 0991 (English); 0845 600 0992 (Welsh language); websites: www.teachertrainingwales.org (available in English and Welsh); www.studentfinancewales.co.uk for information about student fees.
- In Scotland – tel: 0845 345 4745; website:, www.infoscotland.com/teaching, www.gttr.ac.uk/teach/Scotland, www.saas.gov.uk.
- Training in Northern Ireland: contact the Department of Education (DENI): tel. 02891 279100: email: mail@frni.hob.uk; website: www.deni.gov.uk/indexteacher_pg.

Is there any help if I want to study Medicine?

There is a special deal for graduates domiciled in England and Wales who are on the four-year fast-track medical programme.

Year one

- You can apply for same support as undergraduates – student loans for fees and maintenance.

From year two onwards:

- Help with tuition fees
- You are eligible for a means-tested NHS bursary
- 50% of student loan.

I want to study Law – what help is there?

With full-time course fees for the Graduate Diploma in Law (GDL)/Common Professional Examination (CPE) about £2,500–£7,000, and the Legal Practice Course (LPC) running at an average of £5,200–£9,000 (but we have heard £10,000 mentioned), most students are going to need some help:

- **Training contract**. This is the best route financially. A firm providing a training contract will generally give a sponsorship for one or two years while you are at law school, which could involve paying your fees and providing a maintenance allowance. But sponsorship is competitive and even the best students can find it difficult to get. There is an increasing number of good people around to choose from. Those who do secure sponsorship would normally expect to complete their training contract with that firm. Occasionally a longer commitment to employment is demanded.

  Clifford Chance, a leading international law firm, recruits 130 trainee lawyers each year. The firm will cover the cost of tuition fees for its future trainees on the GDL and LPC and will provide a maintenance grant during this period. This is also a valuable time in which you can build networks before commencing your actual training contract.

  For sponsorship information see the CSU publication *Prospects Legal*, available from your university.

- **Vacation Placement Programmes.** A number of firms run these programmes for second-year undergraduates (or final-year if you are a non-lawyer), when they will size you up for a training contract. To get accepted for a placement programme is in itself an achievement, but it is certainly no guarantee of success.

- **Law Society Bursary Scheme**. Available for students taking CPE/GDL and LPC. They are very limited, competitive and include hardship criteria – but worth trying. The bursary is made up from a variety of funds and grant-making trusts which have been grouped together under an umbrella scheme. Applications for awards for 2008–09 were invited in March 2008. More information and application form available from the Law Society's Information Services hotline – 020 7316 5772 or email: bursaryapplications@lawsociety.org.uk. See also www.lawsociety.org.uk.

- **Law Society Diversity Access Scheme**. This aims to provide support to those with talent who will have to overcome particular obstacles to qualify as a solicitor. These could relate to social, educational, financial or family circumstances or to disability. For further details see www.lawsociety.org.uk or email: dascheme@btinternet.com.

- **Local authority grants**. Local authorities are not obliged to fund GDL or LPC students, and rarely do, but they do have discretionary funds available for a wide range of courses and, providing you meet their criteria for awards, you could strike lucky. There are no hard-and-fast rules, as every local authority has its own policy. Your local authority may well issue a leaflet giving information on study areas eligible for financial support. Enquire at your local education authority. Failing that, contact the Law Society (website above).

- **Loans**. If all other lines of attack have failed there is always a loan (see pages 202–4).

Laura's story

Laura is studying at the College of Law (London).

'Most of the top law firms recruit for training contracts two years in advance, i.e. in the third year of uni or at the beginning of the GDL. This can lead to the bizarre situation I found myself in where you get a job in a law firm before you have even started studying law!

'Competition for places at the top firms is extremely stiff: applicants are all expected to have at least a 2:1 degree, As and Bs at A-level and a lot more besides – they must have something extra to make them stand out.

'Despite maintenance grants and the funding of law college fees by law firms, it is quite usual for students to finish law college with up to £30,000 of debt. Many take professional studies loans of up to £20,000 because the maintenance grant usually only covers rent in London and little else! It can be quite stressful to be in so much debt, but I think most people view it as an investment – in themselves. The debt repayments can be quite crippling when you are a trainee, but are less significant on qualification as there is usually a big pay rise when you qualify. The debt is manageable, but it may not be great if you suddenly decide after law college or the training contract that law is not for you!

'For the top law firms, the recruitment process is long and laborious, involving long and testing application forms. If your application is successful, there are usually up to three interview stages, which include verbal reasoning tests, a team exercise, a written exercise and interviews with partners.

'The careers department in my college was fantastic and gave one-on-one advice and guidance about firms, how to tailor application forms to present yourself in the best way, and they also provide mock interviews and feedback from other students.'

Further information for law students

- For the most comprehensive information about firms offering sponsorship see www.prospects.ac.uk or ask your university for details.
- *Lawyer 2B* is a dedicated magazine for law students and those considering a career in or around the legal profession. A sister publication of *The Lawyer*, it provides news, comment, features and careers advice in an informal yet informative style. It is published five times a year and is available free from most UK law schools. In addition to the magazine, the *Lawyer 2B* has launched a new website. www.lawyer2b.com which gives breaking news along with features, comment and advice to reinforce the information in the magazine.
- For vacation placements and mini-pupillages look at the Prospects website: www.prospects.ac.uk.
- For general information see www.lawsociety.org.uk. Click on Student Guide.

Other professional qualifications?

Accountants, engineers, actuaries – all usually join firms that specialise in that kind of work. The firm will pay for your training and pay you while you are being trained.

I want to study in the United States

It's not cheap. Tuition for one nine-month academic year in state universities ranges from $4,000 to $13,000 and in private universities from $8,000 to $35,000. On top of that you will have living expenses, which vary tremendously: from $7,000 to $20,000. Don't automatically rule out the more costly courses, as the university may offer financial help through:

- ⊙ scholarships or fellowships
- ⊙ teaching/research assistantships
- ⊙ a loan.

Awards from bi-national exchange programmes, foundations or corporations etc. may also be available. See the appendix in the Fulbright Commission guide to Postgraduate Study in the US, available from the Fulbright Commission (details on page 102), or log on to www.fulbright.co.uk.

See page 207 for studying abroad – what to read, who to contact.

Extra funding

Are there any other funds I can apply for?

There may be. But not all councils and funding bodies give them and these are under review.

Child Tax Credit

Available to students with dependant children and paid by the Inland Revenue. The amount you get will depend on circumstances. Call 0845 300 3900 (Northern Ireland 0845 603 2000) 8am to 8pm for more details, or visit www.inlandrevenue.gov.uk and check out how much you could get.

Access to Learning Fund

Usually given as a grant to students with higher-than-expected costs and according to need; part-time students can apply if studying at least 50% of full-time course. Contact your university.

Help for the disabled

The Disabled Students' Allowance for postgraduate study offers up to £10,000 pa for full- or part-time students on a course that requires first-degree entry. See *Bridging the Gap*, free from the DIUS Publications Department.

Are funding arrangements the same for all parts of the UK?

No. For residents in Scotland, Wales, Northern Ireland, the Channel Islands and the Isle of Man, funding arrangements are slightly different.

Advice note

Seeking a career in the legal profession? Check out *Graduate Prospects Law Directory*. With some 80 employers advertising 2000 training contracts, the publication also includes valuable insights into the broad spectrum of potential career paths. Website: www.prospects.ac.uk.

It's a fact

By far the most popular master's degree is an MBA. Around 10.5% of master's qualifications awarded in 2005 were in Business Studies.

Over all, more women (53.3%) took master's degrees, and around 52.7% of master's qualifications were the result of full-time study. 50.9% of master's graduates were over 30.

(HECSU (Higher Education Careers Services Unit) What do Master's Graduates do? report, 2007)

What do master's graduates do?

According to a recent HECSU report, of those who completed their studies in 2005:

- 22% worked in management positions six months after completing their course
- 12.5% went to work as education professionals
- 9% were employed as business and finance professionals
- 7.1% became health professionals
- 5.8% worked as social and welfare professionals
- 11.9% were in general professional and technical occupations.

Unemployment amongst master's graduates was 4.2%; far lower than the 6% of first-degree graduates who were unemployed.

(HECSU What do Master's Graduates do? report, 2007)

Loans

OK, so nobody is going to fund me – can I get a loan?

Yes, but not the student loan. There are four excellent alternative schemes.

1. The Career Development Loan

Available only to those taking vocational training of up to two years. You can borrow up to £8,000 and not less than £300. The loan is designed to cover course fees (only 80% given if you are in full employment) plus books, materials and living expenses where applicable. The loan is provided by the banks (Barclays, Co-operative, the Royal Bank of Scotland) and can be for a full-time, part-time or distance-learning course. Interest on the loan is paid by the government while you are studying and for one month after your course has finished (or up to six months if you are unemployed when repayment should start). Phone 0800 585505 for a free booklet on Career Development Loans; line open seven days a week 8am–10pm.

Cash crisis note

Career Development Loans: though you can only get a CDL for two years, if your course is longer, it may be possible to take out a loan just for the final two years.

2. The Business School Loan Scheme

If you want to take an MBA, the Association of MBAs (AMBA) should be able to help. It runs a special scheme to assist graduates and other suitable applicants to study for a master's degree in Business Administration. The scheme is run in conjunction with NatWest Bank. To take advantage of the scheme you need to have a bachelor's degree or other suitable professional qualification, a minimum of two years' relevant work experience or five years' experience in industry or commerce, and to have secured yourself a place on an MBA course at a business school that is on the Association's approved list. Maximum loan for full-time students is two-thirds of present or last gross salary, plus tuition fees for each year of study. Preferential interest rates are given during the course. Repayment starts three months after completion of your course and you have up to seven years to pay it off. See www.mbaworld.com.

Our business schools are on the up and up.

International business school ranking

Where the top UK schools come in the world's top 100

	2008	2007
London Business School	2	5
University of Cambridge: Judge	10	15
University of Oxford: Said	19	19
Manchester Business School	22	22
Lancaster University Management School	22	28
Warwick Business School	29	36
Cranfield School of Management	30	37
University of Strathclyde Business School	30	–
Imperial College London: Tanaka	35	56
City University: Cass	41	73
Edinburgh University Management School	44	54
Leeds University Business School	48	93
Bradford School of Management	53	70
University of Bath Management School	69	73
Nottingham University Business School	76	93

FT (Financial Times) Business School Ranking

3. Law School Loans

Assisted by the Law Society, a number of major banks run a special scheme to help students fund law school courses. The loan, which currently stands at up to £25,000, is given at very favourable rates. For more details and an application form contact the banks directly.

4. Postgraduate Loan

What loans do banks offer to postgraduates?		
Bank	**Course area**	**Amount offered**
Barclays	Career Development Loan (for vocational training lasting at least one week)	£300 min; £8,000 max.
Co-operative	Career Development Loan	£300 min; £8,000 max.
HSBC	Professional Studies Loan	Course fees and living expenses up to a total maximum of £25,000. Additional funding available in one year to cover large purchases, e.g. car, providing within the maximum total of £25,000.
	Medical, Dental, Veterinary	Up to a maximum of £25,000. From 4th year. Available to UK residents only.
Lloyds TSB	Further Education Loan only available to existing current account customers studying full-time for a professional qualification: Architect, Barrister, Chartered Engineer, Dentist, Doctor, Optometrist/Optician, Pharmacist, Solicitor, Surveyor or Veterinary Surgeon	up to £10,000 at a preferential rate. Can delay repayments for 48 months and can take up to 5 years to repay.
	Graduate Loan	Up to £10,000 (minimum loan £1,000). Option to delay repayments for the first 3 months, after which payments can be spread over a maximum of 5 years. Typical APR 8.4%.
NatWest	Professional Trainee Loan: for Barrister, Solicitor, Doctor, Dentist, Pharmacist, Vet, Chiropractor, Optometrist, Osteopath, Chiropodist/Podiatrist, Physiotherapist	Up to £20,000 for full-time students (full-time trainee solicitors and barristers can borrow up to £25,000. Part-time trainee solicitors and barristers can borrow up to the cost of course fees).
	NatWest College of Law Loan	Up to £25,000 for full-time students (part-time students can borrow up to the cost of course fees). No repayment for 4–9 months after study, tranche drawdown option available.
	MBA Loan	Borrow up to two-thirds gross pre-course salary plus course fees up to 80% (less any grants). Repayment holiday for 3 months after completion of course. Tranche drawdown option available.
	Graduate Loan (any purpose)	£1,000 to £15,000 if graduated in last 3 years and have full-time job or job offer.
	Interest-free Graduate Overdraft Repayment Plan	Interest-free loan to repay your student overdraft – up to £2,000 in the first year, £1,000 in the second year, £500 in the third year after graduation.
Royal Bank of Scotland	Law student Loan (GDL/LPC full-time or part-time)	Up to £15,000 repayable over 7 years (conversion courses limited to £5,000).
	Healthcare, Chiropractic, Dentistry, Veterinary, Osteopathy	Up to £15,000 repayable over 7 years.
	Career Development Loan	£300 to £8,000
	Graduate Loan (any purpose)	£1,000 to £15,000 for those who have graduated in last 3 years and who have full-time job or job offer.
	Interest-free Graduate Repayment Loan	Up to £2,000 in the first year after graduation, £1,500 in the second year and £1,000 in the third year. Whole sum must be repaid 3 years from graduation.

> ## Cash crisis note
>
> If you have just graduated and already have a loan to pay off, think twice before getting even further into debt.

> ## Advice note
>
> Want to know more about the cost and routes to funding for postgraduates? Log on to www.prospects.ac.uk and access Funding for Further Study. The guide is designed to cater to the needs of the myriad of people who might consider participating in further study. Information on how to secure employer sponsorship makes it as relevant to those returning to study as those going straight from university; and it also offers specific advice for both international students and those with disabilities.

Overseas Students

What help is there for students coming to the UK from abroad?

There are scholarships specifically for overseas students, but there aren't very many, so apply early.

The Overseas Research Students Award Scheme (ORSAS) was set up to attract high-quality international postgraduate students to the UK to undertake research. The scheme is administered by individual universities on behalf of the Department for Innovation, Universities and Skills. Awards provide funding to pay the difference, in most cases, between the fees charged by academic institutions to international students for tuition and those charged to home/EU students. Awards do not cover maintenance or travel expenses. For full information visit www.orsas.ac.uk, which includes information on eligibility, the application process and the universities taking part in the scheme. If you cannot find the information you need, email orsas@hefce.ac.uk or the university where you intend to study.

The best source for finance is your own home government. Failing that, try the British government through the British Council, the Foreign and Commonwealth Office or the Overseas Development Agency schemes.

International Students House provides accommodation bursaries for postgraduates from developing countries who are studying in London. Students should already have won a scholarship to cover fees. Last year some 40 bursaries were given. It also administers the Mary Trevelyan Fund, a hardship fund that will give up to £1,000 to London-based final-year postgraduates and undergraduates from developing countries who are facing financial difficulties. Last year this scheme was undersubscribed. Contact: Chris Hutty, International Students House, 229 Great Portland Street, London W1W 5PN. Tel: 020 7631 8369. See also www.ish.org.uk, which includes details of accommodation and links to a cost of living site. (Also see *Sources of Funding for International Students* in the book list below.)

There are also the Commonwealth Scholarship Plan, the UN and other international organisations. Some universities give awards and scholarships especially to students from abroad – but each university needs to be contacted individually. Some charitable trusts also cater for foreign students. EGAS (see details on page 172) might be able to help you winkle them out, or check for yourself in appropriate directories (see further information in this chapter). EU students can compete for UK postgraduate awards already listed in this chapter, but on a fees basis only.

As a student from abroad, what is it really going to cost?

Fees – there is no set rate of fees for postgraduate courses. In the past there has been a recommended minimum, but each institution can charge what it wants. Fees for overseas students are generally substantially more than those for home students. EU nationals are generally eligible for UK home student rates. Science courses are usually more expensive than those in the arts. For average overseas postgraduate fees in 2007–2008 see page 179.

Living expenses – International Students House recommend that you will need around £10,000 to live in London excluding fees. Our research in Chapter 1 will give you some idea of what things in Britain are likely to cost.

Further information for foreign students studying in the UK

- ⊙ *Sources of Funding for International Students,* free from the British Council Information Centre, Bridgewater House, 58 Whitworth Street, Manchester M1 6BB. Tel: 0161 957 7755. Email: generalenquiries@britishcouncil.org.
- ⊙ *The International Student's A–Z:* A guide to studying and living in England, Wales or Scotland (3 editions). Published annually by International Students House, 229 Great Portland Street, London W1W 5PN. Tel: 020 7631 8369.
- ⊙ Association of Commonwealth Universities scholarships: www.acu.ac.uk.

Who to contact/what to read

- ⊙ *Postgraduate Directory.* Free from your careers service.
- ⊙ *Prospects Postgrad Magazine*: options for further study and research. Free from your careers service.
- ⊙ Prospects website – it's massive: www.prospects.ac.uk.

Studying abroad – what to read, who to contact

- *Directory of Study Abroad Programme.* Website: www.studyabroaddirectory. com.

- *Scholarships and Funding for Study and Research in Germany,* German Academic Exchange Service, 17 Bloomsbury Square, London WC1A 2LP. Tel: 020 7235 1736.

- *Beginners' Guide to Postgraduate Study in the USA.* Information on applying, tuition fees, etc. Educational Advisory Service, Fulbright Commission, Fulbright House, 62 Doughty Street, London WC1N 2JZ. Tel: 020 7404 6994. Include an A4 SAE with 48p stamp. Email: education@fulbright.co.uk. Website: www. fulbright.co.uk.

★ **Book-buying/course equipment universities**

	Weekly spend
Leicester	£14.30
Nottingham	£14.10
London	£12
Coventry	£11
Aberdeen	£10.70
Birmingham	£10.40
Cardiff	£10.20
St Andrews	£10.10
Cambridge	£9.90
Belfast	£9.90

- Try the UK Embassy or High Commission of the country where you are interested in studying: they may well have guides on awards and assistance offered.

- See also www.intstudy.com and www.studyoverseas.com.

10

Making the money go round

Banking and budgeting

In this final chapter, we try to give you some advice on how to manage your money, with the help of students, a bank student adviser who has first-hand knowledge of some of the financial difficulties students get themselves into, and how best to help them.

Problems and predicaments

My rent is over £70 a week. There's gas and electricity and telephone on top of that; I'm not making ends meet.

I've got an overdraft of £3,000, the bank is charging interest; if I've got an overdraft how can I pay the interest charges?

I thought: "£1,500, wow!" at the beginning of the term and blew the lot in the first few weeks. I haven't even the money for my train fare home.

I'm a Geography student and have to go on a compulsory trip. Where on earth am I going to find £120?

I know now that I shouldn't have bought the car and spent all that money on booze, but ...

A bank student adviser's view

A student loan of over £4,600! It certainly sounds a lot, but is it really? If all you are receiving is the standard funding for students then you haven't got wealth beyond your dreams, just the absolute minimum for survival. Bear that in mind right from the start and every time temptation looms, then you shouldn't go far wrong. There will always be those who like to live on the edge – spend now and cope with debt and disaster later. Most students who get into debt are genuinely surprised at how easily the money 'just slipped through' their bank account. Debt has a way of just creeping up on you if you let it. So be warned.

Budgeting – what it is and how you do it

The principles are incredibly simple. Putting them into practice is, for many people, incredibly hard. It is a matter of working out what your income and expenses are and making sure the latter doesn't exceed the former. It may sound rather boring, but it's a lot better than being in debt. The students quoted earlier obviously didn't budget.

Student advice

Take out a certain amount of money each week and keep it in a glass jar; then you can see it going down.
2nd year English Language student, Lancaster University

Save coppers and small change; you'll be surprised how much you save – providing, that is, you don't cheat.
1st year student, Birmingham

Check your bank account constantly, daily if necessary, on the internet, that way you can track where the money is going.
2nd year student, Durham

Where to keep your money – bank, building society, under the mattress?

Before you can start budgeting you need to choose somewhere to keep your money. In fact the Student Loan Company won't pay out your loan unless you have one. We would recommend either a bank or a building society. They are generally quite keen to attract students' accounts because they see students as potential high-earners as you'll see from page 213 when we look at the enticing freebies they all offer. These are worth studying, but shouldn't be the deciding factor. More important is to choose a bank or building society that is located close to your home or place of study. While these days you can use the cash-dispensing machines in most branches of most banks and building societies, they haven't yet invented a machine that can give advice.

Cash crisis note

Beware the private-enterprise cash machines; they generally charge for withdrawals, sometimes as much as £2. Not a good deal if you are only drawing out £10. Most banks' cash machines are free to users whether you are a customer of that bank or not. The machine will always tell you if it is making a charge, so always check.

What type of account?

There are a number of different types of account. At the bank you'll need to open what's called a current account so you can draw money out at any time. Many banks offer accounts specially designed for students, so it's worth checking with them what they have. Some current accounts give interest – not as much as a savings account, but every little helps. Check your bank for interest rates.

A building society current account is very similar to a bank account. They, too, give instant access to your money, and also pay interest on any money in your account. How much depends on the going rate and your building society.

Look for 'free banking' – this means that you don't pay charges when in credit or within your interest-free overdraft.

Caution

- Don't keep your cheque guarantee card and chequebook together. If they're stolen, somebody could clean out your account.
- Keep your Personal Identification Number (PIN) secret. Never write it down or tell it to anyone else.
- Cheques take three days to clear from an account. So don't go on a mad spending spree if you find you have more money in your account than you thought. The read-out on the cash machine may not be up to date.

Shariah compliant

There are a number of banks that offer Shariah compliant accounts, including HSBC. Their Amanah Bank Account provides all the functionality you would expect from a leading current account, but the funds held by the bank are kept separately from conventional funds. However, you would not be entitled to the special student incentives mentioned later in this chapter – at the moment. But things could change!

Shop around

If you are looking for a bank account shop around and compare the banks and what they can offer you in terms of overdrafts etc. If you want an overdraft, the simplest way to compare charges is to ask for the EAR – Effective Annual Rate. This is a standardised way of expressing the total cost of borrowing if you were continually overdrawn for a year. It is, they advise, also worthwhile asking the following questions:

- ⊙ How much interest will I earn if I am in credit?
- ⊙ Do I get a free overdraft facility? If so, how much?
- ⊙ If I want to arrange a larger overdraft, will I be charged an arrangement fee?
- ⊙ What will the interest rate be on my overdraft?
- ⊙ If I am overdrawn without consent, how much will I be charged for:
  - ⊙ the unauthorised balance
  - ⊙ the bounced cheques?
- ⊙ Ease of getting an overdraft?
- ⊙ Rates of interest charged if overdraft goes beyond limit, and ease of extending it?
- ⊙ Interest rates on graduate loans – some are much better than others?
- ⊙ What happens to your overdraft once you graduate?
- ⊙ Proximity to university/lodgings of local branch?
- ⊙ Reciprocal cash point facilities close to your institution – otherwise you could be charged for making withdrawals?

What will *you get when you open an account?*

When you open an account you may receive some or all of these services and facilities:

- ⊙ **Chequebook**, which you can use to pay big bills and for large purchases.
- ⊙ **Cheque guarantee card**, which could be for up to £100. Some banks limit it to £50 for students. This states that the bank will guarantee your cheque up to the amount shown on the card, so the shop where you are making your purchase will let you take the goods away there and then. This is often incorporated into your cash card.
- ⊙ **Cash card**, which enables you to withdraw cash from a cash machine, and may offer additional payment functions.
- ⊙ **Debit card** (SOLO, Switch, Maestro or Delta) which will automatically debit your account for goods bought when passed through a terminal at the point of sale.

- **The three-in-one card**. Most banks and building societies combine the facilities mentioned above into multifunctional cards which act as cheque guarantee cards, give access to cash machines and can be used as debit cards so you can purchase goods and services without writing a cheque.
- **Account number**, which you will need for any correspondence with your bank.
- **PIN**– this is your own Personal Identification Number, which you will need to remember and use when getting money from the cash dispenser.
- **Paying-in book** containing paying-in slips, probably with your branch name printed on them, which you can use when paying in cheques and money. Just fill in the slip and pass it to your bank. Most banks provide pre-printed envelopes, which you can pick up in your branch and then post through a letter box in the banking hall. You can also pay in cheques through some cash machines.
- **Statements** sent to you at regular intervals (we would advise you to ask for them monthly). The statement will give details of the money going in and out of your account – an essential part of budgeting properly.
- **Internet banking**.
- **24-hour telephone banking** which allows you to keep in touch with your student account and credit card account day and night.
- Student Contents **Insurance**.
- You may also be able to apply for a credit card, but think about it seriously before doing so, it could mean more debt.

Overdrafts, loans, freebies

Which bank? What's the carrot?
What will they do for me?

Banks are the student's friend

Despite all the talk of students and their financial difficulties – our research shows that most students are likely to be in debt to anything up to £20,000 or £30,000 even by the time they qualify – banks are still falling over themselves in an effort to gain your custom. Nearly all offer students some kind of carrot to get them to open an account, and promise some kind of interest-free loan which for most students is an essential part of their funding package. How generous you might think. Banks aren't charities. Their reasoning isn't difficult to fathom. They are in the business of long-term investments. Students are the country's potential high earners. Statistics show that people are more likely to change their marriage partner than their bank. The strategy is: get 'em young and you've got 'em for life.

So what's on offer?

Overdraft

The most useful offer made by banks to students is the interest-free overdraft. Our research showed that 66% of students took advantage of this. As you will see from our chart on the next page, it could add another £1,000–£2,000 to your spending power. But it eventually has to be paid back. And don't assume it is yours as a right: you must ask first. Most banks also offer special arrangements for paying the overdraft off once you graduate. Again, check what these are before you step on the slippery slope to debt. How long will they give you to pay it off? What will the charges be then? How long does the interest-free loan last? These are the questions to ask.

Freebies

Most banks keep their new student offer under wraps right until the very last minute – largely so that their competitors can't top it with a better inducement. This means the new offer is on the table from around June/July. Some banks have a closing date for their main offers, which could be as early as November, when the first loan cheques have been happily banked. The offer is generally open only to first-year students. Before giving you the benefit of their freebies, the bank of your choice will ask for some proof of your student status such as your LA award letter or your first term's loan cheque.

To give you some idea of what you can expect, and to check the next round of offers, we looked at how students fared in 2007–2008.

Last year, the Lloyds TSB offer of £75 cash (£25 paid into account after opening and a further £50 if you don't go overdrawn in your first year), NatWest's offer of a free five-year student railcard worth £100, and 12 free cinema tickets from Barclays seemed like the best freebies at first glance. But who is offering the best deal depends on what you are looking for – see our comparison chart.

What's the best banking buy?

Compare the current facilities offered by some of the major banks. Note student packages are usually revised each summer, so check with the banks for the latest.

What's the best banking buy?

Compare the current facilities offered by some of the major banks. NB Student packages are usually revised each summer, so check with the banks for the latest information.

	Abbey	Bank of Scotland	Barclays	Halifax	HSBC	Lloyds TSB	NatWest	Royal Bank of Scotland
Free banking	Yes	Yes	Yes	Yes	Yes	Yes	Yes	Yes
Interest on current account	Yes, paid monthly.	Yes, paid quarterly.	Yes, paid monthly.	Yes, paid monthly.	Yes.	Yes, paid monthly.	Yes.	Yes.
Free overdraft	1st year: £1,000 / 2nd year: £1,250 / 3rd year: £1,500 / 4th/5th year: £1,800	1st–5th year and 1 year postgraduates: £2,750	c £200 on opening account. Up to: 1st year: £1,000 / 2nd year: £1,250 / 3rd year: £1,500 / 4th year: £1,750 / 5th year: £2,000	Up to: 1st year: £2,750 / 2nd year: £2,750 / 3rd year: £2,750 / 4th year: £2,750 / 5th year & postgraduate £2,750 (1 yr)	1st–3rd year: £1,500 (tiered in 1st year) 4th–6th year: to £2,000	Up to: 1st year: £1,000 / 2nd year: £1,250 / 3rd year: £1,500 / 4th year: £1,750 / 5th year: £2,000	Up to: 1st year: £1,250 / 2nd year: £1,400 / 3rd year: £1,600 / 4th year: £1,800 / 5th year: £2,000	Up to 1st year: £1,250 / 2nd year: £1,400 / 3rd year: £1,600 / 4th year: £1,800 / 5th year: £2,000 – possible extension to £2,500
Student adviser	No.	Yes, major campus branches/university towns.	All branch advisers can help.	Yes.	Call centre advisers available 24 hrs.	Yes.	Yes.	Yes. In most branches.

Student insurance	No special package.	See freebies.	See freebies.	Four levels of posessions cover from £2,000 to £5,000.	Student Posession Insurance.	Student Belongings Insurance.	Student Posession Insurance.
Freebies	Commission-free travellers' cheques and foreign currency. 25% off AA membership for one year. 20% discount on Card Care Insurance. Bank of Scotland Current Account Visa Debit card. 24-hour telephone and internet banking.	12 free cinema tickets. Online shopping discounts at Barclays and Me website.	Commission-free travellers' cheques and foreign currency. 25% off AA membership for one year. 20% discount on Card Care Insurance. Halifax Current Account Visa Debit card. 24-hour phone and internet banking.	Refund of your £15 UCAS application fee. Fee-free credit card with £500 limit. Banking 24/7 via internet banking. Transfer to Graduate service at the end of Student Service.	Up to £75 cash, (check details). Free NUS Extra card worth £10. Free mobile phone insurance worth up to £90, YHA membership worth £10, 35 free music downloads. AA driving school – offer worth up to £29 and more.	Free 5-year Young Person's Railcard worth £100. And 10% savings at Waterstones. Plus free mobile phone banking, and more.	Scotland £100 cash or Travel Package worth £149. England – travel package worth up to £165. Commission-free travellers' cheques. Discounts on books, CDs, videos, computer games, concert tickets, travel and more.

Graduates

There are other benefits to be considered once you graduate, such as covering your student bank overdraft and finding the money to pay it back, and terms for paying it back, and finding the money to tide you over while you get started in work. You may also be thinking of undertaking further study – here the banks will help too.

	Abbey	Bank of Scotland	Barclays	Halifax	HSBC	Lloyds TSB	NatWest	Royal Bank of Scotland
Paying off undergraduate overdraft	Interest-free advance overdraft of up to £2,000, decreasing to £500 pa over 3 yrs.	Interest-free overdraft 1st year £1,500, 2nd yr £1,000, double if pay £5 monthly charge.	Can keep student account for a year after graduating.	Interest-free overdraft 1st year £1,500 2nd year £1,000.	Interest-free overdraft Yr 1 £2,000 Yr 2 £1,000 Yr 3 £1,000.	Interest-free overdraft Yr 1 £1,000 Yr 2 £1,000 Yr 3 £500.	Interest-free overdraft £2,000 in Year 1, £1,500 in Year 2 and £1,000 in Year 3.	Can keep student account for a year after graduating.
Low-cost graduate loan	Up to £10,000 (minus any interest-free overdraft).		Up to £10,000.	Up to £25,000 at preferential rate. Range of repayment periods.	Up to £10,000 at preferential rate.	Up to £15,000 at preferential rate over 7 years (5 years for loans of £10,000 or more).	Up to £15,000.	£1,000–£15,000 at 2.5% over base rate with 7 years to pay if amount £10,000 or over.
Professional study loan e.g. for Medicine, Dentistry, Optometry, Veterinary Science or Law	No.		Career Development Loan £8,000 max.	Considered on individual basis. Excellent rates given.	Further Education Loan up to £10,000 – to existing Lloyds TSB current account holder.	Up to £20,000 (Barristers/Solicitors up to £25,000). MBA Loan available.	Up to £15,000.	
Career development loan	No.	Yes, up to £8,000.	No.				Yes, up to £8,000.	

But should one be bribed into choosing a bank? Forward-thinking students may well decide that interest-free overdraft facilities carry more weight in making the choice than a paltry one-time cash offer. Here you would do well to look carefully at the small print before making a decision. Some banks offer more in the second and third years. But do you want that kind of temptation?

> *I went for the freebies – rather than the most sympathetic bank manager – bad move when debt loomed.*
> 3rd year student, Glasgow

What is a bank student adviser?

A student adviser ('student champion' at RBS) is somebody in the campus branch of the bank, or the branch closest to your college, who has been earmarked to deal with student problems. They are usually fairly young, and they are always well-versed in the financial problems students face. Certainly you will find them sympathetic, and full of good advice on how to solve your particular problems. But you won't find them a soft touch, as one student adviser pointed out: 'It's no good us handing out money like confetti – it just builds up greater problems for the student later on.'

What is a low-cost graduate personal loan?

This can be a life-saver for the newly qualified graduate. It is a special personal-loan scheme offered by some banks to graduates to help tide them over the first few months while they get settled into a job. Most banks offer anything up to £10,000, some up to £15,000 and more, and some up to 20% of your starting salary. A graduate loan can be individually negotiated. The loan could be used to pay for suitable clothes for work, a car, advance rent – whatever you need. But remember: nothing is for free; you will have to pay interest, and if you already have a student loan and a substantial overdraft, this might be just too much debt. The graduate loan should not be confused with the many other types of loan banks offer to postgraduates to assist with study. (See Chapter 9.)

Banks' websites

Check out the banks' websites for the latest information and offers.

Abbey	www.abbeynational.co.uk
Bank of Scotland	www.bankofscotland.co.uk
Barclays	www.barclays.co.uk
HSBC	www.banking.hsbc.co.uk
Lloyds TSB	www.lloydstsb.co.uk
NatWest	www.natwest.com
Royal Bank of Scotland	www.rbos.co.uk

Cash crisis note

Never run up an overdraft without asking the bank first. They are much more sympathetic if you put them fully in the picture. And unless they know you are a student, you could find you miss out on the interest-free loan. Talk to your bank's student adviser – ideally before you hit a problem.

I ended my first term at uni £300 overdrawn. What a shock! How did it happen? It's only too easy if you don't keep a close watch on your account. I now bank on line so can check-up all the time. Okay, so I do have an overdraft, but at least I know.
2nd year Languages student, Durham.

Your income – how much?

It's all very well to have an official piggy bank in which to keep your money, but where is the money going to come from and how much is it likely to be? If you have read the rest of this book, you should by now have some idea how much you are likely to have as a student. We have listed some of the likely sources in our budgeting plan. With a little ingenuity you may have discovered others.

A step-by-step budgeting plan

1. Take a piece of paper and divide it into three columns (see page 220). On the left-hand side write down your likely income sources and how much they will provide, for example:
   - maintenance grant
   - student loan
   - fee loan
   - parental contribution
   - bursary
   - money from Access to Learning Fund
   - money earned from holiday job
   - money earned from term-time job
   - sponsorship
   - interest-free overdraft

2. The trouble with budgeting, especially for students, is that money generally comes in at one time, often in large chunks at the beginning of a term, and your outgoings at another. When you work you will probably find it easiest to budget on a monthly basis, but as a student you may have to do it either termly or yearly depending on how the money comes in.

3 In the middle column write down your fixed expenses – things that you have to pay out – like rent, gas, electricity, telephone, food etc. Don't forget to include fares. Now total them up.

4 Subtract your fixed expenses from your income and you will see just how much you have, or haven't, got left over to spend. Draw a line under the list in your right-hand column and now list your incidental expenses – things like socialising, clothes, the cinema, hobbies, birthdays etc. This is your 'do without' column: the area where you can juggle your expenses to make ends meet.

5 Apportion what's left over to the things listed in this final column, making sure you've got at least something left over for emergencies. Do the figures add up?

6 Seems simple enough and logical on paper. But of course it doesn't work quite as easily as that. There's always the unexpected. You can't get a job. Your car needs a new battery. People use more gas than expected. Did you really talk for that long on the phone?

7 Having worked out your budget, use the final column on your budget sheet to fill in exactly how much your bills do come to. In this way you can keep a check on your outgoings and how accurate your predictions were, and do something before the money runs out.

If you are having difficulty putting together a budget, look at the student examples at the end of Chapter 1, page 28.

Hot tip from a burnt student

'There are so many hidden costs at uni – expenses pop up all the time. It's impossible to budget at the beginning of term, which makes financial management a nightmare – sports levies, balls, tours, travel, books – and that's just for starters.'

2nd year Music student, Durham

Income		Outgoings		
			Predicted	Actual
Grant	£	Fees	£	£
Bursary	£	Rent/college board	£	£
Parental contribution	£	Gas	£	£
Fee loan	£	Electricity	£	£
Student loan	£	Telephone	£	£
Sponsorship	£	Launderette/cleaning	£	£
Job	£	Food	£	£
Access to Learning Fund	£	Fares while in college	£	£
Other	£	Fares to college/home	£	£
		Car expenses	£	£
		Books/equipment	£	£
		Compulsory trips	£	£
		TV licence	£	£
		Student rail/bus card	£	£
		Broadband	£	£
Total:	£	Total:	£	£
		Socialising	£	
		Hobbies	£	
		Entertainment	£	
		Clothes	£	
		Presents	£	
		Holidays	£	

What is a standing order?

Regular payments such as rent can be paid automatically from your bank account through a standing order. You just tell the bank how much to pay out and to whom, and they will do the rest. The system is ideal for people who are bad at getting round to paying their bills. Oops, forget to pay the electricity and you'll soon know. Standing orders are not so easy to organise when you are in shared accommodation with everyone chipping in to pay the bill. However, we did discover one student household in Durham which had a special bank account just for bills which they all paid into.

What is Direct Debit?

With a Direct Debit set up on your account, the bill is again paid automatically, but it works in a different way. The bank of the organisation you are paying the money to will collect the money direct from your account. This is an ideal way of paying when the amount being paid out is likely to change.

Cards and the catches

Credit cards

These are an easy way to pay for things but can also be an easy way to get into debt. When you have a card such as Mastercard or Visa you are given a credit limit. This means you can make purchases up to that sum. Each month you receive a statement of how much you owe. If you pay back the whole lot immediately there are no interest charges. If you don't, you will pay interest on the balance. There can be an annual charge for credit cards. You can use your card in the UK and abroad at most shops and many restaurants. They are a way of getting short-term credit but are an expensive way of borrowing long term. On the plus side they are a way to spread payments or ease temporary cashflow problems. Living, as most students do, from two addresses, make sure you don't miss a monthly bill that needs to be paid.

Store cards

Many stores, such as Marks & Spencer, offer credit cards that operate in much the same way as described above, but can only be used in that particular store or chain of stores. Although most stores will check your credit rating before issuing you with a card, they are still too easy to come by – get a stack of them and you could find you're seriously in debt. A store card is quite different from a store loyalty card – the type issued by Boots, Tesco and many other organisations. These give you points for everything you buy in that store, which you can save up and use to purchase products. A good thing to have if you are a regular customer.

Debit cards

You've probably seen the Switch/Maestro card in action, as most stores and garages have the system installed. By simply passing your debit card through a Switch/Maestro terminal, the price of the purchase you are making is automatically deducted from your account. What could be easier? Details of the transaction will show up on your next statement. Some stores will offer you 'cash-back' on a debit card, which could save you a trip to the bank.

Safety check

Most banks and building societies will not send plastic cards or Personal Identification Numbers to customers living in halls of residence or multi-occupancy lodgings, because they could go astray or sit unclaimed in the hallway for days. All too easy to steal. You may have to collect them from a branch nearby.

Cash crisis note

While most big stores and pubs will not charge for giving cash-back, some of the smaller stores may. Always check.

What if the money runs out?

Help, I'm in debt!

Don't panic, but don't sweep the matter under the carpet and try to ignore it, because it won't go away. In fact it will just get worse. Get in touch with the student welfare officer at your university, the student adviser at your local university branch or your bank manager. Or all three. Through experience they will be able to give the best advice and help. Impoverished and imprudent students are not a new phenomenon.

> *I needed £200 to put down as my deposit for renting a house next year, but I hadn't got it, so I went round to my bank and they extended my overdraft.*
>
> 1st year Urban Planning Studies student, Sheffield

Caution

Don't borrow from a lot of places. If you've got an overdraft and a student loan, that's probably enough.

Getting an overdraft

If you are struggling, don't turn your back on the interest-free overdraft facilities that most banks offer students and are considered by many students to be an essential part of their income – helping to fill that financial black hole between loan payments. As you can see from our chart on page 214, free overdraft facilities vary enormously, as do the amounts you can borrow – up to £2,750 in your first year.

If you go over your overdraft limit, get on the phone or call in immediately to your bank. Many of the clearing banks have campus branches or at least a branch in the town geared to dealing with students. They'll probably be sympathetic and come up with a helpful solution.

A planned overdraft

'I'm going for an interview and need something to wear.'

This is not an unusual request from students in their final year – jeans and a scruffy T-shirt rarely make a good impression. Banks are very good at coming up with a plan to help you out with an obvious or specific need. After all, an interview success could mean you'll clear your overdraft that much more quickly.

An overdraft is often the cheapest way of borrowing, even if it is not part of the special student package. There are charges and interest rates, which need to be checked out. The advantage of an overdraft is that you don't have to pay it back in fixed amounts, though the bank has the right to ask for its money back at any time.

Borrowing on credit

'Haven't got the money at the moment so I'll buy it on Mastercard.'

Easily done, but be warned – though Mastercard/Visa is excellent as a payment card, credit can cause problems. If you don't pay off your bill by the date given on your statement, you will have to pay interest and, compared with other sources of borrowing, this is very high. Unlike your friendly bank, credit card companies are not the sort of people you can negotiate with, and are very likely to sue. Don't see them as another source of income.

Thrift tips

Leeds University Union Welfare Service suggests these ways of managing your money:

- ⊙ Get value for money – use markets or large supermarkets for fresh fruit and vegetables. Your local corner shop may be convenient, but is often more expensive.
- ⊙ Make the most of student discounts for coach and rail travel, clubs, restaurants and hairdressers.
- ⊙ Use the library rather than buying books – has your uni got a second-hand bookshop?
- ⊙ Withdraw only the amount of cash you actually need on a weekly basis from the bank – otherwise it will disappear.

Personal loan

This is quite different from an overdraft. It is usually used when you want to borrow a much larger sum, over a longer period – say several years. It differs from an overdraft in that you borrow an agreed amount over a set period of time and the repayments are a fixed amount, generally monthly. You might take out a loan to pay for your course fees, but not for short-term credit to tide you over until your next grant cheque arrives.

A bank manager's view

'The problems students have are very real. As a bank manager, all too often we find we are just picking up the pieces when things have gone too far. Debt brings stress, and that will affect your ability to study. Come sooner rather than later.'

Don'ts

(Which unfortunately some students do!)

- ◉ Don't fall into the hands of a loan shark. Any loan offered to students, except from a recognised student-friendly source, e.g. banks, building societies, parents or the Student Loans Scheme, should be treated with the utmost caution and suspicion. It's bound to cost you an arm and a leg, and lead to trouble.

- ◉ Don't run up an overdraft with your bank without asking first – even the much-vaunted interest-free overdraft offered by most banks to students should be checked out first, otherwise you might find you are being charged. They need to know you are a student.

- ◉ Don't forget to pay your gas and electricity bills. Make them top priority. A week or two on bread and (cheap) jam is better than having to pay court costs.

- ◉ Don't pawn your guitar, only to find you can't afford to get it out to play at the next gig.

- ◉ Don't try 'kiting'. The banks have got wind of what's been going on, and you're bound to be found out and in real trouble. For the uninitiated (like this author), kiting is the dishonest practice of making the most of the time lapse between people reporting that their credit card is missing and it being recorded as stolen. Be warned: it is a criminal offence, and could end up increasing your debts – or even worse.

- ◉ Don't get blacklisted with the bank. 'Kiting' is a sure way of getting a bad record. Running up an overdraft is another.

- ◉ Don't see credit cards as another source of income.

Savings?

Most books on budgeting give lengthy advice on saving. We think it unlikely that students will do more than just make ends meet, and even that will be a struggle. However, if you do find that you have some surplus cash, or are in that lucky position of being able to do without the student loan and decide to take it out as an investment, you could put it in an ISA, or open a savings account at a bank, a building society or the Post Office. Check out the interest rates and the terms and conditions. Many high-interest accounts give limited access to your money – so watch out.

A final word of advice from a student

'Before starting a degree, students don't realise just how tough it's going to be. You think, how on earth can anybody be so irresponsible as to get into £22,000 worth of debt? But once you are into university life, you know only too well. Despite the hardship, don't be put off; university is excellent – an incredible experience not to be missed!'

Top Tips for students

Most banks close to universities have student advisers. Barclays has a national network of over 200, whose full-time job is to advise students on how best to manage their money while at university. This is their list of top tips on managing your money. Some have already been suggested by students elsewhere in this book, but repetition can't hurt if it keeps you out of debt.

- Don't wait until you get to college to open an account. Open one at your local branch. You will need it in order to apply for a student loan.

- Once you know how much you will have to live on per term, ask your bank for advice on budgeting. Don't be worried about going back for further guidance if you're finding it hard to cope.

- Limit your borrowing to a few sources. Spreading debts around too much makes it difficult to keep track of them and can only create problems later.

- Be cautious about how much money you borrow on your overdraft, even if it is interest-free.

- Arrange to have your monthly statements sent to your term-time address to help you monitor your budget.

- Try to limit your trips to the cash machine to once a week, otherwise you could easily lose track of how much you are spending.

- Insurance is vitally important, but ask your parents first if you can be included on their house insurance.

- Wait until you arrive at university before buying expensive books and equipment; then you will know what you really need. Ask around for places offering the best deals, such as your university bookshop, or buy second-hand textbooks from students in the years above you.

- As your loan comes termly, it is often a good idea to get your loan money paid into your savings account and then transfer money over perhaps every week or every month. This will help you budget and spend within your means.

- Familiarise yourself with the student services available to you at your university. Student support centres are in place to help you with all aspects of student life, including your finances.

- Keep checking your account to ensure all payments are made.

- Always deal with bills and statements as they arrive – try to avoid putting them to one side or forgetting to pay bills. We recommend paying by Direct Debit if possible.

- If you've got problems, remember that your bank's student adviser is there to offer advice and support. Don't ignore a problem, hoping it will go away by itself – because it won't.

Index